THE
POMEGRANATE
AND THE ROSE

The Story of Katharine of Aragon

By Winifred Roll

PRENTICE-HALL, INC.
Englewood Cliffs, New Jersey

En priant tous qui voirres ceste hystoire
Qu'ilz excusent mon simple entendement.

I beg all who see this story
To excuse my humble ability.

(probably Bernard André—translated by J.
Gairdner—in the Memorials of Henry VII)

The Pomegranate and the Rose: The Story of Katharine of Aragon
by Winifred Roll
© 1970 by Prentice-Hall, Inc.
Library of Congress Catalog Card Number: 70-105861
Printed in the United States of America • J
ISBN 0-13-686238-1
Prentice-Hall International, Inc., London
Prentice-Hall of Australia, Pty. Ltd., Sydney
Prentice-Hall of Canada, Ltd., Toronto
Prentice-Hall of India Private Ltd., New Delhi
Prentice-Hall of Japan, Inc., Tokyo

Second printing...........October, 1971

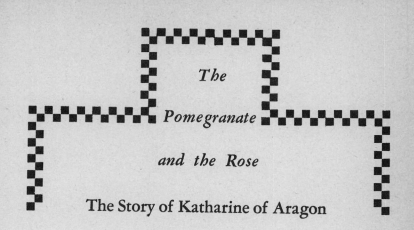

The Pomegranate and the Rose

The Story of Katharine of Aragon

Miniature of Katharine of Aragon.
By Lucas Horenbout [?]
(National Portrait Gallery, London)

Miniature of Henry VIII.
By Lucas Horenbout {?}
(Fitzwilliam Museum, Cambridge)

■▪■▪■▪■▪■▪■▪■ *Preface* ■▪■▪■▪■▪■▪■▪■

Much is known and much has already been written about Henry VIII's first wife, Katharine of Aragon, but what has been said before has often been biased by the religious and moral standpoint of the author and by the attitudes of the period in which he lived. I have tried to write without prejudice and without preconceptions as to who was good and who was bad. I have made no attempt to create atmosphere for which there is no evidence.

I have ignored the rumors and let the facts, which are fascinating, speak for themselves. The historical material available, though sometimes contradictory, is, however, so vast that the very act of selection can result in considerable differences of emphasis. Where there is a gap I have not filled it in; where the evidence is conflicting I have stated the opposing points of view.

There are more official papers dealing with Henry's separation from Katharine than there are for any other period of her life. The comparatively brief account given in this book paints, I believe, a correct picture and could also be a prelude to more reading in depth. It should be remembered that all negotiations about the so-called "divorce," as indeed is true of all events in her life, took place against a background of wars and threats of war, of intense diplomatic activity and of alliances and counter-alliances which are scarcely touched upon here.

I have paid special attention to some of the minor characters in the drama of Katharine's life as details about them are not easy to find—e.g., Elizabeth Blount, Henry VIII's first known mistress; Henry Fitzroy, Henry VIII's illegitimate son; and Vives, one of the first philosophers to concern himself with female education in England. The more famous, such as Thomas Wolsey, Thomas More, Thomas Cromwell, etc., have not lacked biographers.

As Katharine lived before the newly-invented printing press had time to standardize spelling, there are several ways of spelling her name. In Spain she was known as *Catalina.* In England she usually signed herself *Katharine* or *Katherine;* somewhat arbitrarily I have chosen the former. Spellings of other proper names are of my own choice though in general I have favored Spanish spellings of Spanish names.

Only contemporary or near-contemporary sources have been used—in particular, the English, Spanish and Venetian Letters and Papers of the period. Spelling has been modernized in all the quotations except in one letter from Katharine which is given as she wrote it. If the reader is encouraged to further research, the Selected Reading List which follows the Notes at the end of the book should prove helpful.

I would like to thank my family and friends for their advice and patience. My particular gratitude is, however, due to Miss Marian King, who first encouraged me to write, and to Mr. Legare Obear of the Library of Congress for his unfailing sympathy and help. I would also like to record my thanks to the librarians and staffs of the British Museum, the London Library and the Widener Library of Harvard University; to the Keeper of the Public Records and to the College of Heralds in London; to Mr. Roy Strong of The National Portrait Gallery; London; to Mrs. Marston of the Kennedy Institute of Politics, Harvard, and to Mrs. Senanayake-van Zeeland for their typing of the manuscript. Finally, I can only hope that the reader of this book obtains at least some of the pleasure I found in doing the research and writing.

■▼■▼■▼■▼■ Contents ■▼■▼■▼■▼■

St. Paul's Cathedral

Sunday, November 14, 1501

As Katharine passed through the triumphal arch and entered the great west door of St. Paul's Cathedral,[1] the trumpeters and minstrels in the gallery above played a great fanfare of welcome. Her dress was of white satin, as became a virgin bride, but it was made in a fashion new to England, with the skirt held out by hoops. On her auburn hair she wore a veil of white silk with a golden border enriched with pearls and precious stones. It covered most of her face and almost reached down to her waist. Her train was held by Lady Cecily of York, sister of the English Queen Elizabeth. She was escorted by the Spanish Duke of Cabra and a sturdy, fair-haired boy of ten, dressed in white velvet—Henry, Duke of York, the King of England's younger son. Behind her was a large retinue of richly-dressed lords and ladies, some of them dark-haired Spaniards and some fair-skinned English.

This was Katharine's wedding day, planned over thirteen years before, delayed time and time again, but at last really taking place. As to whether she was beautiful or not, opinions of the day differed. But she was young and small, appealing and attractive to the crowds which had turned out to greet her and take part in the festivities. No one can know what thoughts were passing through her mind as she prepared to walk up the aisle in the grand procession. It is possible, however, that she felt both relief and apprehension—relief that the last six months of arduous traveling were over and apprehension of what the future held in store.

It had been May when she said good-bye to her mother in Granada. Since then she had ridden over the hot, dusty roads of Spain and twice attempted the stormy seas separating her from the coast of England, which she had almost given up hope of seeing. In later years she was to say that this perilous crossing was an evil omen of what lay ahead of her. Katharine had been ill in Spain, both ill and frightened on the sea-crossing. Even after she was safe on dry land in Plymouth, it had taken her another five weeks of slow travel over rough English roads to reach London. There had been little time to rest and prepare herself for this great day which had been so long awaited and the details of which had been so minutely prepared.

Katharine was accustomed to royal grandeur and display, to pomp and ceremony. Her mother, Isabella, one of the best-dressed women in Europe, had also dressed her children in gorgeous clothes for state appearances. But the spectacle before her this day was truly magnificent even by Spanish standards. Henry VII, stingy as he was reputed to be, had more than relaxed his austerity for this great occasion, the marriage of his eldest child Arthur, Prince of Wales, to Katharine, Princess of Spain.

In the distance, a great rose window with seven tall windows beneath glowed at the east end of the vast Gothic cathedral. A long pathway of wood, five feet high and twelve feet broad with railings at each side, all covered with red worsted cloth, stretched the length of the nave in front of the Princess. It ended in a higher platform, surrounded on all sides by steps, the "high place" where the Archbishop of Canterbury was ready to receive her. Nineteen bishops and abbots were standing on the steps so as not to block the view from the congregation in the body of the church. The King and Queen were already in a little room over the north side of the high place, hidden from sight as they did not want to distract attention from the bride and bridegroom. The Lord Mayor and his company were on the south side.

The high walls of the cathedral were hung with rich tapestries. The November light outside was transmuted by the stained glass windows into glimmering jewels. The candles flickered, shedding their soft glow over the magnificent scene: the English court clad in costly apparel, silks and velvets embroidered and sparkling with precious stones; the Archbishop, bishops and abbots in their sumptuous, bright-colored vestments; and the Lord Mayor, resplendent in crimson velvet, accompanied by his sheriffs and aldermen in scarlet, wearing their gold chains of office. A living English tapestry stretched before Katharine. To the fanfare of trumpets she stepped forward over the red carpet to take her place in this tapestry, happily ignorant of how woven with sorrow her part in it was to be.

As she reached the high place, the trumpets stopped and the retinue was still. Prince Arthur, a slim pale boy of fifteen years, a few months younger than Katharine herself, and also dressed in white satin, had entered by a door in the north wall and was awaiting her. The banns were read. The Duke of Cabra gave her away, and the young couple were solemnly married by the Archbishop of Canterbury.

After the ceremony, which lasted more than three hours, the Archbishop, the bishops and abbots, the noble lords and then the noble ladies went in procession over a blue carpet laid on the marble floor of the choir to the high altar. The minstrels again struck up their joyful music as, hand in hand, Arthur and Katharine slowly followed. By the great carved screen leading to the choir they paused. They turned first to the south, then to the north, so that all could see them. But to them it must have been as if a sea of faces lay before them, so many people had crowded into the church. They entered through the door in the screen flanked by stone statues of former kings of England. They passed by the handsome carved stalls in the choir and the tomb of John of Gaunt, their common ancestor, where eight large tapers burned day and night, to kneel together before the high altar. When Mass had been sung, Arthur bestowed upon his wife her wedding portion, a deed to entitle her to a third of the revenue of Cornwall, Wales and Chester.

Arthur then left by the north door in order to be able to greet his bride in the Bishop of London's Palace. Katharine, again accompanied by the Duke of York, joined the procession going back through the nave. As they came out of the west door they were greeted by a magnificent pageant where former kings of England, Spain and France appeared in royal splendor. Also watching the spectacle were those citizens who had been unable to enter the crowded cathedral. Wine had been flowing freely from the conduits in the streets during the long ceremony and continued to do so all day, thus contributing much to the gaiety of the throng.

When the pageant was over, the procession continued across the yard to the Bishop of London's Palace where further festivities had been prepared. The Lord Mayor and many noble lords and ladies dined in the great hall where they were served with twelve dishes at the first course, fifteen at the second, and eighteen at the third course. The Princess and her company dined in another chamber where they were given the most delicate dainties that could be obtained in the whole realm of England and entertained by all manner of diversions.

At five o'clock in the evening the bridal pair were blessed and bedded according to the custom of the age for people of noble birth. In the words of the chronicler,[2] "After the congruent usages and customs in marriages of persons of noble blood, their said bed and lodging was blessed with the effusion of certain orisons thereunto limit and appropriate by the Bishops and Prelates there present . . . *and thus these worthy persons concluded and consummated the effects and complement of the sacrament of marriage."* *

* See footnote: Chapter 6: *The Court at Black Friars.*

1

Princess of Spain

1. *The European Background*

Katharine, daughter of Ferdinand and Isabella of Spain, and Arthur, son of Henry VII of England, were both born at the end of the fifteenth century, a period of great change in Europe. The Middle Ages were dying and modern Europe was taking shape. A New Learning was spreading from Italy; new lands were being discovered overseas; and new forms of government were developing. A new spirit of criticism also arose which was to question the power of the Holy Catholic Church. It was the time of the Renaissance and the period when the seeds of the Reformation were being sown.

Of course, there had always been change. The development of societies and nations never stands still. Some periods of time show little advance, some even regression, but there are milestones in history, important events which serve to mark the culminating point of gradual change. The milestone often said to distinguish this new age from the so-called Dark Ages preceding it is the fall of Constantinople to the

Turks in 1453. The great classical scholars who had been living in Constantinople were driven out. They came to Italy, bringing with them their ancient Greek and Latin manuscripts and an appreciation of the classical culture which had disappeared from Europe when Rome fell to the barbarians. The Renaissance had, however, started before 1453. The arrival of the scholars from Constantinople only gave a fillip to a movement which had begun, chiefly in Florence, about a hundred years earlier. Petrarch, Boccaccio and Dante in Italy, Chaucer in England, were among the forerunners of the new Humanism, as this revival of interest in art, letters, philosophy and science was called.

At the time of Katharine's birth, the Renaissance was in full swing. Raphael, Botticelli, Michelangelo, Ghirlandaio, Titian, Giorgione and Bellini, Leonardo da Vinci, Ariosto, Machiavelli and Copernicus were all alive. Their Humanist influence had already begun to spread to Spain and to the rest of Europe which were now ready to receive it. The less the nations had to cope with internal strife, the more time they had to devote to pursuits of the mind, to embark on less warlike adventures and to develop trade.

This was also the era of the great discoverers. Christopher Columbus had been in Portugal in 1486 when Bartholomew Diaz returned from his voyage round the Cape of Good Hope which opened up the eastern route to India for the Portuguese. Four years later, having persuaded Ferdinand and Isabella to finance him, Columbus set sail in search of a western route to China and Japan. As we now know, he landed in the West Indies. It was not Cathay but the New World he had discovered. However, though he was given a glorious welcome in Spain on his return, which Katharine must have heard about and may have witnessed, he was never to benefit personally from his discovery. He died neglected and the Crown of Aragon and Castile inherited the treasures of the Indies. But the way was now open for other adventurers to search for new lands and, above all, new sources of wealth. Amerigo Vespucci, carrying out some of the plans made by Columbus, landed on the north coast of South America at about the same time as Cabot reached Newfoundland from England. The year 1485 also saw the birth of Cortez, whose discovery of Mexico was to make Spain even richer than before.

In the days of medieval feudalism, the royal dukes and barons, the bishops and other church dignitaries had ruled over their vast estates from their own personal courts. With the help of their own private armies, they had waged war on each other and often possessed more real power than the king to whom they owed allegiance. But this power was now breaking down. The nobles were losing their authority and the king was beginning to take control. As a result, nations were becoming important as nations. Italy alone remained divided. City states such as Florence, Milan, Mantua, Ferrara, as well as the Papal States, still continued as separate entities.

The most important nations were France, the Holy Roman Empire, Spain and England. But Brittany was then still separate from France, Scotland from England and, as it still is today, Portugal from Spain. France and Brittany were united in 1491 when Charles VIII married the Duchess Anne. Together, the two countries then became perhaps the strongest in Europe. As their barons had been subjugated earlier than in other countries, the French kings had also had more time to consolidate their power. The Holy Roman Empire which had declined since the days of Charlemagne was beginning to revive under the rule of Maximilian I. It was known as the Hapsburg Empire after the name of his family. It consisted chiefly of parts of Germany, Austria, Hungary and, through Maximilian's marriage, Burgundy.

When Katharine was a child, Maximilian reigned over the Hapsburg territories with only the title of King of the Romans. He was not made Emperor until 1503. By his marriage to Mary of Burgundy he had two children, Philip and Margaret. Louis XII had succeeded Charles VIII as King of France and was much feared by Maximilian and the rulers of both Spain and England for the power he had already gained in Europe. Katharine's parents, Ferdinand and Isabella, ruled over the whole of Spain except the Kingdom of Granada in the south, which was held by the Moors, and the tiny Kindom of Navarre in the north, which was held by the French; in addition, Ferdinand was King of Naples and of the Two Sicilies. Henry VII had just ascended the English throne. It is with these two countries, England and Spain, and their royal families that we are particularly concerned. Three of the royal children are the chief characters in this story—Katharine, Arthur, and Henry VIII.

Children were of great importance to the royal houses of Europe, not only to ensure the continuation of the dynasty and the policies of the reigning monarch, but also as a means of cementing alliances with other nations. Marriages were arranged with other royal children, often when they were still in the cradle. The children were pawns in the royal game of diplomacy. Only rarely were they able to exercise personal choice in the selection of their partners. Suitability of those to be betrothed was determined by politics. This attitude was summed up in the family motto of the Hapsburgs which may be translated as, "Let others wage war; thou, happy Austria, wed," though, in fact, both wars and marriages were common to all the royal families of Europe. The idea of dynastic marriages was not new, but it became an increasingly important factor in the policy of the day as nations themselves became more important and it was necessary to regulate the balance of power.

Five of the children born to Ferdinand and Isabella lived to become part of the dynastic schemes of their parents, though some of them only briefly. By means of the marriages arranged for them, Spain became allied to Portugal, Austria, the Netherlands and England. But the schemes did not work out quite as expected. After the deaths of Ferdinand and Isabella, Spain as such lost national importance and became part of the empire of their grandson Charles V.

Henry VII of England and his Queen Elizabeth had four children whose marriages were carefully planned in an attempt to maintain the power of the House of Tudor in Europe. Both their sons were eventually married to Katharine in order to consolidate the Spanish alliance. One daughter married into Scotland and the other into France. However, only one of these marriages was to achieve the desired effect. The alliances made with France and Spain came to nothing. But the marriage Henry VII arranged for his daughter Margaret with James IV of Scotland ultimately brought about the real union of England and Scotland. But this is looking far ahead, nearly seventy years after the death of Katharine herself. What we must now consider is what had been happening in Spain about the time of her birth.

2. Spain

Spain was then inhabited by both Moslem Moors and Spanish Catholics. The Moors had come from North Africa in the eighth century. They had overrun the country and settled there, pushing the former inhabitants into the northwest corner of Spain. In the course of time, the Spaniards had gradually gathered strength again and begun in their turn to push the Moors further and further south. The reconquest was, however, slow, for Spain became divided into kingdoms which warred against each other as much as against the Moors. In the fifteenth century, the most important of these Catholic kingdoms were Aragon and Castile. In 1469, Isabella of Castile married her cousin Ferdinand of Aragon when she was eighteen years old and he nineteen. By this act the unification of Spain was begun; it was to be completed in 1492 when together *Los Reyos Catolicos,* the Catholic Monarchs, finally conquered Granada and overcame the last of the Moors.

Isabella, however, had not become Queen of Castile without a struggle. The direct heir to the throne was her half-niece Juana la Beltraneja, but a large faction in the kingdom refused to acknowledge her and supported Isabella's younger brother instead. Isabella first fought on his behalf but, when he was killed in battle, she was persuaded to become the Pretender. She succeeded only because Juana was declared illegitimate. Isabella then had to fight the Portuguese, who invaded Spain in support of Juana. But these early battlefields were Isabella's proving ground where she learned much about soldiering and diplomacy which was to stand her in good stead later in life. It was at this time that her appearance in armor first became familiar to her subjects.

Various obstacles also impeded Isabella's marriage to Ferdinand. There were other suitors, including a Prince of England (probably the Duke of Gloucester who became Richard III); and, although the ordinary people favored Ferdinand, he was not the choice of the King of Castile. Moreover, there was no love lost between the nobles of the two kingdoms. The story was told that Ferdinand had to disguise himself as a mule driver in order to travel safely to Valladolid where Isabella was staying. Once they were united, however, Isabella and Ferdinand became the most powerful monarchs Spain had ever known. They did not always agree but, whatever their domestic difficulties, they managed to present a united front in public. Isabella's vision was aided by Ferdinand's guile and both were ruthless in their efforts to make Spain safe for Catholicism and a power to be reckoned with in Europe. Here alone in all Europe the Reformation did not penetrate and any questioning of the established faith was dealt with forcibly by the Inquisition.

The Inquisition was aimed at those who did not believe in, or practice, the Catholic faith—that is to say, the unconverted Moors and Jews, both rich and powerful sections of the community. The state treasury was empty because of the expense of the long drawn-out wars and more money was urgently needed. It was possible at that time to raise money by confiscating the property of criminals. By creating a new class of criminal, a new source of revenue could be obtained. A notice was therefore fastened on all church doors to say that sinners must confess within fifteen days. Anyone who did not confess to the sinfulness of his former religion was regarded as a sinner and a criminal. The penalty was either imprisonment or burning at the stake. Those who were condemned and those who fled the country in order to escape punishment forfeited their possessions to the Crown.

Torquemada was made head of the investigations and his name has become inseparable from the tortures which were inflicted under his authority. The Inquisition was not new but it was given newer and fuller powers at this time. Many people objected, including the Pope, but Ferdinand and Isabella overruled their objections. Two thousand people are said to have been burned. Many escaped the penalty by fleeing the country, leaving behind their worldly wealth but taking with them their culture and learning. When it was suggested that Spain could not afford to lose so many people, Isabella replied that it was better for the country to be depopulated than to be polluted by heresy. No mention was made of the financial gain to her coffers. Ferdinand and Isabella also tried to encourage other rulers to set up courts of Inquisition. One was indeed set up England, but it was operated with less enthusiasm and less cruelty than in Spain.

Although the Moors were the Infidels against whom Catholic fervor was roused, it must not be thought that they were backward in culture or education. To appreciate this, one has only to look at their monuments which have survived to the present day, such as the Palace of the Alhambra or the Mosque in Cordoba. They had a university, a fleet, an army. Their numerals superseded the Roman letter numerals and we still use them. If cleanliness is a sign of civilization—it was certainly an accompaniment of Roman civilization—it was shown by the number of public baths found in Moorish cities. The comparative dirtiness of the conquerors has been said to be a direct reaction against the cleanliness of the conquered. It has also been said—though with what truth is open to conjecture—that Isabella herself had only one bath in her life and that was on the eve of her marriage.

3. The Fall of Granada

The last great campaign against the Moors began in 1490 when Ferdinand, accompanied by his twelve-year-old son Juan, besieged the city of Granada. The rest of the province had already been subdued and many refugees had taken shelter behind its walls. Ferdinand's army of 50,000 (some historians say even more) camped on the plain within sight of the red walls and towers of the fortress on the hill. The strength of the battlements gave no indication of the deli-

cate beauty of the Alhambra Palace behind. Ferdinand at
first made no attempt to draw the enemy into battle. During
the winter he prepared for a campaign similar to one he had
already conducted at Ronda, to starve the city into surrender.
As soon as spring came, he started to lay waste the countryside around, collecting the spoils for the use of his own army
and thus depriving the besieged Moors of the supplies they
so badly needed.

At this time, Isabella and the royal children, accompanied by their ladies-in-waiting, came to join Ferdinand
and live in the camp. Isabella was in armor and rode around
superintending operations, cheering the soldiers by her presence. Katharine, then about five years old, lived in one
of the elegant pavilions near her mother. One night, the
hangings of Isabella's pavilion accidently caught fire. The
flames quickly spread to the neighboring tents and both she
and the royal princesses were in danger of their lives. Soon
the whole camp was alight and in great confusion. No one
knew what had happened and thought that the Moors had
come upon them unnoticed. It seems the Moors were equally
bewildered at the sight of this vast bonfire in the enemy's
camp which they knew they had not kindled, for they did
not take advantage of the enemy's disarray to launch an
attack. However, once Ferdinand realized the true situation,
he and his army used all their efforts to quench the fire,
which eventually burned itself out. The next morning, when
they looked around, the camp was destroyed together with
many valuables belonging to the nobles, but no lives had been
lost.

To prevent the possibility of such a thing happening
again, Ferdinand and Isabella decided to build a permanent
camp. In the short space of three months a new city of stone
was built. It was made in the shape of a rectangle and

its two main streets intersected in the middle to form a cross. They called it Santa Fe. Meanwhile the Moors were beginning to feel the effects of the famine imposed upon them by Ferdinand. In October, they started to sue for peace. The negotiations were complicated by differences of opinion in Granada but eventually were successfully concluded. On January 2, 1492, the siege was over.

On this day, the Spanish army formed itself into a great procession with Ferdinand and Isabella at its head. They marched out of Santa Fe and took up their positions at the foot of the hill while a column under the leadership of Cardinal Mendoza went ahead bearing Ferdinand's silver cross and the royal standards. At the same time, the Moorish King, with his family and fifty retainers, came down from the castle. He stopped when he reached the main part of the Spanish army and as he handed over the keys to Ferdinand, he said, "They are thine, O King, since Allah so decrees it: use thy success with clemency and moderation".[1] He then continued sadly on his way. The story is also told that he drew up his horse on a hill at a place now called *El Ultimo Sospiro del Moro* (The Last Sigh of the Moor) to take one last look at the beautiful city he would never see again. When his mother saw the tears which welled in his eyes, she said, "You do well to weep like a woman for what you could not defend as a man".[2]

Meanwhile, the Catholic Monarchs with their children and the rest of the army waited until the sign and token of the cross had been raised on the highest tower of the Alhambra and the standards of St. James and the banners of Ferdinand and Isabella were flying from every turret and pinnacle in the city before they too went forward in all their splendor to take possession. A herald then proclaimed from the top of the high tower:

Saint James, Saint James, Saint James, Castile, Castile, Castile, Granada, Granada, Granada: by high and
mighty power, Lord Ferdinand and Isabella, King
and Queen of Spain, have won from the Infidels and
Moors the city and realm of Granada. . . .[3]

Over seven hundred years of Moorish rule ended on this
day. The news was received with great joy throughout the
Christian world and the event was celebrated both by the
Pope in St. Peter's, Rome, and by the Archbishop of Canterbury in St. Paul's, London.

Katharine and her brothers and sisters were present at
the ceremony in Granada but the younger ones could not
have appreciated its exact significance. In the summers that
followed, however, the fairy-tale architecture of the wonder-
ful palace, the gardens and courts full of the scent of orange
and myrtle and roses, the sound of fountains and running
water, the breathtaking views of the Sierra Nevada framed
in the Moorish windows, could not have failed to delight
them. Isabella herself loved Granada so much that she
chose it for her last resting place.

The Fall of Granada was the event which marked the
end of Moorish rule in Spain but, in fact, the Moors held out
for some time afterward in isolated pockets so that Ferdinand
and Isabella could not altogether relax their vigilance. The
main force of the enemy was broken, however, which enabled
the Catholic Monarchs to turn their attention to other things
than war. As they proceeded to strengthen the courts of the
Inquisition, expel the Jews, finance Columbus and expand
the machinery set up to govern that part of the country
already under their control, they also were able to take their
part in maintaining the balance of power in Europe. They
had more time to further the marriage alliances they had
planned for their children.

4. *The Spanish Royal Family*

Katharine was the youngest of five children of Ferdinand and Isabella. She was born on December 15 (or 16), 1485. In the spring of that year her father had led his army against the Moorish enemy in the picturesque hilltop town of Ronda in the southern part of the province of Granada. By May he had destroyed the town and had come to join Isabella in Cordoba to celebrate the victory. Together, they and the royal children and the court journeyed northward to Alcala de Henares,⁴ where they wintered in the palace of the Archbishop of Toledo to await the birth of the child Isabella was expecting.

There was then no permanent capital or seat of government in Spain as London and Paris had become in England and France—Madrid did not become the capital until 1560. The seat of government was where Ferdinand and Isabella chose to reside and they were always moving from one place to another. When they moved, their ministers, state papers and officers of their household traveled with them. There were several reasons for this peripatetic life. As long as the fighting continued, Ferdinand and Isabella had to be in the south. But they could not ignore the rest of the country. They had to ensure that their laws were obeyed and that order was maintained. Only with their united rule had comparative peace come to the north and they did not want to lose it. But there were also the same reasons that made other royal households of the period change their places of residence from time to time. As sanitation was primitive, elementary hygiene demanded that a large number of people should not live too long in one place. It was also necessary to change residences in order to obtain new food supplies since in general the court lived off the land around the palace.

The Spanish royal children were thus all born in different places. Their early lives were spent either in luxurious tents near the battlefields or, when there was no fighting, in castles in different parts of Spain. When Katharine was born, her eldest sister Isabel, was already fifteen; her only brother Juan, was seven; Juana was five and Maria three years old.

From contemporary accounts we have some idea of the appearance of the family. Ferdinand was considered hand- some when he married. He had a smiling face. His skin was bronzed and he had a high forehead. His hair was dark and his eyes were brown, with a slight squint in the left one. His frame was sturdy and muscular and he was slightly shorter than Isabella, who herself was not tall. She was quite a different type. Her hair was reddish-blonde and her eyes between blue and green—"the handsomest lady whom I ever beheld," said one of her household flatteringly, though not necessarily truthfully. Both were excessively religious, but Isabella more so than Ferdinand.

The eldest daughter was tall and thin and probably suf- fered from tuberculosis, a prevalent disease at the time. It is likely that her brother Juan and Henry VII of England and his son Arthur were all tubercular. Isabel was as pious as her mother but less active and forceful both in character and religion. She preferred the quite contemplative life and would rather have lived in a convent than marry into Portugal. Juana has been described both as the beauty of the family and as lacking in physical charm. From the por- traits now thought to be of her, it is difficult to tell which opinion is true. She had dark hair and eyes and is thought to have resembled her father; she had the same slight squint in one eye. Katharine was a sturdier child, though not very tall. She had fair hair tending toward red and in general was more like her mother. We do not know what Maria looked like. Juan, as heir, was brought up apart from the rest of the family. He had his own royal court with his own officers and household. Isabella's pet name for him was "my angel," perhaps referring to his fair hair and fragile appearance for he seems to have been delicate. It is doubtful, however, whether he was really a good-looking boy for he had something wrong with his lower lip. He also stuttered.

Isabella never received any formal education during the turbulent days of her youth. She had passed the early part of her life in a convent and was certainly well-versed in all religious matters. She had also learned how to sew and embroider and how to ride horseback, but she knew no language other than Castilian, the form of Spanish which was to become the official language of Spain. Ferdinand had even less learning though he became extremely experienced in politics and warfare. Ferdinand and Isabella, however, were determined that their children should have the best education of the day. This was the age of great teachers, and both the Spanish and English royal children were to benefit.

Scholars were brought from Italy to teach at the Spanish court. Among them was Alessandro Geraldini, who became Katharine's tutor and stayed with her for many years. Foreign books were also welcomed and were allowed into the country free of duty. Ferdinand and Isabella saw that the New Learning would help prepare their children for the parts they were to play on the European stage. In addition to the domestic arts, including sewing and embroidery which were always to be a comfort to Katharine, the girls probably learned Latin, philosophy, grammar, theology, music and some languages, though Katharine does not seem to have been proficient in any European language but her own when she first arrived in England. She had, however, corresponded with Arthur in Latin.

The children were all brought up in the Catholic faith and made to perform its rites with the same fanatic zeal as their parents. Juana was the only one who would not conform and as a result was severely punished by her mother. She was reputed to be the most brilliant of the children and perhaps for that reason dared to question Isabella's crusading beliefs. The age was a tough and harsh one and many cruelties were perpetrated in the name of the Catholic Church. It is unlikely that the children were entirely unaware of what had happened to the infidel in their midst, but they must have accepted these acts as natural phenomena of the times. Pity and charity were kept for the poor, not for the heretic.

5. *Marriage Plans for the Family*

By the time Katharine was three years old, marriage plans had been made for all the children except Maria. The eldest sister was the first to leave home. The Spanish royal family all took part in a magnificent ceremony in the vast Cathedral of Seville when Isabel, then about nineteen years old, attended by seventy maids of honor, was formally betrothed with great pomp to Prince Alfonso of Portugal. She had been pledged to him when a baby as the price of peace between the two countries and the time had now come for the promise to be fulfilled. In the autumn, she said goodbye to her family and, escorted by the Cardinal of Spain and a train of nobles and ladies, made her way into Portugal. The wedding took place in November. Eight months later, Alfonso was thrown from his horse and killed. Isabel came home to Spain, seeking in her grief to retire into a convent.

The Spanish court went into mourning with her, only casting it aside to celebrate the march into Granada. The Portuguese, however, were as anxious as her parents to continue the alliance. So, before long, Isabel was going obediently, if unwillingly, back to Portugal to marry Manuel, her late husband's cousin and heir. As the price of her return, the Spanish Monarchs extracted from the Portuguese the promise that they would expel any Jews who had taken refuge in their country when driven out of Spain by the Inquisition.

About the time Isabel's betrothal took place in Seville, Maximilian suggested a marriage alliance between his son Philip the Handsome and one of the Spanish Princesses, Juana or Maria. They were then considered too young to leave home, but the idea was not forgotten. Several years later, a double alliance was made with the Hapsburgs. In 1496, after a betrothal ceremony in Valladolid, Juana was taken to the coast and seen on board ship by Isabella and the other children. With a great armada, she sailed across the same sort of stormy sea in the Bay of Biscay that her youngest sister was to brave five years later. After a long rough crossing, she reached the coast of Flanders. She married Philip in the fall with none of her own family present. The following spring, the ships returned to Spain bringing with them Maximilian's daughter Margaret. She was then married with great pomp to Juan, heir to the kingdoms of both Aragon and Castile.

Although Katharine was named after Isabella's partly English grandmother,[5] Isabella could not already have been thinking of an English marriage alliance for her daughter. Henry VII had only been crowned six weeks before Katharine's birth and his son Arthur was not born until nine months afterward. Almost immediately the idea seems to have arisen in both countries to arrange a match between the two children. Before Katharine was two years old feelers had been put out from England. In 1487 or 1488, Ferdinand and Isabella sent Dr. Roderigo Gonsalez de Puebla, with Juan de Sepulveda to assist him, to England to open negotiations. After having received the ambassadors in London, Henry VII sent them into the country to visit Arthur, who was at that time about twenty months old. They were shown the infant dressed, undressed, awake and asleep. Dr. de Puebla reported back to Spain, "He appeared to us so admirable that, whatever praise, commendation, or flattery anyone might be capable of speaking or writing would only be truth in this case." [6]

When Katharine was three years old, a delegation from England arrived at the Spanish court to continue the negotiations. The English ambassadors were Thomas Savage and Richard Nanfan, attended by one of the King's Heralds. On the way, they were joined by Dr. de Puebla and de Sepulveda. They traveled in the depths of winter and, as always seemed to happen in the rough seas between the two countries, had a perilous and stormy journey in their little top-heavy sailing vessels. They left London on December 21 and did not reach Spain until February 16. They were held up by snow when they landed and then had difficulty in locating Ferdinand and his court. They had to wait three more weeks before they finally had an audience with the Catholic Monarchs in their large and imposing castle at Medina del Campo.

Roger de Machado had the task of keeping the record of the visit. It has come down to us as he wrote it, rather verbose and in French.[7] He gives a very detailed description of the splendid reception they were given and obviously had a keen eye for clothes which he describes in much detail. Perhaps he knew that the ladies of the English court would be all agog to know what was being worn in Spain:

March 14, 1489

Richmond rode before the Ambassadors wearing a rich coat of arms richly embroidered with the arms of England. . . . It was about seven o'clock in the evening before the said ambassadors were sent for, and the daylight was failing, but they were sent for with a great attendance of torches. . . .

They found the kings in a great room seated under a rich cloth of gold of state; and in the middle of this great cloth of state was an escutcheon quartered with the Arms of Castile and Aragon. And the King was dressed in a rich robe of cloth of gold, woven entirely of gold, and furred with a rich trimming of fine sable; and the queen was seated beside him dressed in a rich robe of the same woven cloth of gold in the fashion of the country. . . . And over the said robe a riding hood of black velvet, all slashed in large holes so as to show under the said velvet the cloth of gold in which she was dressed. . . .

The said Queen wore round her waist a girdle of white leather made in the style that men usually wear: [of] which girdle the pouch was decorated with a large ruby the size of a tennis ball, between five rich diamonds and other precious stones the size of a bean. And the rest of the girdle was decorated with a great number of other precious stones.

She wore on her neck a rich gold necklace composed entirely of red and white roses, each rose being adorned with a large jewel. Besides this she had two ribbons suspended each side of her breast, adorned with large diamonds, rubies, pearls, and various other jewels of great value to the number of a hundred or more. Over all this dress she wore a short cloak of fine crimson satin furred with ermine, very handsome in appearance and very brilliant. . . . Her head was uncovered except only a little "coiffe de plaisance" at the back of her head without anything else. Truly as I believe, and also as I heard it said at the time, I

estimate the dress that she then wore at the value of
two hundred thousand crowns of gold.

Two hundred thousand crowns was the sum which had
been agreed upon for Katharine's dowry.

There were many more receptions and Isabella's clothes
were always as sumptuous as those described. She never wore
the same dress twice. Jousting, dancing and feasting were
provided as entertainment, but Machado was not as en-
thusiastic in his descriptions of these as he was of the
fashions.

The ambassadors saw Prince Juan, then not quite eleven
years old, and the Princess Isabel, who was about seventeen
at the time. At last, on March 24, they met Katharine in the
company of her sisters:

> . . . all of these dressed in cloth of gold. They were
> attended by fourteen maidens, the eldest of them not
> more than fourteen years old. It was a beautiful sight
> to see the richness of their dresses. . . . And on the
> 25th day of this same month of March the said Kings
> made another festival in honour of these ambassadors,
> to wit, a bull fight. . . . And it was beautiful to see
> how the Queen held up her youngest daughter, who
> was the Infanta donna Katharina, Princess of Wales;
> and at that time she was three years of age.[8]

From this time she was known in Spain, as well as in
England, as Princess of Wales.

Other entertainments followed, but business was eventually
discussed on March 26 and 27, when there was some tough
negotiating about the amount of the dowry and the general
terms of the alliance. When the talks were over, the ambassadors escorted Ferdinand, Isabella, Juan and the four
Princesses out of town before they themselves left on their
homeward journey.

By September 1497, Ferdinand and Isabella were content. Isabel, Juan and Juana were married where their parents wanted them to be. Katharine's betrothal to Arthur had been reaffirmed in England the previous month when the Spanish ambassador had stood proxy for her. Maria was the only one of the children for whom no arrangements had yet been made. These marriages clinched the alliances with Portugal, the Empire and England. France, the enemy, was surrounded by allies of Spain.

This peak of contentment however, did not last long. As fast as the marriages had been made, they came toppling to disaster. Isabella's health also started to fail at this time, so she was consequently less able to bear stoically these blows of fate. First Juan died in Avila, just six months after his marriage, probably from tuberculosis, though sexual excess has also been suggested as a cause of his early death. Ferdinand was with him at the end, but Isabella was too ill to make the journey. His widow, Margaret, was pregnant so there was still hope that there would be a grandson to take Juan's place as heir to Castile and Aragon. Early the following year, a son was born to Margaret, but their hopes were dashed when the child was born dead. Margaret had failed them, so she returned home. There were no other royal Spanish sons to whom she could be married.

In August, Isabel came home from Portugal in order to be near her mother when she had her baby. After having given birth to a son, she died in her mother's arms. The child was named Miguel. He was left by his father in the care of Isabella, who found consolation and pleasure in his presence. Not only was he her only grandchild, but he was also the heir to the thrones of both Portugal and Spain. In May 1499, Isabella set out for Granada, taking with her Maria, Katharine and Miguel. Isabella was still feeling ill. She was not yet fifty but this was considered old in those days. She had, however, enough of her old spirit left to engineer yet one more marriage. The following year Maria was sent to Portugal to marry King Manuel, her late sister's husband. This alliance became even more important to Isabella when shortly afterward her grandson Miguel died. But, though both Maria and Manuel survived to produce several children, the marriage did not succeed in uniting the two countries. Eventually, one of Maria's sons inherited the Portuguese throne. Isabella's hopes for succession to the throne of Aragon and Castile depended on a child she had never seen and never would see who had just been born in Flanders to Juana and Philip—the future Emperor Charles the Fifth. Later, Charles married one of Maria's daughters and Maria's son and heir married one of Charles's sisters, but the countries remained separate.

Juana's story is perhaps the most tragic of all the tragic stories attached to Isabella's children. She had never been on good terms with her mother and had often been severely punished for being stubborn and disobedient. She, therefore, left home willingly to marry Philip even though she had never seen him. She then fell passionately in love with him. Philip, however, was not in love with Juana. He was unfaithful and cruel, greedy only for her inheritance when eventually, after the deaths of her brother Juan, her sister Isabel and Isabel's son, she became next in line to the thrones of Castile and Aragon. In fact, Philip died before she did, but not before he and Ferdinand had both conspired against her. She spent most of the rest of her life locked in lonely castles, said to be mad. Whether she had gone mad at an early age and was badly treated because of this or whether the treatment she received turned her mad we shall never know. But her eldest son, Charles, continued the cruel treatment after Ferdinand died, until there was no doubt that she was insane. He then governed Spain in her stead. From the age of 30, when Philip died, to the age of 76, when she at last died herself, Juana never knew freedom. Ironically, she was the only one of Isabella's children who lived to be old.

But Isabella was to know nothing of this. She heard disturbing reports of Juana's behavior, but there were at any rate apparently healthy grandchildren as a consolation. Grief-stricken as she was at the deaths which had overtaken her family, she was perhaps glad to have her youngest child still by her side.

6. *Farewell to Spain*

Katharine was the only daughter left at home in the sorrowing Spanish court. In England they had long been waiting for her arrival. Her marriage by proxy had taken place several times but still her departure was delayed and the argument about her dowry continued. In England, the legal age at which a girl could marry was when she had finished her twelfth year; for a boy it was when he finished his fourteenth.[9] The real marriage, therefore, could not have taken place before Arthur's fourteenth birthday on September 22, 1501. To be on the safe side they obtained a special dispensation from the Pope, but it turned out not to be necessary.

In spite of having given their consent many times, Ferdinand and Isabella were not altogether convinced that the English alliance was the ideal one for Katharine. They wavered over the contract, sometimes encouraging it, sometimes seeming about to discard it. They wanted England as an ally against France but were not sure how reliable Henry VII was or how securely he held the throne. Not until other contenders had been subdued and the Earl of Warwick, his adversary with the strongest claim, executed in 1499, were they prepared to let Katharine leave. By then, the Catholic Monarchs were overwhelmed by the series of domestic tragedies which had overtaken them and Isabella's health had quite broken down. Perhaps too she was afraid to let her last child go to this unknown country which, from the reports of her ambassadors, did not sound very attractive.

One of her ambassadors, Don Pedro de Ayala, wrote in 1498:

> The King of England is less rich than generally said. He likes to be thought very rich, because such a belief is advantageous to him. . . . The King himself said to me, that it is his intention to keep his subjects low, because riches would only make them haughty. . . . He is disliked but the Queen beloved, because she is powerless. . . . The King looks old for his years, but young for the sorrowful life he has led. . . . He likes to be much spoken of, and to be highly appreciated by the whole world. He fails in this because he is not a great man. Although he professes many virtues, his love of money is too great.
>
> Though it is not my business to give advice, I take the liberty to say that it would be a good thing if she were to come soon, in order to accustom herself to the ways of life in this country and learn the language. On the other hand, when one sees and knows the manners and the way of life of people in this island, one cannot deny the grave inconveniences of her coming to England before she is of age. You know the reasons. They are many. But the Princess can only be expected to lead a happy life through not remembering those things which would make her less enjoy what she would find here. It would, therefore, still be best to send her directly, and before she has learnt fully to appreciate our habit of life and our government.[10]

Dr. de Puebla, the other ambassador, reported that the King and Queen of England "wish that the Princess of Wales should accustom herself to drink wine. The water of England is not drinkable and even if it were, the climate would not allow one to do so." He then added some words of comfort: "The English are of a very changeable character, and it is difficult to negotiate with them. As soon, however, as they have bound themselves by a treaty, they keep it and are very reliable." [11]

Henry VII's well-known eye for a pretty girl was apparent in the message: "The King and Queen wish very much that the ladies who are to accompany the Princess of Wales should be of gentle birth and beautiful or at least that none of them should be ugly."[12] It could be expected that if the ladies were attractive they might also find English husbands and so help to cement the alliance.

When Katharine was twelve, she and Arthur were allowed to write to each other. As neither knew the other's language, they had to correspond in Latin. Their stilted letters sound more like exercises than spontaneous effusions of love though this is in part due to their being read in translation. In a letter dated October 5, 1499, Arthur wrote from Ludlow:

> Most excellent and illustrious lady, my dearest spouse, I wish you very much health, with my hearty commendation.
>
> I have read the most sweet letters of your Highness lately given to me, from which I have easily perceived your most entire love to me. Truly those your letters, traced by your own hand, have so delighted me, and have rendered me so cheerful and jocund, that I fancied I beheld your Highness and conversed with and embraced my dearest wife. I cannot tell you what an earnest desire I feel to see your Highness, and how vexatious to me is this procrastination about your

coming. I owe eternal thanks to your excellence that
you so lovingly correspond to this my so ardent love.
Let it continue, I entreat, as it has begun; and, like as
I cherish your sweet remembrance night and day, so
do you preserve my name ever fresh in your breast.
And let your coming to me be hastened, that instead
of being absent we may be present with each other,
and the love conceived between us and the wished-for
joys may reap their proper fruit. . . .[13]

The marriage settlement had been a matter of considerable
debate between the representatives of the two wily Kings
ever since the negotiations had started. It was decided in the
end that Katharine's portion should be 200,000 golden
crowns, half of which was to be paid *after* the real marriage
had taken place and the other half within two years. Ferdinand wanted to pay in crowns of Castile and Aragon, not in
English money as this was subject to fluctuation. There was a
further complication as to whether her plate and jewels
should be included or not. In return, Katharine was to receive
one third of the revenues of Wales, Cornwall and Chester.
Ferdinand and Henry also inserted clauses ensuring the
alliance of Spain and England against France should the
need arise.

Dr. de Puebla began to fear that the negotiations would
never end. Soon, however, it became clear that Katharine
would definitely be coming to England and endless preparations were made to receive her. She was expected first
at the end of July, then the end of September, then in June
of the following year. But her own health and her mother's
were giving them trouble and still she did not leave.

Dr. de Puebla reported on the lavish welcome being prepared for her in England and the vast amount of money that
was being spent. But Isabella in her grief and ill-health did

not react very favorably toward these planned extravagances. Gone were the days of dresses valued at 200,000 crowns; now she wore only black robes. Her reply from Granada was simple and moving:

> I am pleased to hear it, because it shows the magnificent grandeur of my brother [the King of England], and because demonstrations of joy at the reception of my daughter are naturally agreeable to me. Nevertheless it would be more in accordance with my feelings, and with the wishes of my Lord [King Ferdinand] if the expenses were moderate. We do not wish that our daughter should be the cause of any loss to England, neither in money nor in any other respect. On the contrary, we desire that she should be the source of all kinds of happiness, as we hope she will be, with the help of God. We, therefore, beg the King, my brother, to moderate the expenses. Rejoicings may be held, but we ardently implore him that the substantial part of the festival should be his love; that the Princess should be treated by him and by the Queen as their true daughter, and by the Prince of Wales as we feel sure he will treat her.[14]

Katharine herself was prepared for the journey with fine new clothes and 35,000 crowns worth of gold and silver plate and jewels. But even so she did not depart in as much grandeur as her sisters had done before her. She took with her as her personal badge the pomegranate, the emblem of Granada. This has been said to be a symbol of fertility, showing wishful thinking on the part of those who chose it.

At last, on May 24, 1501, still not feeling well, Katharine left Granada. She said good-bye to her mother, whom she was never to see again, and set off on her long, slow journey. Isabella was not strong enough to accompany her. Ferdinand had just come back from Ronda on May 15 where he had

had to put down an insurrection. Katharine had waited in order to say good-bye to him too. For two months, she and her train of one hundred and fifty attendants filed northwestward across Spain in the heat of the summer until they reached Corunna on July 20. With her was Donna Elvira Manuel, who was to stay with her in England and be her companion, and an archbishop with two other prelates, who were to take the place of her parents at the wedding. Besides these, her tutor (Geraldini), her ladies-in-waiting (presumably young and good looking as requested), her doctor, cupbearer, cook, barber, steward, butler and every other servant she might need went with her.

She stayed a month in Corunna where the ships were awaiting her and then, on August 21, she left her native country and set sail for England. Four days later she was back a little further along the coast, in Laredo. Rough seas had driven them ashore and one of the ships was missing. Here she stayed sick and miserable until Henry, tired of waiting, sent one of his sailors, Stephen Brett, to pilot them across the Bay of Biscay to England's southern shore.

On September 26, they set sail again but only to meet more terrible storms. The wind and the waves battered their little ships and Katharine, although she had been brought up to be brave, was sick and terrified. At last, after six days at sea, they sighted the English coast. Plans had been made to welcome Katharine at Southampton, but Brett was glad to land her party where he could. On October 2, 1501, they docked at Plymouth and Katharine first set foot on English soil.

Thought to be Katharine of Aragon as a young girl. By Michel Sittow.
(*Kunsthistorisches Museum, Vienna*)

Now thought to be Katharine; formerly thought to be Juana. Certainly one of Isabella's daughters in Spain. By Juan de Flandes. (*Thyssen-Bornemisza, Lugano*)

Spain at the time of Katharine's birth.

Queen Isabella of Spain, mother of Katharine of Aragon. Artist unknown. (*Queen's Collection. Copyright reserved*)

King Ferdinand of Spain, father of Katharine of Aragon. Artist unknown. (*Queen's Collection. Copyright reserved*)

The Alhambra Palace in Granada, where Columbus is said to have been received by Ferdinand and Isabella. (*Spanish Tourist Office*)

Juana of Castile, sister of Katharine. By Juan de Flandes. (*Kunsthistorisches Museum, Vienna*)

Philip the Handsome, son of Maximilian and husband of Juana. By Juan de Flandes. (*Kunsthistorisches Museum, Vienna*)

Europe at the end of the Fifteenth Century.

2

Princess of Wales

1. The Tudors

Our King, he is the rose so red,
That now does flourish fresh and gay.
Confound his foes, Lord, we beseech,
And love his grace both night and day.
Anon.

Katharine must already have been told something of the English royal family and the history of the country where it was intended she should spend the rest of her life. England was now at peace after thirty years of civil war. The year of Katharine's birth had been the year in which the War of the Roses ended and Henry VII ascended the English throne.

The Wars of the Roses had their origin in a struggle for the throne between descendants of two sons of King Edward III—Edmund, Duke of York, and John of Gaunt, Duke of Lancaster. The House of York had taken as its emblem the White Rose and the House of Lancaster had chosen the Red

Rose. The war actually started when an attempt was made by the Yorkists to oust the Lancastrian King Henry VI from his throne. A bitter contest had continued between the two Houses until, in 1485, the Yorkist King Richard III was defeated and killed in the Battle of Bosworth Field by Henry Tudor, leader of the Lancastrians by tenuous right. Richard III had previously alienated so many of his followers by his cruelties that they had deserted and fought against him. In return for their support, Henry had promised that if he was successful he would unite both Houses by marrying Elizabeth of York.

Henry did not in fact marry Elizabeth until he was firmly established as King in his own right. Although it had never been customary in England for women to inherit the throne, Elizabeth could have been considered to have a stronger claim as she was directly descended through the male line from Edward III's son, Edmund, Duke of York. Henry, on the other hand, although descended from an older son of Edward III—John of Gaunt and his third wife—traced his descent through his mother and also came of a doubtful line: John of Gaunt had not married his third wife, Catherine Swynford, until after the birth of their children. The children were eventually legitimized but their descendants were prevented by an act of Parliament from inheriting the throne.

Henry's ancestry on his father's side was partly royal, but again was illegitimate. His father claimed descent from a semi-mythological Welsh King, Cadwallader. More immediately, he was descended from Owen Tudor, a Welshman of humble origin who had come to England to the court of Henry V. After the death of the King, the widowed Queen had borne Owen Tudor two sons who were brought up at court. Their father was driven away and was killed in the

Wars of the Roses, fighting on the Lancastrian side. One of the sons, Edmund, was created Earl of Richmond and married Margaret, daughter of the important Beaufort family. He too was killed fighting against the Yorkists just before the birth of his son who, after inheriting the title of Earl of Richmond, ascended the English throne as Henry VII.

Elizabeth's girlhood was spent in times of great danger. When Richard III usurped the throne after the death of her father, Edward IV, she and her sisters were taken by their mother to live in sanctuary in Westminster. Elizabeth's brothers—Edward, the rightful king, and Richard, Duke of York—were imprisoned in the Tower of London where they disappeared. There is some mystery as to the exact fate of the young princes. It is generally believed that they were murdered on the instructions of their uncle Richard III, but it has also been suggested that Henry VII may have been responsible. Richard promised that the lives of Elizabeth and her mother and sisters would be spared, so they came out of sanctuary. The legend is that Elizabeth was then kept in the castle of Sheriff Hutton in Yorkshire together with her kinsman the Earl of Warwick. After the Battle of Bosworth Field, she was brought to London to marry Henry VII, a marriage that she very much desired.

The union of the Red and the White Roses did not mean, however, that England was immediately at peace. There were several conspiracies producing Yorkist pretenders to the throne, the most important of whom were Lambert Simnel and Perkin Warbeck; the former claimed to be the Earl of Warwick and the latter the Duke of York, who had disappeared in the Tower. But Henry managed to overcome all opposition. In his efforts to maintain his own authority he eliminated the nobles he thought dangerous, including the Earl of Warwick.

It is possible that Warwick was beheaded to please Ferdinand and Isabella, who were anxious to see the English throne secure for their daughter. Shortly after his execution, they received a report from their ambassador in England, Dr. de Puebla, to inform them that this was now the case:

> This kingdom is at present so situated as has not been seen for the last five hundred years till now, as those say who know best, and as appears by the chronicles . . . so that not a doubtful drop of royal blood remains in this kingdom except the true blood of the King and Queen, and, above all, that of the Lord Prince Arthur.[1]

Katharine was to say later that her marriage was doomed because it had been made in blood.

Dr. de Puebla, however, was not quite accurate. Several descendents of Edward IV were still alive. The Queen had sisters. More important, she had a cousin, the Earl of Suffolk, who was destined to be a thorn in Henry's side. He became head of the Yorkist movement and fled to Europe just about the time Katharine came to England.

2. *The English Royal Family*

In 1501, Henry VII was forty-four years old and his Queen ten years younger. Henry was said to look more French than English. He also spoke French fluently as much of his youth had been spent in France. He was slim and of medium height. He had dark shoulder-length hair, small heavy-lidded eyes, a narrow face and a stern, thin-lipped expression. In the words of a ballad of the day:

> His face is white, the wart is red
> Thereby you may him ken.
>   Anon.

In his youth, he was reported to have been handsome, with pale gold hair and lively blue eyes. Now, he was sallow, prematurely old and afflicted with pains in his joints. His hair was thin and white, his teeth few and black. Before he died—from tuberculosis, according to the King of France— Dr. de Puebla said he had become fat.

Elizabeth was reputedly beautiful, with fair complexion and yellow hair. She seems to have been pleasant, quiet and self-effacing, though it is difficult to know now what she was really like. It was customary to describe all members of the royal family in glowing terms regardless of truth. Elizabeth herself did not have much money although her husband amassed riches. She sometimes had to sell her plate or borrow money in order to pay her expenses and to help her sisters, who were also poor. She had her dresses turned and repaired and made many other small economies. But, she paid sixteen shillings for a parrot (a large sum in those days), which must then have been a rare novelty and a smart thing to possess.

It is difficult to imagine what feelings Henry VII and Elizabeth had for each other. Yorkists had been killing Lancastrians and Lancastrians Yorkists for so long that there must have been a great deal of mutual distrust at the beginning. However, they seem to have adapted themselves to the situation. When Katharine joined the family, they had already had seven children, but only four of them were still alive. Arthur, the oldest, had just celebrated his fifteenth birthday on September 20. He was the offspring of both York and Lancaster, an heir to please both houses. In him lay the hope of peace for England. The name he was given favored neither side. It recalled only the Celtic legends of his father's ancestors, the days of glory when the exploits of King Arthur and the Knights of the Round Table signified greatness for

England. It was an irony of fate that he should always have been weak and ailing and altogether unsuited to live up to his grand name.

Arthur automatically became Duke of Cornwall at birth. Three years later he was also created Prince of Wales, the title given to the heir to the English throne from the time of Edward I until today. He was not educated with his brothers and sisters because it was usual for the eldest son to have his own court and household. At an early age he was sent to live in Ludlow, near the Welsh border, as titular head of the King's Council which administered that region. In appearance he was slim and pale. His hair was fair. He was quiet and studious by nature.

Margaret was born on November 29, 1489, in the Palace of Westminster. Not much is known about her as a child. In a poem written to celebrate her betrothal at the age of twelve, Walter Ogilvy, a Scot, described her rather extravagantly as being beautiful, courteous, clever, charming, elegant, graceful, witty and modest; her eyes were lively; she was tall, had fine hands, golden hair and a persuasive tongue. Margaret was present at Katharine's wedding festivities, but not long afterward, she left for Scotland to marry James IV. Her path did not cross Katharine's again for many years.

Henry was born in Greenwich on June 28, 1491. He was, therefore, five and a half years younger than Katharine. From his portraits as a child, Henry seems to have been a sturdy boy. His behavior, too, was always that of a strong and healthy person, especially by contrast with Arthur. He had a round face, little eyes and small full lips; his hair was red-gold, his complexion fair.

Although he was the second son, many titles were heaped upon Henry in the first years of his life. By this means his father consolidated more power into his own hands and less into the hands of his nobles. The young prince was made

Warden of the Cinque Ports and Constable of Dover Castle; he became Earl Marshall, Lord Lieutenant of Ireland, a Knight of the Bath and Warden of the Scottish Marches; and, before he was five years old, he was given the Order of the Garter, England's most famous order. He was also created Duke of York.[2]

Mary, the youngest child, was born about 1496, also in Greenwich. She was still only a child when Katharine first met her. Later, Katharine came to know her well and was always very fond of her. Mary was also Henry's favorite sister. We have no clear idea of her appearance at this time, but we do know that she was said to be extremely beautiful when older. There had also been three other children but they had died either at birth or soon afterward.

3. The New Learning

The court of Henry VII was the first English court to feel the influence of the Renaissance. His children were the first English royal children to be educated in the new Humanism, as Katharine and her brother and sisters had been in Spain. Henry VII, brought up as Ferdinand and Isabella had been, either on the battlefield or in hiding, had little formal learning. He was none the less keen that his children should have the advantages of education.

The spread of the New Learning had been helped by the invention of printing which had taken place in Europe early in the fifteenth century. In England the first printed book was made by Caxton in 1477. He is thought to have learned the art of printing in Cologne where he lived for a year. Over a hundred books came off his press during his lifetime. It is interesting to note that one of the early ones was Malory's *Morte d'Arthur,* which must have appealed to Henry who always stressed his Celtic origins.

European scholars were encouraged to come to the English universities, but England also produced her own Humanists who had traveled to foreign universities and been influenced there by the New Learning: William Grocyn, the Greek scholar; John Colet, Dean of St. Paul's, who founded St. Paul's School; Thomas Linacre, who studied medicine as well as Greek and founded the College of Physicians. Linacre taught Latin to Prince Arthur and Princess Mary and, among his more eminent pupils, were Thomas More, England's most famous humanist, and Erasmus, the great Dutch scholar. Erasmus, then comparatively unknown, had come to England in 1499. He had been invited by one of his former pupils, William Blount, Lord Mountjoy, who at this time was an older companion of Prince Henry. Later, he was to serve in Katharine's household.

England also played her part in the financing of explorations in the New World. Although Henry VII had not supported Columbus when his help had been requested before that of Ferdinand and Isabella, he had financed the first expeditions of Cabot. Cabot sailed the Atlantic in search of Brazil, but instead discovered Newfoundland and New England which he declared desolate and useless. Stow, the historian, told the story of three men who were taken in Newfoundland by Cabot. They were clothed in beasts' skins, ate raw fish, and spoke such a language that no man could understand them. Two years later, two of them were seen in the King's court at Westminster clothed like Englishmen, indeed indistinguishable from Englishmen.

4. *Tudor England*

Katharine's first act on her arrival in England[3] was to go to church to thank God for bringing her safely to land. It must have taken her days to get used to the feel of dry land again, to accustom herself to the motion of riding a horse instead of waves. But the worst of her journey was over. The rest of it was made in easy stages, deliberately slow in order that the preparations for the wedding could be finished in London before she arrived. She rode only a few hours a day or was carried in a litter, a kind of covered chair suspended between two horses, one in front and one behind.

Even without newspapers, knowledge of her arrival quickly spread. She received a genuine welcome from the people of Plymouth and from all the country folk along her route. They gathered together to look at their new Princess and her dark-haired, brown-skinned retainers in their foreign attire. Katharine's own coloring was not so different from that of English girls, but the fashion of her clothes was completely strange. The gentry brought her gifts. Church bells were rung and bonfires were lighted to greet her. Tongues chattered in a language she could not understand, but it was not hard for her to see that kind and welcoming words were being uttered.

When Isabella was informed that at last her daughter had safely arrived in England, she was told that "the Princess could not have been received with greater joy had she been the Saviour of the world." [4] Katharine was never to lose the affection and goodwill of the ordinary people whom she charmed before they could know anything of her upright character and steadfast ways.

This was her first experience of a foreign land. In her own country she had traveled in the height of the summer through barren, mountainous regions where the sun was scorching even though snowcapped peaks towered over the winding roads. She had ridden through the valleys and over the plains, but always within sight of the mountains and always in the dry, dusty heat. She was used to the long dry summers of Granada and Seville and the long cold winters of northern

Castile. But the cloudy skies, the misty sun, and rainy days of
England were new to her. There were no mountains, only
gentle hills. The countryside was abundantly covered with
forests and now in October the leaves of the trees were full
of autumn colors. The grass was still green, not parched and
brown; many sheep grazed in the fields, for wool and wool-
len cloth were England's greatest industry.

The towns and villages were small and scattered and every
village had its manor house and church. The old castles were
large and strong, but the newer palaces were more graceful,
built as homes not fortresses. Middle-class houses were
framed in timber which was sometimes filled in with rose-
colored brick in a herringbone pattern, sometimes with flint,
sometimes with plaster. Often three stories high, they over-
hung the narrow streets and from the latticed windows
rubbish was tipped into the gutter which ran down the middle. The people set great store by their gardens, which lay
behind their houses, full of fruit, herbs and flowers. The
poorer cottages were built of wood and clay, described by
the Spaniards as hovels made of sticks and mud. Fires were
frequent and dangerous but gradually declined in number as
brick began to take the place of wood and plaster.

After the Wars of the Roses, England was a safer place to
live in. Increasing foreign trade made the country richer. As
a result people were beginning to make their homes more
comfortable. The unhealthy habit of leaving bones and dirt
upon the floor, covering them up from time to time with
clean rushes and sweet-smelling herbs to kill the smell, was
gradually abandoned. Carpets came into fashion. The bare
walls were covered with paneling or hung with tapestries,
and glass took the place of oiled cloth in the windows. As
glass was only made in small pieces, it was generally cut into
diamond shapes and encased in lead, in the same way as

stained glass in church windows. Furniture had formerly been very limited, chiefly benches, stools and trestle tables with one big dresser to display the gold and silver plate. Now it became more plentiful and more comfortable. People also began to eat off pewter plates instead of wooden trenchers, though the nobility still used gold and silver plate. Big fires of wood and sometimes coal blazed in huge fireplaces on the wall of the great hall, but not all rooms were heated. At night, the houses were lighted with oil lamps or homemade candles. Beds were comfortable, made of down, feathers, wool, hair or straw. The pillows were soft. The sheets were made of linen and the coverings and canopies were often very elaborate. Sanitation, however, still remained primitive.

The people of England were tall and well-built. The men wore doublets lined with fur which reached from their shoulders to halfway down their legs. Their hair was short and their caps decorated with one or two ornaments. An English gentlewoman usually wore over her shift a cloth petticoat lined with gray squirrel or some other fur and over the petticoat a long gown also lined with fur; the train of the gown was carried over her arm. The women covered their hair completely either with a complicated sort of velvet cap with flaps hanging over their shoulders like two hoods and two more hanging down the front, or with a kind of kerchief in muslin or some other fabric. Their stockings were black and their shoes thick-soled of different colors.

There was a big distinction between the lives of the rich and the lives of the poor, whose hard lot was only ameliorated by the kindness and charity of those better off than they were. The poor worked hard and long and had few pleasures; they were, however, quite well-fed. A laborer's day lasted from sunrise to sunset, winter and summer. As artificial light was inefficient, people generally went to bed early and got up early. Mealtimes were, therefore, different too. A large dinner was served at the early hour of ten o'clock in the morning. A similar supper was eaten between four and seven in the evening. A typical repast for a noble household consisted of soup, meat and poultry, followed by game, followed by sweets and fruit, all washed down by ale and wine.

Reading had not yet become a general pastime as the printing of books was still a recent invention. By day, the nobles amused themselves with hunting, hawking, jousting and tennis. They played chess, backgammon, dice and cards. At night, they amused themselves with dancing, singing and music. They watched or played in masques and mummeries, early forms of plays and ballets. The ladies also took part in such of these activities as pleased them. The ordinary people thronged to watch the magnificent spectacles put on by the King and nobles in their palaces—and sometimes were called upon to help pay for them. They were also entertained by strolling musicians and traveling actors who performed miracle plays in the streets on movable carts. Other popular amusements were wrestling, bearbaiting and cockfighting, often provided as distractions at big fairs. Football was a rough game played through the streets with everybody taking part and many being hurt. Many punishments were administered in public and had become a kind of horrible entertainment, too. Surrounded by crowds of people, traitors were executed, heretics and witches burned, poisoners boiled alive, and minor crimes punished by whipping or ducking.

The English also had some more agreeable characteristics which were thought noteworthy by foreigners. Erasmus wrote to a poet frend of his:

> The Erasmus you once knew is now become almost a sportsman, no bad rider, a courtier of some practice, bows with politeness, smiles with grace, and

all this in spite of himself. . . . Did you but know the blessings of Britain, you would clap wings to your feet, and run hither.

To take one attraction out of many; there are nymphs here with divine features, so gentle and kind. . . . Besides, there is a fashion which cannot be commended enough. Wherever you go, you are received on all hands with kisses; when you take leave, you are dismissed with kisses; if you go back, your salutes are returned to you. When a visit is paid, the first act of hospitality is a kiss, and when guests depart, the same entertainment is repeated; wherever a meeting takes place there is kissing in abundance; in fact whatever way you turn you are never without it. . . . If you had once tasted how sweet and fragrant those kisses are, you would indeed wish to be a traveller . . . for your whole life in England.[5]

This particular habit had already attracted the attention of other visitors:

Their habits touching their wives and daughters are excessively simple. Throughout the island, when a person is invited to a friend's house, upon his arrival he kisses the lady, and in this fashion is welcomed as a guest. And even in every street they permit their friends to use this freedom with their wives.[6]

But another side of the picture was presented by a Venetian who, in 1510, wrote of the cold-heartedness of parents toward their children, the want of tenderness in husbands toward their wives and the mercenary way in which marriages were contracted.

Illnesses of all kinds were plentiful, but medical care elementary. The chief cures were purging and bleeding. Every kind of skin disease was called leprosy; sufferers from it were outcasts who had to carry a wooden clapper so that people could avoid them. Many children never lived long enough to become adults. Adults died young. Few people lived to be more than fifty so that to be forty-five was to be old. Society was a young one and therefore inclined to be freer and less set in its ways. When children became soldiers, went to a university or married at fifteen, they were obviously considered responsible at an earlier age than they are today.

A short time after Henry VII ascended the throne, England was afflicted by a new and terrible disease called the sweating sickness, which recurred from time to time and killed many people. It seems to have been a particularly virulent form of influenza:

> For suddenly a deadly and burning sweat invaded their bodies and vexed their blood with a most ardent heat, infested the stomach and the head grievously: by the tormenting and vexation of which sickness, men . . . were so painfully panged that if they were laid in their bed, being not able to suffer the importunate heat, they cast away the sheets and all the clothes lying on the bed. If they were in their apparel and vestures, they would put off all their garments even to their shirts. Others were so dry that they drank the cold water to quench their importune heat and insatiable thirst. . . . All in manner as soon as the sweat took them or within a short space after yielded up their ghost. So that of all of them that sickened there was not one amongst an hundred that escaped.[7]

Anyone who survived the illness twenty-four hours was likely to live, though it was possible to catch it again. The only cure suggested was to lie still in bed, take no meat and drink warm drinks in moderation.

In religion, England was Catholic, as was all Europe. There was, however, a greater freedom of thought and spirit of criticism than in Spain. The King and Queen were devout and so were the people. They believed and practiced the doctrines of the Church. Any criticisms they had were leveled at the worldly priests who ministered to them. The higher dignitaries of the Church had come to be indistinguishable from other nobles of the land. They also lived in big houses, ate well and grew fat and kept large retinues of servants. The Church was blamed only for being rich and its clerics for paying no attention to their own spiritual lives. The inhabitants of London complained, for example, about the excessive fees charged by curates for tapers at mass, for conducting marriages and burials and for other duties they performed. The citizens still wanted these services, however; it was not a question of doing away with them.

5. Journey to London

Some of these aspects of life in England Katharine already knew, some she could see for herself, and some she had still to discover. Meanwhile, a whole host of new faces were there to greet her. Lord Willoughby de Broke, steward of the King's household, was in charge of the reception arrangements and he, together with the Earl of Surrey and the Duchess of Norfolk, had come with a large company of countesses, baronesses and many other honorable gentlewomen, to escort her on her way. But Henry VII had also sent the Spanish ambassador, Don Pedro de Ayala, who he thought would be more likely to cheer the young Princess than his colleague, Dr. de Puebla. He may already have been known to Katharine. He certainly spoke the same language and could help interpret for her. Sixty lords and ladies of Spain with almost as many from England had to be housed and fed and entertained every day and night as the long procession moved slowly over the unpaved roads by way of

Exeter, Honington, Crokehome (where Katharine lodged in the parsonage), Sherborne Abbey, Shaftesbury Abbey, Ambresbury Abbey, Andover (where she stayed at the Angel Inn), Basingstoke and Dogmersfield. Some of the places where Katharine stayed were run like royal palaces with many servants and an overabundance of food, but everywhere she was received with friendliness and great hospitality.

When Henry heard that Katharine had arrived in England, he immediately sent to Ludlow to inform Prince Arthur. He also wrote a letter of welcome to Katharine in French:

> [Your late] arrival here in our realm is to us . . . so very agreeable, that we cannot well say or express the great pleasure, joy [and] consolation which we have from it, and especially [in the hope] of seeing your noble presence, which we have often desired, both for the great graces and virtues which we hear it has pleased [God] to give to your person, as also for the mutual amity, confederation, and good alliance between our good cousins the king and queen of Spain [your] parents and us, which at this time will be by you . . . greatly augmented.
>
> . . . . .
>
> [Madam,] I [beseech you that] it may please you to regard us henceforward as your good and [loving] father, as familiarly as you would do the king and queen your parents, for on our part we are determined to treat, receive, and favor you like our daughter, and in no wise more [or less dearly] than any of our own children. . . .[8]

Although Henry VII no doubt received reports from the representatives he had sent to meet Katharine, he nevertheless thought that he and the Prince should see her for themselves. On Thursday, November 4, he set out in the company of several dukes, earls and barons from his castle at Richmond. Delayed by bad weather and muddy roads, he spent the night at Chertsey. The next day dawned cloudy as usual, but the sun came out a little later so he and his followers rode off to Easthampstead in Windsor Forest. Here Prince Arthur came with his suite to salute his father and they all passed a pleasant evening together. On Saturday morning the King and the Prince proceeded separately to Dogmersfield [9] in Hampshire, where Katharine was expected. Henry first met Don Pedro, who had ridden ahead of the Spanish party, and demanded that he and Arthur should see the Princess immediately on her arrival. He was told that it was not proper, according to Spanish etiquette, for them to see the bride until after the wedding. Perhaps Henry was suspicious that Katharine was not as handsome as she had been described; he took counsel with his followers and then insisted that they should see her. There was no gainsaying him.

Katharine and her party arrived at the Bishop of Bath's palace in Dogmersfield about noon. They had just retired to their rooms when, between two and three o'clock, Henry, still in his muddy riding clothes, presented himself. The Archbishop of Toledo and other dignitaries who had come with Katharine received him and managed, through interpreters, to convey the message: "Tell the King of England that the Princess is resting. She can see no one." Henry's reply was peremptory. "Tell the Lords of Spain that the King will see the Princess, even were she in her bed." He waited awhile and Katharine came to meet him in her "third chamber" where "were used the most goodly words uttered in the language of both parties." [10] The King was satisfied with what he saw and took his leave.

Arthur reached Dogmersfield later in the day. Together, he and the King went to Katherine's chamber where the young couple met for the first time. History cannot relate what they felt. All we know is that, though they had already been betrothed several times by proxy, on this occasion they were betrothed in person.

After supper, Henry VII and Arthur again came to visit her. Katharine called in her minstrels and the whole company was entertained by music and dancing. Katharine danced with one of her ladies to show them Spanish dances. Arthur danced with one of the English ladies. Arthur and Katharine could not dance together, even if etiquette had permitted them to do so, as they only knew the steps of their own countries.

The next day, King Henry and Prince Arthur left Dogmersfield and rode first to Windsor, then to Richmond where the Queen was staying. Henry told Elizabeth the story of his meeting with Katharine and said how much he had liked her appearance and behavior. They then made their separate ways to Baynard's Castle, the chief royal palace in London.

Katharine and her party traveled more slowly and by a different route. On Monday, November 8, she stayed in the village of Kingston-on-Thames where she was met by three or four hundred people, all gaily dressed in the red and black livery of the Duke of Buckingham, who was at their head. He received her with a speech of welcome in Latin. On Tuesday, the company arrived at Kennington, the Archbishop of Canterbury's palace, near Lambeth, where Katharine stayed for three days until the final arrangements for her entry into the City of London were complete.

On the morning of Friday the 12th, after she had dined in Lambeth, Katharine made her long-awaited entry into London. She and all her retinue from Spain gathered on St. George's Fields, just south of the River Thames. Another large company was waiting to escort her, among whom were the Archbishop of York with many bishops and other dignitaries of the Church and a large number of noble lords with their knights and squires, all well horsed and richly clothed. Some of them she had already met, such as the Duke of Buckingham and the Earl of Surrey, but some were strangers. Chief among them was ten-year-old Prince Henry, Duke of York and younger brother to Prince Arthur. He was to ride at her side all day. At this time they could not even speak to each other as they had no common language.

Katharine rode on a mule, richly trapped, with Prince Henry on her right and the Legate of Spain on her left. Her gorgeous dress was in the Spanish fashion. Her fair auburn hair hung loose over her shoulders; she wore a broad hat like a cardinal's tied with a gold lace and under it a carnation-colored coif (a sort of cap) covered the top part of her head. About her were English and Spanish footmen also richly appareled; behind came eight English and Spanish ladies, riding two by two but back to back, for the Spanish and English rode sidesaddle on opposite sides of the horses. They were followed by the rest of the gaily-arrayed procession.

They moved along the south bank of the River Thames toward London Bridge. For Katharine, and for most of the Spaniards with her, this was their first view of London, England's largest city. It then had a normal population of perhaps seventy-five thousand, but on this occasion its numbers were swelled by visitors from every part of the realm. Every lord, both spiritual and temporal, was keeping open house with lavish feasting and every servant was decked out in his master's livery.

Katharine and her followers could see on the other side of the river, Westminster, with its abbey and palace and law courts separated from London by large houses with gardens running down to the river. The city itself, encompassed by high and thick walls on three sides, looked prosperous and festive.[11] Among the timbered buildings with overhanging gables arose innumerable church towers and spires. Dominating them all was St. Paul's Cathedral bearing an eagle and a cross on its lofty spire. Baynard's Castle was on the waterfront, and beyond it lay the grim fortress of the Tower, which sometimes served as royal palace and sometimes as prison.

The procession crossed old London Bridge between its double row of gabled houses and was then halted by a pageant, the first of many that had been rehearsed to welcome Katharine. She did not understand the words that were addressed to her, but was perhaps entertained by the spectacle. St. Katharine and St. Ursula greeted her in the first pageant. In the fifth one, God himself gave her good counsel and emphasized how important it was for England that she should bear children to reign in the land. At this stage, the procession was also watched by the King, Prince Arthur, and their attendants who were stationed in the window of a merchant's house. The Queen watched from another room with the two little princesses, Margaret and Mary, and their ladies-in-waiting.

The muddy streets had been spread with gravel to prevent the horses from slipping. Wine flowed freely from the conduits to cheer the citizens who had turned out to greet their new Princess. The people lined the streets and on every window ledge and battlement stood the Yeoman of the Guard. The Lord Mayor in crimson satin, followed first by the Recorder in black velvet, then by two sheriffs and twenty-three aldermen in scarlet, rode forth on horseback to welcome Katharine to their city. They were followed by the King's Heralds, in their coats of velvet and cloth of gold blazoned with the royal coat of arms, who made way for the procession to pass.

Among the spectators was Thomas More who was to be

one of Katharine's staunchest supporters in later years. In a letter to one of his friends, he afterward gave a most glowing account of Katharine's entry into London and, in less favorable terms, a description of her Spanish escort:

> Katharine, the most illustrious daughter of the King of Spain and bride of our most noble Prince, has just entered the City where she was received with more pomp and ceremony than we can remember ever having been given to any one before. Such was the magnificence of her English escort that it was impossible not to be lost in admiration. But as for her Spanish retinue, it was beyond belief of God or man. I am afraid you would have burst out laughing if you had seen them, so ridiculous were they. . . . They were deformed, mutilated, barefoot, Ethiopian Pygmies. If you had been there you would have thought they had escaped from the infernal regions. But their mistress, believe me, pleased everybody with her appearance. Nothing was lacking in her that could make a young girl beautiful. . . . May this much celebrated marriage bring England good fortune.[12]

At the entrance to St. Paul's Churchyard, Katharine was met by the Archbishop of Canterbury and the choir of the Cathedral. She followed them into St. Paul's up to the altar where she knelt in prayer. She was then escorted into the Bishop of London's Palace on the north side of the churchyard. There she passed the night and prepared herself for the marriage ceremony which began at ten o'clock the next morning.

6. Marriage Festivities

The day after the wedding, Katharine stayed quietly with her ladies in the Bishop of London's Palace. Up to this time, she had been served her food in the Spanish manner.

Now she was served in the English fashion as became an English princess. The King and Queen were in residence a short distance away at Baynard's Castle and Prince Arthur seems to have been with them. Most people were released from duty for the day to recover from the excitement and fatigue of the wedding ceremony. But the King's mother entertained the chief notables from Spain at dinner and the Earl of Derby invited them for supper.

The next day the festivities started again. Katharine and her retinue joined the royal family at Baynard's Castle. The whole company then went down to the waterside where more than forty barges garnished with streamers and pennants awaited them. Accompanied by minstrels playing on their trumpets, clarions, recorders and reeds, they came up the Thames to Westminster Bridge where they disembarked. In Westminster Hall, there was an impressive ceremony to make new Knights of the Bath. Afterward, a grand entertainment had been arranged with jousting and tilting and pageants in the great courtyard, for when real battles were not being fought, the nobles loved the mock combat of the tilting yard. They dressed up in their heavy and beautifully-wrought armor and played at fighting to amuse the ladies and other spectators. At night there was feasting in the Hall accompanied by masques. Ships and dragons, silken tents and giants, castles and lions, beautiful maidens—a sort of Mardi Gras procession—were carried round on carts.

Sometimes all the ladies sat together; sometimes Katharine sat at the high table with the King. Arthur was placed either at a side table with the other royal English children and various noble lords and ladies or with his father when the sexes were separated. He never appears to have been seated near Katharine. On several evenings the company got up to dance between the entertainments. On one occasion, Prince Arthur danced with his aunt, Lady Cicely, who had carried

Katharine's train. Katharine and one of her ladies, dressed in Spanish costumes, performed dances from their own country. Prince Henry, not to be outdone, danced with his sister Margaret, then twelve years old, in a very lively fashion. He became so hot and excited that he threw off some of his outer garments. "Perceiving himself to be encumbered with his clothes, suddenly cast off his gown, and danced in his jacket with the said Lady Margaret in so goodly and pleasant manner that it was to the King and Queen right great and singular pleasure." [13]

On the Saturday following the wedding, the English weather lived up to its November reputation. It rained so heavily that it was not possible to have any outdoor festivities. But on Sunday, after going to church, the assembled company started again with their round of pleasure, which continued for another four days. When the jousting was over, Katharine was given the honor of awarding the prizes of precious stones to the lords and knights who had done well in the tournaments. On Friday the 19th, all the company departed from Westminster Bridge by barge in as great state as they had come. The music played again as the King, the royal family and the guests were conducted up the river to Richmond Castle.

Here, the Spaniards went hunting and were entertained with all the games that were provided in the grounds of the palace—chess, cards, dice, bowls, archery and tennis, as well as the usual tournaments and masques.

When the festivities ended on Sunday, November 28, the Spanish guests were speeded on their way with gifts. Henry had stipulated that, though Katharine could bring as many visitors as she liked to the wedding, she was not to keep many retainers with her in England. He said he did not want the same thing to happen as had happened in Flanders with her sister Juana's retinue. Juana's retainers had never been paid, so they had either starved or left her. In other words, once the wedding was over, Henry VII was going to be responsible for the upkeep of as few Spaniards as possible.

After the guests had departed, Arthur sat down and wrote a letter [14] to Ferdinand and Isabella to say that he had never felt so much joy as when he saw the sweet face of his bride. He promised them that he would try to make her a good husband.

There was some unpleasant haggling over Katharine's dowry at this time. It was, to put it briefly, a question of whether the jewels and plate Katharine had brought with her could be considered as part of her dowry if she herself used them. One of the two Spanish ambassadors, Dr. de Puebla, seems to have been the principal cause of the argument. Unfortunately for Katharine, she was not able to let him, her chief lady-in-waiting or her treasurer negotiate, but had to deal with the King herself. Very soon she became aware both of the meaner side of Henry VII's nature and of the doubtful honesty of Dr. de Puebla. Perhaps she did not find it strange, as Ferdinand had similar qualities. What is surprising is that she herself could remain straightforward and honest when surrounded by so much deceit.

Arising from this squabble was the question as to where she should now live—in Ludlow with Arthur or in London with the English court. She, either diplomatically or more probably in innocence, refused to decide when the question was put to her. As her own advisers could not agree as to which was the best course, she left it to the King to decide. While the marriage negotiations were in progress, Henry VII had told Dr. de Puebla that he would keep both Katharine and Arthur at court for a year. By the time Katharine arrived in England, however, both children were considered to be of age. Arthur was definitely to go back to Ludlow but it was not clear what Katharine's movements were to be. It would seem that Henry VII really wished her to accompany Arthur but pretended that he would like her to stay at court.

The other Spanish ambassador, Don Pedro de Ayala, wrote a long letter to Ferdinand and Isabella describing the situation. From this letter it is clear that Arthur, for some unspecified reason which the King had explained to Don Pedro, could not live together with Katharine. Either the Prince of Wales was too young or too sick. Don Pedro's advice was that Katharine should stay with the King and Queen. We know from earlier letters that he liked the Queen. He thought she could comfort Katharine and be a friend to her. He believed that the Princess would more easily bear both being separated from Arthur "and their abstinence from intercourse if she remained with him [the King] and the Queen, who could alleviate her sorrow *for being separated from the Prince, a thing which it would be much more difficult to bear if she were living in his house in Wales,* adding many other reasons the King himself had given me only a few days before for retaining the Princess during the next two years near his person." [15] However, after four days discussion, Henry gave his decision and no one dared to disagree. The young couple left together on December 21. Henry wrote to tell Ferdinand and Isabella what had happened but without going into detail. Arthur and Katharine spent the Christmas holidays about forty miles from London on their way to Ludlow.

7. *Death of Arthur*

Ludlow Castle was the chief residence of the Prince of Wales. Arthur had lived there most of the time since he was a young child under the guardianship of Sir Rhys ap Thomas, a Welsh hero who had fought valiantly in support

* Author's italics. See Epilogue.

of Henry in his early struggles for the English crown. The
castle, though it had been fortified against the unruly Welsh
barons of an earlier day, had a pleasant charm. Built of deep
red brick, it stood on a little hill overlooking a forested and
fertile countryside. The life of the miniature court there had
its limitations as it was so far from London but was no more
primitive than in any other English castle of the day. Arthur
also possessed other houses in the area, such as Bewdley and
Tickenhill, which they visited from time to time. But Katharine was never to see the countryside at its best. She arrived
in the winter. In the spring she was ill and by the summer
she had left.

Ludlow was also the seat of government for Wales, which
was administered by an advisory council of ten men under
the titular direction of Prince Arthur. One of his chief advisers was Sir Richard Pole, whose wife Margaret was a
cousin of the Queen and a sister of the Earl of Warwick who
had been executed shortly before Katharine's arrival in
England. Although Margaret was twelve years older than
the Princess, there developed between them a loyal friendship which was to last the whole of Katharine's life.

It is not known how the Prince and Princess of Wales
spent their days. The Spanish and English households existed
side by side under the same roof. There was some inter-
mingling, for Henry VII, as an economy measure, had ordered them to take their meals together. But whatever time
Katharine and Arthur were able to spend in each other's
company was short. The sweating sickness ravaged the area
in the spring. Both Katharine and Arthur were ill and it is
likely that they were infected by this plague. Arthur, already
weakened by tuberculosis, did not survive. It is not known
which disease killed him. On April 2, 1502, sixteen-year-old
Katharine, not yet five months married, became a widow.

Arthur had a funeral as grand as, and even more prolonged than, his wedding festivities. He lay in state in Ludlow Castle for three weeks before he was taken to Ludlow Church, where his heart was reputedly buried. The funeral procession then set off for Worcester Cathedral. Many nobles of the land had been sent by Henry to take part in this sad journey which took place in the worst weather possible. One day was described by a witness as being "the foulest cold windy and rainy day I have ever seen." The cathedral was almost empty during the ceremony as so many people were suffering from the epidemic.

The King and Queen were at Greenwich when Arthur died. Sir Richard Pole hardly dared to inform them of the death of their eldest son, but it had to be done. One Tuesday morning early in April, the King's "Ghostly Father," a Friar Observant, knocked at the King's chamber door somewhat before the usual hour. When Henry VII knew who it was, he asked for him to be shown in. The Father asked everyone in the room to leave. Having made his obeisances, he then broke the sad news.

The King was overcome with grief and immediately sent for the Queen. When she saw how distressed he was she comforted him in spite of her own overwhelming sadness. She begged him to remember his duty to God, to himself as King, to his country and to her. She went on to say that his mother had had only one son whom God had preserved. Henry had had two sons, one of whom still lived, and two fair princesses. And, she added, both she and the King were young enough to have more children. The King recovered himself and thanked her for her comforting words. The Queen then went back to her room where she gave way to her own grief. She was so upset that her ladies sent for the King to come and comfort her. The King hastened to her side and reminded her of the wise counsel she had given him. He said they should both thank God that they still had one son.[16]

This story puts the relationship of Henry VII and Elizabeth in a good light. Whatever feelings they might have had for each other as representatives of rival houses early in their lives seem at this moment of grief to have been quite forgotten. They already had had seven children, two of whom had died in infancy. Now Arthur, their eldest, in whom had lain so many hopes for the future of England, was dead too. Their sorrow drew them together.

In February of the following year, the Queen gave birth to another daughter in the royal apartments of the Tower of London. The child was named after the Queen's sister Katharine, who was with her at the time. Perhaps Elizabeth was also thinking of Arthur's widow, now back in London. A week later, on her thirty-seventh birthday, the Queen died and the child did not long survive her. Prince Henry was still the only son and heir to the throne.

3

Princess Dowager

1. *The Young Widow*

When Katharine was well enough to travel, clad all in black, she was brought from Ludlow in a litter draped with black and hung with black valances, paid for by the Queen. Her household followed her and they were all established in Durham House, which was situated in the Strand a mile from St. Paul's Cathedral. Its gardens ran down to the river and it was generally approached by boat. It was one of the imposing houses Katharine would have seen when she first looked across the river before her state entry into London six months earlier. Built by a Bishop of Durham about the middle of the fourteenth century, Durham House was a large Gothic building with pointed windows and lofty marble pillars. Many notable people were to live there after Katharine, including Sir Walter Raleigh a century later. He had his study in a little turret overlooking the Thames with a view as pleasant as any in the world, according to one of his visitors. Perhaps Katharine, too, went up there sometimes and looked out at the boats and life on the river, an outside life in which she was not allowed to join.

Katharine lived in Durham House for almost four years, though sometimes she was invited to court. From letters she and the Spanish ambassador wrote, we know she was at various times at Greenwich, Ewelme, Woodstock, Richmond, Westminster, Eltham and Fulham. But, wherever she was, as long as Donna Elvira was in charge—which was until Katharine was nineteen years old—she lived a life of almost complete seclusion. Her period of mourning was protracted and she had little contact with the English. Some people at court thought this retirement unnecessary, as did Katharine herself. Dr. de Puebla reported accordingly to Isabella late in the year 1504, but Donna Elvira was still not permitted to give Katharine any more liberty. The segregated life gave Katharine little opportunity to speak English. Ambassadors sent by Henry VII to Spain in 1505 were asked by Ferdinand:

> "Can my daughter speak any English?" and we said that her grace could speak some and that she understood much more. . . . The King said, "Forsooth I love my said daughter entirely, for ever she hath loved me better than any of my other children and I am greatly desirous that she shall be an English woman and to learn for to speak English; and so I have written to her by divers of my letters that she should apply for her to learn that language." [1]

To comfort her in a foreign land, Katharine had only her religion, her music, her embroidery and conversation with members of her Spanish household. The only ray of hope for her future was the suggestion that she should marry the new Prince of Wales. But he was only eleven years old and she was sixteen and a half. No matter how big, handsome and charming he was, he must still have seemed like a child to her. Even if the prospect that she might still become Queen of England was some compensation—after all she had come to England for this purpose—she cannot have been made any happier by all the haggling and arguments which were to precede the actual marriage.

Originally, one hundred and fifty Spanish officers and servants had been delegated to attend upon Katharine in England. This number was cut down to fifty-eight and of these it is not known how many actually went with her to Ludlow nor how many were allowed to stay with her when she became the Dowager Princess of Wales. It is likely that their number was reduced then and even more reduced a few years later. Even so, her household was no mean one, even if not as magnificent as the royal court in which Katharine had been brought up nor as important as the one she and Arthur had so briefly ruled over in Ludlow. Those who stayed with her seem to have served her loyally though they were underpaid and often quarrelsome. Only toward the end of her widowhood did her household get out of control.

Some of the ladies-in-waiting who had come over with Katharine from Spain would have liked to marry English noblemen. Katharine was distressed that she had no money to give them, for without a dowry it was practically impossible for them to find husbands. One of her closest friends was Maria de Rojas, who was said to have shared her bed after Arthur's death. Another was Inez de Venegas, who, regardless of dowry managed to marry Lord Mountjoy and so was able to continue seeing her mistress. Maria de Salinas, who was to become Katharine's greatest friend during the rest of her life, is not thought to have come over to England at the same time as the others. She was, however, already part of the household by 1505, at which time Katharine was still short of money and reported that she was unable to pay her. There was also in her service Francesca de Caceres, whom Katharine did not like. She later married the merchant Francis Grimaldi and intrigued against her mistress by spreading gossip about the private life of the Spanish household.

Katharine cannot have been happy at Durham House. Her adolescent years were inexpressibly dull and monotonous. There was no gaiety and no social life for her in her own home or at court. The ladies attending her fared better, for some of them were able to find husbands. Katharine obeyed and respected her governess, Donna Elvira, who was of her mother's generation. It is obvious, however, that she intensely disliked her parents' ambassador, Dr. de Puebla, from the beginning. Katharine suffered from what could be called cultural shock. She had been transplanted from Spain to England, where the language, customs and climate were altogether different. She had been taken away from her parents; she particularly missed her mother to whom she had been very attached. She had been given a taste of freedom and then had it snatched away. She was oversheltered and isolated so that she did not have a chance to grow up like other girls. As she lived among Spaniards, she could not come to terms with the English way of life. She was no longer completely Spanish; neither was she English.

Katharine was living in what seemed to her dire poverty among an ill-paid quarrelsome household. Such money as she received was doled out by her parents or Henry VII as alms and not as her right. She had come down in the social scale. She was no longer living the life of a daughter of the King and Queen of Spain at their court; nor was she wife of the future King of England holding a court of her own. It is not surprising that she became ill. But her health always seems to have been poor. Even in Spain she had suffered from fevers and these were to continue all through her life in England.

After Arthur died, there are in the records no letters of love and pity for Katharine from anybody in Spain or in England. It was not Katharine's feelings that concerned her parents; it was the loss of the hundred thousand gold escudos they had paid as dowry, and the fear that the Anglo-Spanish alliance might break down. Ferdinand and Isabella were having trouble with the French over Naples and were particularly anxious that England should be on their side.

2. Marriage Negotiations Again

The first act of the Catholic Monarchs was to send a new ambassador to England—Ferdinand de Estrada. He was given very precise instructions. He was to make sure that Henry VII returned the dowry. He was to demand that Katharine should be given properties equal to one-third of the revenue of Cornwall, Wales and Chester, which had been promised to her by Arthur on their wedding day. He was to pretend to arrange for Katharine to return home immediately. They hoped by this means to frighten Henry into falling in with their wishes.

But Estrada also had secret instructions to try to arrange as quickly as possible a marriage between Katharine and Arthur's younger brother, Henry, the new Prince of Wales. He was at the same time to negotiate a favorable new marriage settlement as well. There were now three Spanish ambassadors in England. The other two, Dr. de Puebla and Don Pedro de Ayala, as well as all members of Katharine's household, were told to obey Estrada as though his orders had been given by Ferdinand and Isabella themselves.

The Spanish Monarchs informed Dr. de Puebla of Estrada's coming on May 10, 1502, as soon as the news of Arthur's death had reached them. They waited two more days before they wrote again to him to say how afflicted with sorrow they were at the news which had brought back so many sad memories of their own former losses. However, they said, it was God's will. Then at last they showed concern for Katharine's well-being. They said they had heard she had been ill; she must, therefore, be removed from Ludlow, an unhealthy spot, with all speed. It is likely that Henry VII and Queen Elizabeth would have brought her away in any case as there was no point in keeping her there once Arthur was dead. They may indeed have made the arrangements before any message arrived from Spain.

Ferdinand and Isabella soon became suspicious that Henry VII might not hold himself responsible for Katharine's support. Perhaps they were warned by Dr. de Puebla, for almost immediately they wrote to him about it. They said that they could not believe that the King of England was capable of exposing the Princess in her time of grief to want and privation. He must pay Katharine her dowry. They had heard that she had been advised to borrow money. This she must never do; nor was she to sell her gold, silver and jewels, nor any part of them. Ferdinand and Isabella were still counting on them to be a substantial part of her new dowry if she married Prince Henry.

It is interesting to note that on one occasion Isabella showed herself willing to part with the jewelry and plate for another cause. In the fall of 1503, the French were threatening to invade Spain. The Spanish Monarchs were in need of two thousand infantry from England to help them repel the invasion. Estrada was instructed to persuade Henry VII to send the soldiers. At the same time, Isabella, with her usual thrift, told him to pay them as little as possible. He was to try to borrow money to pay them. In case that was not possible, Isabella sent him a letter of credit for 10,000 ducats. As a last resort, Katharine was permitted to raise money by selling her dowry. The army was obviously of vital importance to her parents at that moment. Katharine was, however, spared the necessity of selling her possessions. The French threat did not materialize.

Ferdinand and Isabella made no attempt to send money to their daughter as they thought Henry VII could not possibly refuse to support her if she obviously had nothing. When, the following month, they heard that some people had advised Katharine not to accept what Henry offered, they must have thrown up their hands in horror. They hurriedly wrote to say that she must accept whatever she could get from him. During these years, Katharine was always short of money. Sometimes her parents sent her a little; sometimes Henry VII gave her some. But she never felt she had enough to pay her servants, buy new clothes, or live as she would have liked.

A battle of wits arose between the Spanish Monarchs on the one hand and Henry VII on the other. At first Katharine herself was no more than a pawn in their game of politics. Both sides were equally wily, equally cautious, equally stingy. Both were willing to negotiate a marriage treaty between Prince Henry and Katharine, though neither would admit it openly to the other. If there was to be no marriage, Ferdinand and Isabella still wanted to have back the Spanish dowry, obtain Katharine's English revenues and really have their daughter come home. As Henry VII was in possession of all three, he was in a much stronger bargaining position.

Ferdinand and Isabella continued to demand, plead, beg and reason that the hundred thousand escudos should be returned. Henry did not refuse them outright but he did not give the money back. Nor did he give to Katharine the revenues she had been promised. He had, however, agreed in principle as early as September 1502 that a marriage treaty should be drawn up, so it would seem that he really wanted the Anglo-Spanish alliance to continue. The following June the treaty was published, stating that Prince Henry should marry Katharine when he reached the age of fifteen, which would be three years later.

The Spanish Monarchs and Dr. de Puebla were in the meantime engaging in a lot of hypocritical double-talk in their efforts to achieve this object. On August 10, 1502, Ferdinand and Isabella again instructed their new ambassador, Estrada, that he should pretend to arrange for Katharine to come home to Spain where the customs of the country would permit her to give vent to her grief:

> You shall say to the King of England that we cannot endure that a daughter whom we love should be so far from us when she is in affliction, and that she should not have us at hand to console her; also it would be more suitable for a young girl of her age to be with us than to be in any other place.[2]

These words which, on the surface seem full of sympathy and motherly concern were vitiated by the carefully detailed instructions which followed. Estrada was to stage a mock departure for the Princess. He was at the same time to try to negotiate that she should stay to marry Prince Henry without letting one set of plans interfere with the other. Isabella thought that Henry VII would speed up his decision if he thought that Katharine might slip out of his grasp. She also mistrusted Dr. de Puebla and feared that he might have come to some secret arrangement with Henry VII.

Although Ferdinand and Isabella badly wanted the English

alliance, they obviously had genuine doubts about how good it was for a young girl's morals to remain in England, which had been described to them as being too free in its manners. Donna Elvira, who had been put in charge of Katharine, was told to guard her even more closely. Isabella believed that if any slur should be cast on her daughter's reputation the marriage would be out of the question.

Estrada's arrival caused a stir in the English household. In spite of instructions that the others should obey him, it was not quite clear who really had the ultimate authority—he, Donna Elvira, Don Pedro de Ayala or Dr. de Puebla. Isabella settled the matter by writing that Donna Elvira was to be in charge as far as Katharine and her staff were concerned; Estrada was to protect Donna Elvira, conciliate her and see that she was obeyed both by Katharine and her followers. He was also in charge of the diplomatic negotiations concerning Katharine's future. If he found Dr. de Puebla untrustworthy, he was to manufacture an excuse to send him back to Spain; if he found him honest and helpful, he was to flatter him and make use of him. In order not to upset Dr. de Puebla's vanity, he in his turn was told to make full use of Estrada and to take him along during all the negotiations. Further to placate Dr. de Puebla, who had always hated Don Pedro, Ferdinand diplomatically chose this moment to summon Don Pedro home. He was then sent as ambassador to Philip and Juana in Flanders—from the troubles of one sister to those of another.

Even though Dr. de Puebla was not considered reliable, he was left in England because he had the ear of Henry VII, who seemed to like him. He was able to report things which someone less close would not have been able to do. He was also useful as he was accustomed to fulfilling the other duties of an ambassador. He was responsible both for the

well-being of Spanish subjects living in England and for
any negotiations concerning the considerable trade that
existed between the two countries.

However, Dr. de Puebla had no better success after Don
Pedro had left. In April of the following year, Isabella wrote
him a very angry letter:

> . . . You wrote to us that if we would command
> Don Pedro de Ayala to come here you would take
> care to conclude this negotiation to our entire satis-
> faction. . . . We now find out that ever since he came
> here our affairs have been conducted in a much worse
> manner than they were before.

She expressed her sorrow and anger at not receiving either
the dowry or the Princess back home. She then informed
him that

> . . . preparation must be made for the return hither of
> the Princess of Wales, our daughter, for there must be
> no delay about her departure on account of them. In
> any case you will come with her, and if you should
> have served us well you will receive our thanks, and
> if not, you shall be made to know that you have not
> served us.[3]

In June 1503, Katharine and Henry were officially betrothed at a ceremony in Fleet Street a day or two after the
marriage treaty had been made public. Queen Elizabeth had
not lived long enough to witness this occasion. She had died
in February but must have known that the marriage treaty
was being negotiated. She was not to know how long it
would be before the marriage actually took place. She was
also fortunately spared the knowledge that immediately after
her death there was a suggestion that Henry VII should
marry Katharine himself.

It took some time for this news to reach Isabella. It shocked her at once into further frenzied letter writing. She wrote to Estrada to express politely her grief and sympathy at the death of the Queen of England and her horror at the thought that the old King should marry her daughter:

> But as this would be a very evil thing,—one never before seen, and the mere mention of which offends the ears,—we would not for anything in the world that it should take place. Therefore, if anything be said to you about it, speak of it as a thing not to be endured. You must likewise say very decidedly that on no account would we allow it, or even hear it mentioned, in order that, by these means the King of England may lose all hope of bringing it to pass, if he have any. For the conclusion of the betrothal of the Princess, our daughter, with the Prince of Wales, his son, would be rendered impossible if he were to nourish any such idea.

She went on to say that, whereas before it might have been a good idea to bring Katharine home in order to hasten the betrothal between her and Prince Henry:

> . . . it has now become a matter of pure necessity that she should depart immediately. For, now the Queen of England is dead, in whose society [the betrothal being concluded] the Princess, our daughter, might honorably have remained as with a mother, and the King being the man he is, even though the betrothal were concluded, it would not be right that the Princess should stay in England during the period of mourning for the Prince of Wales.[4]

Estrada was told to arrange for a Spanish merchant fleet in Flanders to sail back home via England in order to pick up Katharine on its way. Isabella did not forget that here again

economy should be exercised. When Estrada was negotiating
the arrangements for Katharine's return on a Spanish boat,
he was told to make the payment for this as small as possible.
However, Isabella felt so deeply about Henry VII's possible
attachment for her daughter that she was willing for Katharine to come home without her dowry if it was absolutely
impossible to obtain both.

In the same letter Isabella also suggested that a better
choice of wife for Henry VII would be the Queen of Naples,
Ferdinand's niece. Henry took the suggestion seriously but it
was two years before he sent ambassadors to Naples to discuss the matter. They were then given a long questionnaire
to fill out so that he could learn every possible detail about
the young woman who might become his wife. Her age,
height, color of her eyes and hair, kind of eyebrows, teeth,
lips, nose, forehead, whether her breath was sweet, what kind
of food she ate, what she drank, and so on for sixteen pages.
But it was all in vain. The Queen of Naples was not interested.

In any case, the suggestion that he should marry Katharine,
if ever seriously made by the King, was not pursued. Katharine remained in England and she and Prince Henry were
betrothed when she was eighteen and he almost twelve years
old. But the fact that the betrothal had at last taken place
did not mean that all difficulties were over. Discussions about
the dowry still continued. For the second marriage it was
again fixed at two hundred thousand escudos of which one
hundred thousand escudos were acknowledged to have been
already received by Henry VII. Ferdinand and Isabella
wanted to pay the other hundred thousand escudos in two
lots: one in cash for 65,000 escudos; the other 35,000 to be
in the form of the jewels and plate still held by Katharine
hopefully for this purpose. Henry, however, did not want the

jewels and plate. He wanted it all in cash. Katharine, as Princess of Wales and future Queen of England, was to receive one-third of the revenues of England, with the proviso that she could never take any of it out of the country.

There was, however, one much greater obstacle to be cleared away before Prince Henry could marry Katharine. It had nothing to do with money. A special dispensation had to be obtained from the Pope to allow him to marry his brother's widow. A marriage between people related in this way was forbidden by the Church. It was known that such dispensations had been given in similar cases, but each case was considered on its own merits. There was always the possibility that this one might be refused. In order to prevent any further questioning, it was therefore necessary to know whether Arthur and Katharine had really lived together as man and wife. Isabella, who knew it was important to know, had first tried to find out in the summer of 1502. There had then been some difference of opinion. Katharine's chaplain, Geraldini, had written a letter to Dr. de Puebla in which he said they had. Dr. de Puebla's actions showed that he believed him. Donna Elvira, on the other hand, said they had not. Isabella wanted to believe her and thought that, as first lady of the bedchamber, she should know. Geraldini was immediately summoned back to Spain on a trumped-up excuse before he could talk any more about it.

The new marriage treaty drawn up between Ferdinand and Isabella and Henry VII included the statement:

> The Papal dispensation is required because the said Princess Katharine had on a former occasion contracted a marriage with the late Prince Arthur, brother of the present Prince of Wales, whereby she became related to Henry, Prince of Wales, in the first degree of affinity, because her marriage to Prince Arthur was

solemnized according to the rites of the Catholic
Church, and afterwards consummated.[5]

In a letter Ferdinand afterward wrote to the Spanish ambassador in Rome, asking him to take steps to procure the
dispensation, he said:

> In the clause of the treaty which mentions the dispen-
> sation of the Pope, it is stated that Princess Katharine
> consummated her marriage with Prince Arthur. The
> fact, however, is that although they were wedded,
> Prince Arthur and the Princess Katharine never con-
> summated the marriage. It is well known in England
> that the Princess is still a virgin. But as the English
> are much disposed to cavil, it has seemed to be pru-
> dent to provide for the case as though the marriage
> had been consummated and the dispensation of the
> Pope must be in perfect keeping with the said clause
> of the treaty. The right of succession depends on the
> undoubted legitimacy of the marriage.[6] *

As may be imagined, Isabella the Catholic, with her fanati-
cal religious views, was particularly anxious to receive this
dispensation from the Pope. She was now nearing the end
of her life, frail in body though still strong in will. She and
Ferdinand had ratified the marriage treaty in September 1503.
About the same time, Estrada had arrived back, his task completed, as they thought. The dispensation was a long time in
coming, partly because of the death of two popes while it
was under consideration. In some mysterious way a copy
reached Spain in time to bring comfort to Isabella. She died
on November 26, 1504, believing that Katharine's future was
settled. A copy did not arrive in England until the spring of
the following year, although it had been promised many

---

* See also Chapter 6: *The Bull and the Brief.*

times by the Pope. The date on both documents was December 1503. It is not known why there was so much delay in despatching them: whether the Pope had doubts, whether he was waiting for payment or whether he was only dilatory.

In the depth of winter, Isabella's remains were taken in procession from Medina del Campo in the north of Spain where she died to Granada. She was buried, as she had requested, under a simple slab of stone in the monastery of San Francisco [7] by the side of the Alhambra. Twelve years later Ferdinand was laid by her side. Peter Martir, the court historian, immediately wrote in praise of Isabella: "The world has lost its noblest ornament." The Mayor of Medina del Campo said her soul had gone direct to Hell for the cruel way she had oppressed her subjects. Ferdinand's statement that she died as "holy and catholic as she lived" strangely enough combined the two opposing views.[8] The cruelties her people had suffered, especially the Jews, had been inflicted in the name of the Holy Catholic Church in the belief that it was God's will that heresy should be exterminated.

3. After Isabella

Isabella's death marked a turning point in the history of Spain's relations with the rest of Europe. It also was to change Henry VII's attitude to the marriage of his son. The Spain that had been united by the marriage of the Catholic Monarchs was now in danger of falling apart again. Ferdinand was no longer joint ruler of the whole country, but King only of Aragon and Sicily. His one son and heir had died seven years before. The three surviving daughters were scattered through Europe—Juana unhappy in Flanders, Maria uneventfully lost to view in Portugal, Katharine a pawn in England. Isabella had tackled the problem of succession, no doubt with some misgivings, when she made her will the month before she died. She bequeathed Castile to Juana's son Charles when he should reach the age of twenty. He was then four years old. In the meantime, Juana was to reign, assisted by her husband, Philip. Ferdinand was appointed regent in case of their absence, or Juana's unwillingness—as Isabella knew how difficult her daughter could be.

Even before Isabella died, Ferdinand and Philip anticipated the struggle for succession and were at daggers drawn. Philip already was calling himself King of Castile and Granada, ignoring—or perhaps claiming—Juana's rights. Each tried to enlist the King of England on his side. Henry, as usual, was cautious. His strength lay in being sought after by both contenders for the crown.

As far as Katharine was concerned, she was no longer so desirable a match for the Prince of Wales. She was now only a Princess of Aragon. More important alliances could be made by other marriages. Henry VII had an eight-year-old daughter, Mary. A betrothal between her and Charles, eldest son of Philip and Juana, brought vistas of endless power. Charles was not only heir to the kingdoms of Castile and Aragon. From his father he would inherit the Low Countries; from his grandfather Maximilian he would obtain Austria. Such a marriage had already been thought of as early as 1500 when Henry VII and Philip had met in Calais. Charles was then only a few months old. Now, however, it had suddenly become a much more interesting and tempting proposition for England. Even though Ferdinand was to marry a French princess and hoped to produce another heir, Charles's eligibility was never much reduced. At the most, a new son for Ferdinand could only inherit Aragon. As it turned out, the child died at birth. Charles remained heir to the vast empire of his four grandparents and the newly found lands in America.

There were also rumors that Prince Henry of England might marry a French princess. Henry VII himself was in the marriage market. The suggestions constantly made by Ferdinand that Henry should start negotiations to marry Ferdinand's niece the Queen of Naples gradually took effect. In the fall of 1504, eighteen months after the death of Queen Elizabeth, Henry began to talk of marrying again. It was another six months before he did anything about it. The fact that it took so long makes one think that it had been no more than a rumor that he had ever considered marrying Katharine. But if he were to marry the Spanish queen, then it was even less necessary for Prince Henry to marry Katharine. As Katharine's bargaining position deteriorated, so did her status in England. After her betrothal to Prince Henry, she had enjoyed a brief period of favor at court. She had scarcely been able to take full advantage of it for Donna Elvira was always with her. Her health, too, though never good, was even worse at that time.

In the summer of 1504, Katharine had been staying with the royal family—the King, the Prince of Wales and Princess Mary—at Windsor and Richmond when she was suddenly taken ill with a fever and stomach upset. She seemed to recover and so accompanied the King and Princess Mary to Westminster. There, she had a relapse. She was taken back to Durham House, where she developed another fever that lasted four weeks. She was also afflicted by a bad cold and cough. Her appetite disappeared and her complexion is said to have changed completely. This could partly have been due to the development of spots and blemishes common to girls of her age. The usual remedies of purging and bleeding were applied, but with no success. Her doctor reported that he had twice tried to bleed her in the leg but no blood came. It is difficult to tell now exactly what her illness was. It has been suggested that she had malaria, at that time a

common English ailment, which would account for her re-
curring fevers.

The King was full of sympathy and wrote her kind letters.
He said he loved her as his own daughter. He sent her one
of his servants who was to do anything for her that she required or would give her pleasure. At that time, for once,
she was not short of money, for Henry also allowed her
£100 a month—a considerable sum in those days—for at
least three months. Just before he was due to leave for Spain,
Estrada wrote a glowing account of the King's character. He
said that Henry VII was very kind to Katharine, and often
came to visit her. He also reported that Henry VII kept the
Prince of Wales constantly by his side and this was a good
education for a young boy. Prince Henry, obviously, had not
been sent to Ludlow as the other Prince of Wales had been.

As Katharine began to recover, she became worried and
slightly petulant. She wrote to Henry VII, whom she had
come to regard as her protector at this time, about her quarrelsome household. At this, the King became a little impatient too. Three days after he had sent a very kind letter, he
wrote abruptly to say he was sorry her servants could not
agree; he regretted he could not help her as they were
Spanish subjects, not English; they were outside his jurisdiction. However, according to Dr. de Puebla he did interfere
in her domestic arrangements to help her, though he did not
wish her to know. Dr. de Puebla also described further kind-
nesses of the King and complained that Katharine was inclined to be extravagant. When Katharine was feeling better,
she was again invited to stay at court, where she was treated
by the King as he treated his own daughter. Since Mary was
then eight and Katharine eighteen years old, this was not as
exciting for her as it sounds, but it did indicate that the King
was kindly disposed toward her.

At this time, Isabella lay dying in Medina del Campo, though no one in England seems to have been aware of it. News took even longer to travel in the winter months. Letters between the two countries sometimes reached their destination in under four weeks in the summer but had been known to take as long as five months in winter. The land route was quicker; but despatches were less likely to be intercepted if sent by sea. Katharine was upset because, she said, her father had not written to her for a year. She did not know that he too was ill. She knew her mother was not well and Katharine wrote anxiously to inquire after her health. She was still writing to her in December. When Katharine eventually discovered her mother was dead she must have felt even more isolated and lonely than before. When she began to feel the full consequences of Isabella's death she was made to feel worse.

The Cortes of Castile was now temporarily without a ruler. It refused to carry out the conditions of a favorable new trade agreement which had been made between England and Spain shortly after the ratification of the marriage treaty. Negotiations about Katharine's marriage were not carried on in a vacuum. They were always closely connected with the commercial arrangements between the two countries. The breaking of the trade agreement caused considerable ill-feeling in England.

Ferdinand, as King of Aragon, tried to make Castile responsible for the payment of the rest of Katharine's dowry— a responsibility Castile was not anxious to assume. During the next four years, Ferdinand was either short of money or pretending to be. He was constantly postponing payment of the other 100,000 escudos which had been promised in four installments. Each postponement made Henry angrier with Katharine. His kindness vanished; his meanness became more obvious. Katharine became genuinely short of money, which must have been even harder to bear after the brief interlude of comparative plenty.

In June 1505, the day before his fourteenth birthday, Prince Henry made a formal renouncement of the marriage treaty before the Bishop of Winchester. He declared that, as he had been contracted in marriage during his minority, he would not ratify the treaty which he then denounced as null and void. This was kept secret at the time. It was a card up Henry VII's sleeve, to be produced if he needed it and the idea was probably his and not his son's. In fact, Henry VII did not officially claim that the betrothal was not legal until September 1507.

Katharine was always inclined to blame Dr. de Puebla and the King of England, not her father, for her unhappiness during the next few years. As far as Dr. de Puebla was concerned, this was not entirely fair. His letters to Ferdinand show he had her interests at heart. Henry VII was not a generous man, it is true, but he probably considered that he had been kind and generous to Katharine. He had brought her and her staff from Ludlow. He had installed them in a large and important house very near to London. He had paid for their upkeep and they had all been fed. We know there were times when he sent comparatively large sums of money and there were occasions when he was kind and considerate. There may also have been some truth in the report that Katharine was extravagant and, as we shall see, her own conduct was not always perfect.

In 1506, Katharine wrote to her father to say that she had no new clothes. It sounds pathetic that a young girl, a princess into the bargain, should have been so poor:

> . . . I am in the greatest trouble and anguish in the world. On the one part, seeing all my people that they

are ready to ask alms; on the other, the debts which I
have in London; on the other, about my own person,
I have nothing for chemises; wherefore, by your
highness's life, I have now sold some bracelets to get
a dress of black velvet, for I was all but naked; for
since I departed thence [from Spain] I have nothing
except two new dresses, for till now those I brought
from thence have lasted me; although now I have
nothing but the dresses of brocade.[9]

But we must remember that dresses of the period were
elaborate and costly, and no doubt intended to last. Katharine
had also brought a good number with her as a bride. Henry
felt no more responsible for providing her with new clothes
than he had done for his wife: Elizabeth had constantly had
her dresses altered and repaired instead of buying new ones.
Henry was undoubtedly stingy, but Katharine was not the
only object of his stinginess.

Henry's attitude was not always determined by affection
or sympathy. In the first place, there was his own deteriorat-
ing health. He also had more important matters to consider
than the petty affairs of quarreling Spaniards. The internal
affairs of his kingdom took up a great deal of his time and
attention. In addition, he had to see his relations with France,
Spain and the rest of Europe in perspective. He had no
desire to be embroiled in any war. England's hope of strength
lay in maintaining the peace that had at last come to her
during his reign.

Sometimes Ferdinand, and Isabella too when she was alive,
exasperated Henry VII beyond measure by their wiliness and
cunning. Unfortunately for Katharine, she was on the spot
to bear the brunt of his irritation. When she asked Ferdinand
or Henry VII for extra money, both usually turned deaf ears
to her pleas. Each thought the other should support her, so

neither of them wished to be seen doing it. Whatever sums of money Henry did allow her, he never paid her her share of the revenues of Chester, Wales and Cornwall, which Dr. de Puebla reckoned at one time at 25,000 escudos. But neither did Ferdinand pay the other 100,000 escudos he had promised. Henry VII must have felt justified in holding back his part of the agreement as long as Ferdinand held back his.

This is not intended to whitewash the character of Henry VII, but to show that it was perhaps not so black as it has been painted. Nor is it to be thought that Katharine's life was an easy one. She deserves a good deal of sympathy but she was not always as badly off as she thought she was. The last four years of Henry VII's reign were the worst for her, but they were also to bring about beneficial changes in her own character.

Henry VII's own nature was changing at this time. As he grew older, his defects became accentuated. The deaths of Arthur and Elizabeth helped, or coincided with, a deterioration in his character. He had always been careful with money. His only extravagances, public spectacles such as those described at the time of Arthur's wedding to Katharine, were designed both to impress the foreigner and entertain the populace. Now, he became a downright miser. His greed for money was shown at least as much, if not more, in his treatment of his richer subjects as in his treatment of Katharine.

He had appointed Sir Richard Empson and Edmund Dudley as his agents to extract every possible penny from men of property in England. These two were the most hated men in the country during the last years of Henry VII's reign. They were the first to suffer the death penalty when Henry VIII succeeded him. But Henry VII, who had claimed the English throne when both the state treasury and his own pockets were empty, died a rich man as a result of his carefulness and extortions of his agents. At his death, he was reputed to have accumulated more gold than any other king in Christendom. He believed that a full treasury was one of the best ways of keeping England strong and independent. More important, a large personal fortune would maintain the Tudor dynasty firmly on the throne which, in his eyes, was the same thing. There was method in his madness.

4. *Emancipation*

Though Isabella's death brought a period of oppression to Katharine, it also led to her emancipation. She seems to grow up in mind as well as in body. This is the first time that Katharine really becomes alive to us. Before, she had been a pawn moved about by other people. Now she took a hand in propelling herself along the board until she was eventually changed into a Queen. When she lived in Spain and during her first four years in England, we only hear what other people said about her. We are told where she was, how she dressed, what things happened to her or around her. Apart from her one little complaint to Henry about her quarrelsome servants and the worry she expressed about her mother's illness, she scarcely uttered a word.

Katharine's first move, however, was not a happy one. Dr. de Puebla was now Ferdinand's only ambassador in England. Donna Elvira, who until this moment had always had Dr. de Puebla's support in running Katharine's private life, suddenly found herself on the opposite side. When Isabella was alive, Donna Elvira acted on her behalf and was responsible to her. With Isabella gone, she felt more power within her grasp. In trying to exercise it, she overreached herself. All Spaniards in diplomatic posts abroad now found themselves divided in loyalty. Some supported Ferdinand, some wholeheartedly supported Philip, and some supported Philip only because he was Juana's husband. One of Philip's outright supporters was Donna Elvira's brother Juan Manuel. He had been for some time at court in Flanders though he was never popular with Juana. He was, however, in close touch with his sister in England and through her he worked on Katharine.

Philip, though he bore his wife no love at all, loved the thought of ruling Castile. In order to achieve this, he had to isolate Ferdinand from the rest of Europe and win over the Castilian nobles to his side. Henry VII's friendship and aid were worth seeking. They were sought through Katharine who, without realizing Philip's purpose, tried then to act on his behalf. When his Flemish ambassadors came to see her in 1505, she was flattered. She felt in touch with her sister and ready to like her brother-in-law. The ambassadors asked her to help arrange a meeting between Henry VII and Philip. She agreed. If this meeting was brought about, she might also see Juana, whom she had not seen since 1496 in Spain when she had been eleven and Juana eighteen years old.

Katharine did not realize that by encouraging Philip she was being a traitor to her father's interests. Dr. de Puebla found out what was happening and secretly explained the diplomatic situation to her. As she was a dutiful daughter, she was horrified to think what she might have done. She tried to make amends. At Dr. de Puebla's suggestion, she wrote a letter to the King to explain. Donna Elvira, however, still tried to bring about the meeting and went ahead with the arrangements agreed to originally by Katharine. Only through Dr. de Puebla's further intervention was she foiled. There was a terrible row and Donna Elvira left—supposedly to have an eye operation in Flanders. But she never came back. Two years later people were still gossiping about her.

Esquival, who had been Katharine's Master of the Hall at
the time, said Donna Elvira had gone away in a horrible
hour, but such things were "better suited for conversation
than letters." [10] Katharine seemed genuinely to regret her
going and never mentioned any quarrel. She still blamed Dr.
de Puebla for everything.

Some four months after the fiasco with Philip, she wrote
to her father both to repeat her complaints about the way she
was being treated and to give her version of Donna Elvira's
departure:

> Your highness shall know, as I have often written
> to you that since I came to England I have not had a
> single maravedi,* except a certain sum which was
> given me for food, and this such sum that it did not
> suffice without my having many debts in London; and
> that which troubles me more is to see my servants and
> maidens so at a loss, and that they have not where-
> with to get clothes; and this I believe is all done by
> the hand of the doctor.
>
> Now, my lord, a few days ago Donna Elivra
> Manuel asked my leave to go to Flanders to get
> cured of a complaint which has come into her eyes,
> so that she lost the sight of one of them . . . she
> laboured to bring him [the eye doctor] here so as not
> to leave me, but could never succeed with him . . . I
> begged the King of England, my lord, that until our
> Donna Elvira should return his highness would com-
> mand that I should have, as a companion, an old
> English lady, or that he would take me to his court;
> and I imparted all this to the doctor, thinking to make
> of the rogue a true man; but it did not suffice me
> because he not only drew me to court, in which I
> have some pleasure, because I had supplicated the king

* 350 maravedis were equal to one escudo, i.e., about one-seventh
of a penny at that time.

for an asylum, but he negotiated that the king should
dismiss all my household, and take away my chamber
[equipage] . . . I entreat your highness that you will
consider that I am your daughter, and that you consent not that on account of the doctor I should have
such trouble, but that you will command some ambassador to come here, who may be a true servant of
your highness, and for no interest will cease to do that
which pertains to your service.[11]

She then gave a reasoned argument why Ferdinand should
send all her dowry in money. The King, she said, already
had enough jewels and those she had would only be valued
below their worth if she tried to offer them to him.

From this letter it is clear that Katharine had now left
Durham House for good and was living at court in reduced
circumstances. She did not know that Prince Henry had
secretly repudiated her in June, but she could tell that the
King was less interested in her. Perhaps he was disappointed
in her. She was also ill again at the time, and her letter
probably exaggerated for that reason. She was feeling slightly
hysterical and helpless and was missing Donna Elvira very
much. Nevertheless, her governess's departure was a good
thing. Now, at last, at the age of nineteen, Katharine was
on her own and obliged to struggle for herself for no one
was sent to replace Donna Elvira.

Ferdinand still failed to send any part of her dowry or
anything else that might have tided her over a difficult period.
He could only offer good advice in his reply, which was sent
to Dr. de Puebla:

You will say on my part to the Princess, my daughter, that it seems to me, she should in all things prove
submissive and in much respectfulness and obedience
to the King of England, my brother, her father, as

I believe she does; for that besides this being a matter of course, he thus will love her more and will do much for her. And since, if it please the Lord, that England is always to be her country, and in it she has to pass her life, both with the King of England, my brother, her father, and with the Prince of Wales, my son, her husband; and since her personal expenditure and that of her establishment, and the salaries of her attendants, are and have to be always at the charge of the said King of England, my brother, her father, it seems to me she ought to try that what concerns her establishment and her attendants should be done and ordered with the consent of the King of England, my brother; because thus will he comply fully, and one may trust [he added hopefully] that he will therein respect his own honor and that of the Princess my daughter, as well as his own peace of mind and that of the Princess, my daughter.[12]

As we shall see, it took some time for Katharine to appreciate this counsel, but in the end she did as Ferdinand suggested and was on much better terms with the King as a result.

In this same year, Henry VII sent ambassadors to Spain to find out what the situation was in regard to the succession in Castile. He was told that some favored Ferdinand because he was considered to be a wise man, and some favored Philip and Juana because they hoped under their rule to have to pay fewer taxes. The ambassadors also reported that some of the nobles wanted Katharine to come home and marry the Duke of Calabria so that after Ferdinand's death they could become King and Queen of Naples. Others wanted Katharine to marry Prince Henry and for them to be as near to the Spanish succession as Juana and Philip were "for every man and woman of the realm that do know my lady the Princess favor and love her more than any other of the King's children." [13]

5. *Philip and Juana in England*

The meeting between Philip and Henry VII that had been foiled by Dr. de Puebla was brought about early the following year by fate and the elements. In order to make sure of his succession in Castile, Philip decided that he and Juana must visit Spain and deal firmly with Ferdinand. They set sail in January 1506. It seems surprising that anyone should ever have traveled by sea in winter when it was so dangerous, but Philip no doubt felt the journey to be very necessary. The storms came up as usual. Philip and Juana and their company were tossed about and battered for nine terrible days after leaving Zealand. To make matters worse, a fire broke out on board their ship, but it was eventually brought under control. Everybody was terrified except Juana, who is reputed to have dressed herself in her court robes and to have surveyed the scene calmly. Eventually they were cast on the English shore at Melcombe Regis, near Weymouth, all of them glad to see dry land again but Philip's advisers also impatient at the delay.

They were to be delayed even more. When Henry VII heard they were in England, he sent to welcome them. He invited them to visit him at Windsor Castle and made it difficult for them to refuse without being impolite. Philip, however, came without Juana, who did not follow him until ten days later. Henry's meeting with Philip was described in detail by an eyewitness. The English nobles, like their King, were decked in gay colors and cloth of gold. The Spaniards were all dressed in black. Philip was said to be "a man of stature convenient, of countenance amiable and lovely, of body somewhat crass and corpulent, quick-witted, bold, and hardy stomacked." [14]

The usual kind of Tudor entertainment reserved for impressing foreigners was laid on. In the new chapel at Windsor, King Henry graciously bestowed upon Philip England's highest honor, the Order of the Garter. He himself put the Garter on Philip's leg and Prince Henry buckled it and made it fast. In return, the Prince of Wales received the highest order that Philip could offer, the Golden Fleece. The King had already been given this order several years earlier.

After mass and then dinner, on the morning of February 1, Henry asked Philip whether it would please him to see the ladies dance as it was Sunday and they could not therefore hunt as usual. Philip accepted the invitation and was led by the King into an inner chamber

> . . . where was my lady princess [Katharine] and my lady Mary, the King's daughter, and divers other ladies. And after the King of Castile had kissed them and communed awhile with the king and the ladies they came into the king's dining chamber, where danced my lady Princess and a Spanish lady with her in Spanish array. And after she had danced two or three dances she left, and then danced my lady Mary and an English lady with her. The lady princess desired the King of Castile to dance, which after that he had excused him once or twice answered that he was a mariner, "And yet", said he, "you would cause me to dance," and so he danced not but communed still with the king. And after that my lady Mary had danced two or three dances . . . [she] played on the lute . . . very well, and she was of all folks there greatly praised that in her youth in everything she behaved herself so very well.[15]

Mary was then ten years old.

Katharine was disappointed that her sister took so long to come, and she was very excited when Juana eventually arrived:

> The Tuesday the 10th of the said month, the Queen of Castile came to the said castle of Windsor . . . and they entered by the little park, and so secretly came to the back of the castle, unto the King's new tower, where, at the stair foot, the king met with her, and kissed and embraced her, howbeit that the king of Castile that there was there present with the king had divers times before desired the king's highness for to have remained in his own lodging, and not to have taken the pains to have gone so far.
>
> And after the king had welcomed her, my lady Princess, her sister, my lady Mary the king's daughter, having many ladies and gentlewomen attending upon them, welcomed her; and so all together went up to the king of Castile's lodgings. And in the ante-chamber the king departed from her, and the king of Castile conveyed the king to his lodging, and so at that time departed.[16]

Shortly afterward Katharine left Windsor for Richmond. The sisters scarcely had time to exchange more than a greeting and do not seem to have been left alone for a moment. Philip and Juana apparently had one of their violent quarrels and Henry VII was advised by his council not to interfere between husband and wife. The King left Windsor the day after Juana's arrival and joined Katharine at Richmond, ostensibly to prepare for Philip to visit them there. Philip stayed at Windsor two more days before riding after them. Juana went in the opposite direction back to the sea and the ships waiting to take them to Spain. It was over two weeks before Philip set off to join her, seven weeks before they set sail. This was the only occasion on which Juana came to

England and the last time she and Katharine were to meet. Some time afterward Katharine wrote to her sister to say how pleased she had been to see her and how distressed at her sudden and hasty departure.

There are many unanswered questions concerning Juana's visit. We do not know why she arrived at Windsor Castle after her husband, why she entered by a back way, why Philip did not want Henry VII to meet her, why Katharine left so soon for Richmond, why Juana returned to the coast alone. More than two years later, Katharine was to say that there were "mysterious causes" with which she was well acquainted, but she gave no indication as to what they were.

Juana may have refused to accompany Philip or he may have refused to take her with him, thinking he might be better able to cut short his visit if he traveled alone. Another suggestion has been made that she was too ill to travel after all the terrors of the voyage. Philip's protest that the King should not put himself out to welcome Juana may have been an act of courtesy or it may have been that he did not want them to meet. He may have persuaded Henry to send Katharine away so that she could not hear from her sister any plans that she might communicate to Ferdinand; Henry VII may also not have wanted Juana to hear Katharine's tale of woe. It is more likely that Philip was deliberately trying to prevent Juana from seeing or speaking to anybody at the English court. In spite of Ferdinand's advice that he should cultivate a better understanding of his wife, whose health depended upon gentle measures being used, Philip was already spreading the rumor that Juana was mad so that he would have an excuse to govern Castile in her stead. It would have been easy enough to provoke Juana into one of her violent moods that might have passed as madness. But if Henry or Katharine had seen her for any length of time and had been able to

speak to her alone, they might have had their doubts. If
Philip's aim was to keep them apart, he was successful.
Henry VII made the most of Philip's enforced visit. He
obtained from him a trade treaty very favorable to England.
Several dynastic marriages were suggested, none of which
in the end took place. Henry VII was to marry Philip's sister
Margaret of Savoy, whose first husband had been Katharine's
brother Juan. She was now a widow in her late twenties,
having already been married three times. Princess Mary was
to marry Charles, son of Philip and Juana. Prince Henry was
to marry Charles's sister, Eleanor. The Earl of Suffolk, known
as the "White Rose," who was at that time seeking refuge
in Flanders, was to be handed over to Henry VII on condition that his life was spared. He was a nephew of Edward IV,
a cousin of Elizabeth of York and a possible Yorkist leader.
He was not a danger, as Perkin Warbeck had been, but he
was a nuisance. Henry VII kept his word: Suffolk was not
executed during his reign though he was shortly afterward.
In return for all these favors, Henry promised Philip what
amounted to aid against Ferdinand, though it was not put
quite so plainly in the agreement.

The same storms that blew Philip ashore in England blew
the huge brazen eagle from the top of St. Paul's spire. As it
fell it destroyed one of the signs in Paul's Yard, which was
also an eagle. Superstitious, as most people were at that time,
Philip thought this an evil omen. The eagle was his father's
emblem and also his. The omen did not lie. Juana, the new
Queen of Castile, continued on her way to Spain with Philip
and they eventually met Ferdinand. Both her husband and
father conspired against her. They came to an apparent agreement which made Philip king and excluded Juana completely. Philip was jubilant, but not for long. Within three
months he was dead. Some said he had been poisoned on

Ferdinand's orders; others said he had caught a chill and died from lack of attention from his doctors. No one will ever know the truth. Whatever the cause, Juana was heartbroken.

Many people thought Juana was insane. Her behavior was undoubtedly odd. The rumors about her grew and were probably spread by her enemies and, in particular, her father, who wanted to reign in her place. She was said to travel around the country at night carrying her husband's coffin with her. It is possible that she was only trying to take his remains to Granada where he had said he wanted to be buried—by Isabella's side. In any case, the reported details were gruesome. Juana was helpless in Ferdinand's hands. He had her shut up in the castle of Tordesillas where sadly she awaited the birth of her sixth baby. When a girl was born, she called her Catalina after her sister in England. Juana was never to rule Castile. Ferdinand governed in her place till his death in 1516. Then her son Charles succeeded him and she was still kept under guard with no better treatment.

6. Katharine the Diplomat

Katharine had, in the meantime, learned her lesson from the failure of her first diplomatic attempt. The two years from 1505 to 1507 show a great development in her diplomatic technique and letter-writing ability. She writes clearly and well, showing complete awareness of the situations she is describing. Writers of diplomatic letters between Spain and England had for some time been using ciphers for their more secret information. Katharine first announced to Ferdinand's secretary, Almazan, that she had managed to decipher despatches unaided in April 1507. By September, she was

writing herself in cipher, saying that Ferdinand and his secretary would laugh at her attempts but that she dare not
write the truth in plain straight Spanish. The two chief subjects of her letters were as usual: Dr. de Puebla, whom she
accused, among other things, of being a vassal of the King
of England; and the dowry which she kept on urging Ferdinand to pay. By May 1507, Ferdinand, who realized that
Katharine had grown into a young woman of ability, had
empowered her to act as his ambassador in England.

Dr. de Puebla had never been as bad an ambassador as
Katharine believed, nor had he ever written anything critical
or unkind about her. However, he was now old and feeble.
By October, Katharine said she could take no more notice
of him as ambassador, "as he does none of the things which
belong to such an office; especially now his illness has laid
him so completely aside that he could be of no use even
though he were to desire it. He is nearer to the other world
than to this."[17] She begged her father to send someone
reliable in his place. Ferdinand's last recorded letter to Puebla was sent in the early part of 1508. By May, he had
fulfilled Katharine's request by sending Gutier Gomez de
Fuensalida as ambassador to England. Katharine was to
regret it.

During most of this time Katharine had been ill. In April
1506, just after Juana and Philip sailed, she wrote that
she had been ill for six months. In October she was ill again.
These illnesses may have been in part psychosomatic. The
story of her ill health continued until April 1507. Then
Katharine's physician wrote to Ferdinand to say that at last
she was cured and felt well for the first time since she had
come to England. Her complexion had regained its normal
healthy color. It is noteworthy that her health returned as
she found a new interest in life and as her good qualities
began to be appreciated.

What was perhaps still more important as a cause of her newfound confidence and health was that she had a new confessor, Fray Diego Fernandez. In April 1506, after four and a half years in England, she had written to Ferdinand to ask him to send her a friar, who was also a man of letters, as a confessor "because, as I have written at other times to your highness, I do not understand the English language, nor how to speak it: and I have no confessor."[18] Without a duenna, without a confessor, she felt lost. Ferdinand, however, was too busy, or not interested enough, to find one for her. A year later, she wrote to say that she had found one for herself.

Fray Diego became not only her confessor, but her chancellor as well. He advised her about worldly matters as well as spiritual ones. He became a figure of great controversy in England. Katharine was devoted to him, too devoted. Deeply religious as she was, she needed spiritual guidance; lonely as she was, she needed a friend. He became that friend and she did everything he said. She even had the courage to sell some of her plate in order to buy him books. Unfortunately for her, he took advantage of his position. Because of him she sometimes behaved in a way that neither Isabella nor Donna Elvira would have approved of. He was a young man and did not apparently have a very good reputation. Katharine, however, was so attached to him she would hear no wrong of him. There was a certain amount of scandal. The new ambassador, Fuensalida, was shocked. In March 1509, he wrote:

> It is more than twenty days since the King last saw the Princess. . . . May God forgive me, but now that I know so well the affairs of the Princess's household, I acquit the King of England of a very great portion of the blame which I hitherto gave him, and I do

not wonder at what he has done, but at what he does not do.[19]

Fuensalida tried to have Fray Diego sent away but only earned Katharine's dislike for his pains. She was adamant and the friar stayed on. She said that if he were to leave her, she would die.

One story told by Fuensalida shows how much influence the Friar had gained over her everyday life:

> Many things happen in her house which have need of amendment, but her Highness is so submissive to a friar whom she has as Confessor, that he makes her do a great many things which it would be better not to do. Lately he made her do a thing which much grieved the King. It was this, that whilst staying in a lonely house which is in a park, the King of England wished to go to Richmond, and sent to say to the Princess that next day her Highness and Madame Mary his daughter should be at Richmond, where he would go before or after them. The Princess obeyed the order, but next day when she was about to start, and Madame Mary was waiting for her with the company deputed to go with them, the friar came and said to the Princess, "You shall not go today." It is true that the Princess had vomited that night. The Princess said, "I am well; I do not wish to stay here alone." He said, "I tell you that upon pain of mortal sin you do not go today."
>
> The Princess contended that she was well, and that she did not wish to stay there alone. The friar, how-ever, persevered so much that the Princess, not to displease him, determined to remain. When Madame Mary had been waiting for more than two hours she sent to tell Madame Mary to go, but that she did not feel well. The English who had witnessed this, and had seen the Princess at mass and at table, rode off

with Madame Mary and went away. . . . They tell me
that the King was very much vexed at her remaining
there. . . . These and other things of a thousand times
worse kind the friar makes her do.[20]

It is difficult for us to estimate now whether Fray Diego
was in fact as bad an influence as Fuensalida thought. Certainly the ambassador hinted at immorality. One thing is
clear however: Katharine's development into an independent
and mature person coincided with his first years as her confessor. It is therefore not unreasonable to suppose that in
some respects he had a good influence on her. Eventually,
however, he had to leave her service because of conduct unsuitable to a priest. But this was not until much later when
she and Henry had been married for six years and when she
was not so dependent on her confessor. The fact that he
stayed on after Henry VIII and Katharine married would
tend to disprove some of Fuensalida's insinuations. Perhaps
some of the wise counsel that Katharine was able to give to
her husband in the early days of their marriage was derived
from her confessor.

7. *Death of Henry VII*

Henry VII meanwhile was still in search of a second wife.
Negotiations for the hand—and dowry—first of the Queen
of Naples and then of Margaret of Savoy made no progress.
Neither wanted to marry him. After Philip's death, Juana
was added to the list. Katharine undertook some of the
negotiations on Henry's behalf. Already she realized that in
return for negotiating his suit in Spain she could obtain
concessions for herself. She openly admitted to her father
that she was baiting Henry with praises of Juana. But she
also asked Ferdinand to consider seriously sending Juana to

England. She urged him to take over the government of Castile himself so as to free Juana. She thought that if she brought about Henry VII's marriage to her sister, he would then have the goodwill to marry her to Prince Henry at last. June 2, 1506, the day the Prince had become fifteen and old enough to marry her, had long since passed.

Katharine even wrote to Juana to plead King Henry's cause, saying that he had fallen in love with her on that brief visit to Windsor Castle with Philip. Ferdinand delayed. He did not want a match which would make an English king ruler over Castile. Ferdinand continued the rumor that Juana was mad, that she would not marry until Philip was buried and that she would not allow him to be buried. The fact that Juana was reputed to be mad did not deter Henry VII. The English had nothing against her madness, de Puebla said, as long as she could still bear healthy children. Katharine, however, had no success in these negotiations. Juana remained at home, as both the Queen of Naples and Margaret of Savoy continued to do, and Henry remained a widower.

Katharine was now living permanently at court while conducting this correspondence. Sometimes she earned the King's approbation, which could almost be measured in the amount of money he gave her. On the whole, however, she was out of favor and penniless. In April 1507, she had bemoaned the fact that she had not seen the Prince of Wales for four months although they were both staying in the same house. After the betrothal between Princess Mary and Charles (which had been discussed by Philip and Henry VII) was announced in December of the same year, she was to see even less of him. The King saw to it that they were kept apart. Prince Henry was then sixteen years old. His limbs were said to be gigantic but he was considered a handsome boy. If one thinks of his enormous frame in later years it is just possible to picture him in this earlier stage. His youth and energy and charm had not yet deteriorated into the gross figure seen in his later portraits.

As long as Ferdinand made no move to pay the rest of the dowry, Henry VII made no move to bring the marriage of the Prince of Wales and Katharine to a conclusion. Ferdinand kept making excuses for not being able to send the money—first Isabella's death, then Philip's, then Ferdinand's absence, then Juana's behavior. Katharine dutifully passed the messages to the King and grew more in his disfavor each time. Even when Ferdinand did send money to England, he did not wish the King to know about it until it was absolutely certain that the marriage was going to take place. When dealing with people of no honor and indifferent character, Ferdinand wrote, one must take care not to be cheated. As part of his bargaining position, Ferdinand also refused to ratify the marriage treaty between his grandson Charles and Henry VII's daughter Mary. It is not surprising that in this atmosphere of mutal distrust nothing happened to further the Anglo-Spanish alliance.

On August 7, 1508, Ferdinand appeared to give in to Henry's demands about the dowry. He agreed to pay all of it in cash. He instructed the Italian merchant Grimaldi, who was living in London, to pay over half of the one hundred thousand escudos still owing, but at the lowest rate possible and to take at least two months before paying. The jewels and plate which Katharine had been forced to hoard for seven years were now given to her outright to use as she pleased. Katharine must have been surprised and elated. This was her own hard-won triumph.

It was some time before any money changed hands, however. The new ambassador, Fuensalida, did nothing to help. Unlike Dr. de Puebla he did not get on well with the

English King, who by now was sick and crotchety. Sometimes Henry would not see Fuensalida for weeks and finally refused to see him at all. The ambassador was too serious in purpose and had no tact. Anxious to do Ferdinand's bidding, he went beyond his instructions. He honestly tried both to help Katharine live in a style he considered more suitable for her rank and to bring about the marriage she so much desired, but he set about this task in a curious way. By trying to interfere in her private life and quarreling with her confessor, he only succeeded in alienating her affections completely. Katharine was now capable of running her own affairs and resented help she thought only hindered her plans.

Late in 1508, it became clear that Henry had not long to live. The Venetians reported that he was dying; the French King said that he was in the last stages of consumption. Katharine too was aware that her long negotiations with Henry VII were nearly over. She wrote to her father that once the old King was dead nothing would stand in the way of her marriage. From this one can only gather that she and Prince Henry had managed to meet in spite of the King's efforts to the contrary and that he was anxious to marry her. The Prince of Wales was now old enough and mature enough to know his own mind and to chafe at restrictions. As the Prince grew in stature and independence, the King appeared to shrink and give up the struggle. Katharine was right in her prediction: on his deathbed Henry VII instructed his son to marry her.

Henry VII, the first Tudor king, died at Richmond on April 21, 1509. He was given a funeral as magnificent as any function he had attended during his life. No expense was spared. He was embalmed and brought to St. George's Fields. From there the procession followed the same route as Katharine's on her first entry into London. This time St. Paul's Cathedral was hung with black and the congregation was in mourning. The only color to be seen was on the King's image which rested on his coffin. The wax effigy was dressed in the King's state robes with a crown on the head, and a ball and scepter in the hands. Katharine and her ladies were given an allowance to enable them to buy clothes suitable for the occasion.

The last rites were performed in Westminster Abbey on May 11. The King was laid to rest by the side of his Queen Elizabeth in the beautiful chapel he had ordered as their joint memorial six years earlier. Torregiano, a famous sculptor, had come from Italy to design it and the cost had at the time been estimated to be £1,258, a sum which it is hoped the King did not begrudge. The funeral was followed by a magnificent feast where the rejoicings over the accession of the new King were greater than the lamentations over the death of the old.

Not least of those to be glad were Henry VIII and Katharine of Aragon. Three weeks later, on June 3, after more than seven years of wretched widowhood, Katharine's marriage to Henry took place quietly in the Church of the Observant Friars near Greenwich Palace.

Ferdinand indicated that some people, such as Archbishop Warham and Katharine's confessor had scruples of conscience as to whether the King would be committing a sin by marrying his brother's widow. Obviously these scruples were silenced and nothing more was said on the subject for some seventeen or eighteen years.

4

Katharine the Queen

1. The Coronation

To Westminster thus 'gan he pass
to take the crown his right,
Where both his Queen and he were crowned,
to England's great delight.

Anon.

On June 29, 1509, three weeks after their wedding, Henry VIII and Katharine were anointed and crowned King and Queen of England by the Archbishop of Canterbury in Westminster Abbey. This was the first of many big spectacles during Henry's reign and a momentous occasion. The day was warm and sunny, and all those taking part in the festivities were sweltering in their robes. But, as the procession moved through the center of the city, there was one sharp, cooling downpour of rain succeeded by sunshine and clear sky. Thomas More, who witnessed this ceremony as he had Katharine's first entry into London, took this as a good omen. He wrote in a poem to celebrate the occasion, that as the sun had dispelled the clouds, so would the new King wipe away the tears from every eye and put joy in the place of distress.[1]

As was customary, the King and Queen had come to the Tower of London from Greenwich by water three days earlier. They were escorted by a large company of gentlemen among whom was the Duke of Buckingham. For the coronation, the streets of the City of London were all hung with tapestry and cloth of gold. Young girls, dressed in white and carrying white tapers, lined the route of the procession. All the populace had turned out. In Cheapside stood the artisans and craftsmen "beginning with base and mean occupations, and so ascending to the worshipful crafts: highest and lastly stood the mayor with the Aldermen." [2]

The King "wore in his upper apparel, a robe of crimson velvet, furred with ermine, his jacket or coat of raised gold, the placard embroidered with diamonds, rubies, emeralds, great pearls, and other rich stones." He was followed by the lords spiritual and temporal, all dressed in scarlet and crimson, in cloth of silver and gold, bedecked with jewels; and behind them came nine children of honor clad in blue velvet "powdered" with fleur de lys. Then came the Queen in her litter "borne by two white palfries, the litter covered and richly appareled, and the palfries trapped in white cloth of gold, her person appareled in white satin embroidered, her hair hanging down to her back, of a very great length, beautiful and goodly to behold, and on her head a coronal, set with many rich orient stones." [3]

The cost of materials for robes and gowns alone was tremendous. Only six weeks earlier, large quantities of black cloth had been needed for Henry VII's funeral. Now, for the coronation, thousands of yards of silk and woolen

cloth in scarlet and red and in green and white (the Tudor
colors) were provided by the Great Wardrobe, as well as
large quantities of velvet for the ladies and gentlewomen
who were to be dressed in the Queen's livery of crimson
velvet. The King's retinue was vast, but Katharine's too was
now large enough to satisfy her pride which had been hum-
bled for so long. In her new household more than a hundred
and sixty people are listed as receiving cloth for new robes
and coats. In the jousts and tournaments and revels which
followed the coronation, the rose and the pomegranate and
the intertwined initials *H* and *K* appeared everywhere. Henry
and Katharine watched from a little house covered with
tapestry decorated with roses and pomegranates. The followers of the nobles were dressed in green and white decorated with roses and pomegranates of gold. In 1517, the
Venetian ambassador, obviously impressed by the richness
of the English court, wrote home to say how it glittered with
jewels and gold and silver and that the gentlemen of the
court wore gold chains fashioned from the initials of the
royal pair.

Today, in the Tower of London, there is still to be seen
very beautiful armor made for Henry VIII and his horse and
decorated with the rose, the pomegranate and the two initials of the royal couple.⁴ In Hampshire, near Dogmersfield,
there is a house called the Vyne, which Henry and Katharine
are thought to have visited together in 1510. A curious carv-
ing in the paneling of one room shows the rose and the
pomegranate growing from one stem. In the chapel of the
same house, there are also stained glass windows over the
altar, showing Katharine on the north, Henry in the center
and what is thought to be his sister Margaret on the south.
One of the ships in the English navy, which could be said to
have been started by Henry, bore the name of *Peter Pome-*

granate. In the early years of his marriage, Henry was proud to be married to Katharine and proclaimed his pleasure by the use of these conceits.

2. The Young King and Queen

Henry was a big, tall youth not quite eighteen years old when he was crowned. Katharine was twenty-three. The difference in their ages did not matter then, for both were young and seemingly in love; they were gay, happy, rich and free. Not only had Henry VII's crabbed restraining hand been removed, but five days after the coronation and the day after Henry's birthday, the Dowager Queen Margaret, Henry VIII's grandmother, died at the age of sixty-eight. The celebrations were dutifully halted for a short time to mourn her but soon started again. And Katharine's *bête noire,* Dr. de Puebla, who had apparently left the country sometime before the wedding, was now also dead. His son witnessed both the marriage and the coronation before returning to Spain to attend to his father's affairs. Fuensalida, who had been unpopular with Henry VII, Katharine and her confessor, as well as practically everybody else with whom he had come in contact, was allowed to stay until the ceremonies were over before being recalled. Katharine again represented Ferdinand's interests in England and continued to do so even after the new ambassador, Luis Caroz, arrived in the autumn.

There was a council to advise the new King, but he was more powerful than its members. They never succeeded in restraining him from anything he wanted to do. In any case, they were divided among themselves, some being pro-French and some pro-Spanish. Chief among them were the Earl of Surrey as Lord Treasurer, Bishop Fox of Winchester as

Lord Privy Seal and Warham, Archbishop of Canterbury, as Chancellor. Wolsey, who had been Chaplain to Henry VII, was made Almoner and a member of the council shortly after the coronation. To the people of England, it seemed as if the Golden Age had dawned, with a golden youth to lead them. The royal court entered upon a period of expensive gaiety and merriment, very different from what had gone before. Masques, revels, feasting, jousting and tournaments became the order of the day, no longer special events for visitors.

The royal coffers were overflowing with the riches accumulated by Henry VII. They were further swelled by Katharine's dowry which Ferdinand no longer had any excuse to withhold. He had paid half when he was sure that Henry VII was dead, half after Katharine and Henry VIII were at last truly married. Ferdinand had also given in over the other bone of contention: He had consented to the betrothal of Mary to his grandson Charles, a consent which, however, he was later to withdraw. Immediately after her marriage, Katharine renounced the whole of her dowry to Henry. Ferdinand and Juana also renounced all claim to any part of it. On June 16, 1509, Henry announced publicly that he had received the whole dower of Queen Katharine. So ended the haggling which had begun in Spain more than twenty years before.

It is interesting to note that the last 100,000 escudos were not sent over to England in coin as the first 100,000 had been in 1501. Ferdinand negotiated the payment with merchants in Spain and sent over by courier their bills of exchange on merchants in England. He said it was safer this way. If he sent the actual money by sea it might arrive too late; if he sent it by land it might be taken by the French. The merchants Grimaldi, Vivaldo and Lomelyn acted as Ferdinand's bankers in England and paid the dowry in coin. The banking system of today was then just beginning.

But this was now all in the past. Katharine was married and established as Queen of England. Her old household, which had been falling apart, was disbanded. She paid her debts to every one of her old servants, even those who at the end had caused her so much trouble and distress. Most of them she sent home, commending them to Ferdinand and asking him to treat them well. Her closest friends, Maria de Salinas and Inez de Venegas, who was now married, stayed on in England.

In order to please the people, Henry VIII dealt severely with the extortioners who had bled the country to feed his father's coffers. The two chief tax collectors, Dudley and Empson, were thrown into the Tower of London and later executed, the first of many bloody deeds which were to mar the gaiety of Henry VIII's reign. Other prisoners, as was customary on the accession of a new king, were released.

There were no longer any dangerous pretenders to the throne. The rival houses of York and Lancaster were united in Henry VIII, who reigned undisputed. "The Rose both White and Red in one Rose now doth Grow," wrote the poet Skelton of his old pupil.[5] Thomas More also wrote a poem in Latin called "On Two Roses which became One"— one rose which combined all the qualities of beauty, grace, loveliness, color, and strength which had formerly belonged to both. But, he went on to say, if anyone was so bold as not to love this rose, he would grow to fear it for it also had thorns.

He was to prove a greater prophet than he thought. The Earl of Suffolk, the last of the dangers from the White Rose side had been handed over by Philip and was still in prison. He remained there for a few more years until Henry

VIII decided that he was better out of the way and had him executed. More cannot have known that the time would also come when he himself would feel the thorns. When he dared to cross his King, he too was sentenced to death. But for the moment everything was perfect for Henry, for Katharine, for Thomas More and for England.

It was fashionable to sing the praises of the king, but at the beginning of his reign, Henry was genuinely popular. Everybody was willing to love him and he was welcomed as a change from his money-grubbing father. It would, however, never have been possible to write during his lifetime, even when it became more or less true, that he was "a big, burly, noisy, small-eyed, large-faced, double-chinned, swinish-looking fellow," [6] as Charles Dickens was to write some three hundred and fifty years later.

Thomas More extolled him partly because he had a special reason for disliking Henry VII, who had sent his father to jail for the nonpayment of a fine of £100. In another Latin poem, he praised Henry VIII for his skill and bravery, the fiery power in his eyes, the beauty of his face with its complexion like roses that could have belonged to a young man or a girl. This girlish appearance which seems so at odds with his portraits was also commented on elsewhere, a few years later:

> The King is the handsomest potentate I have ever set eyes on; above the usual height with an extremely fine calf to his leg, his complexion very fair and bright, with auburn hair combed straight and short in the French fashion, and a round face so very beautiful that it would become a pretty woman . . . his throat being rather long and thick.[7]

Lord Mountjoy also expressed his pleasure and excitement

in a letter he wrote to his old friend and teacher, Erasmus,
begging him to come and live in England:

> I have no fear, my Erasmus, but when you heard that
> our Prince, now Henry the Eighth, whom we may
> call our Octavius, had succeeded to his father's throne,
> all your melancholy left you at once. . . . Oh, my
> Erasmus, if you could see how all the world here is
> rejoicing in the possession of so great a Prince, how
> his life is all their desire, you could not contain
> your tears for joy. The heavens laugh, the earth exults,
> all things are full of milk, of honey, and of nectar.
> Avarice is expelled from the country. Liberality scat-
> ters wealth with bounteous hand. . . .[8]

Katharine too was beloved by the people, but rather for
her good qualities than her good looks. And her popularity
was to endure. Thomas More in his Coronation poem praised
her devotion, dignity, unselfishness, eloquence and loyalty
before going on to say that in her expression and in her
countenance, there was a remarkable beauty uniquely appropriate for one so great and so good. A few years later,
Erasmus said she was "a miracle of learning" and not less
pious than learned.[9] No one else but More suggested that
she was beautiful. Her eyes, complexion and smile were
praised, but otherwise she does not seem to have been
remarkable in appearance. There are, unfortunately, no undisputed portraits of her at this time of her life to allow us
to make our own judgment.

After her death, her story was told in verse in the *History of Grisild the Second* by William Forrest, chaplain to
Katharine's daughter Mary. He had known her in her lifetime and was naturally biased in her favor. He described
her appearance:

>She was right comely and cheerful with all;
>In voice, somewhat big sounding she spake.
>In stature but mean, and bonarly [pleasing] withall;
>Her color sanguine. . . .[10]

Besides praising her patience and humility, Forrest also said Katharine was devout and contemplative, kind to rich and poor, generous in the giving of alms and helpful to scholars at Oxford and Cambridge.

3. The First Years of Marriage

In the early days of their marriage, Henry and Katharine were fond of each other and both of them enjoyed the free, gay life. Henry wrote to tell Ferdinand how he was diverting himself with "jousts, birding, hunting and other innocent and honest pastimes," [11] as well as visiting different parts of his kingdom. Then, in case he gave the wrong impression, he added that he did not on that account neglect affairs of state. Caroz, the new Spanish ambassador, however, reported differently. He said the English bishops had told him that the King was young and did not care "to occupy himself with anything but the pleasures of his age. All other affairs he neglects." [12]

Both Katharine and Henry told Ferdinand separately how happy they were, though in rather formal terms. They used the language of diplomacy in writing to the head of a foreign state. They did not forget that Ferdinand was King of Aragon and a much older man, as well as being Katharine's father. A month after their marriage, Henry wrote: "And as regards that sincere love which we have to the most serene Queen, our consort—her eminent virtues daily more and more shine forth, blossom, and increase so much, that, if we were still free, we would yet choose for her our wife before all other." [13]

Henry VIII as a young man. Artist unknown. (*Recently acquired by National Portrait Gallery, London.*)

Henry VII, father of Henry VIII. Artist unknown. (*Nostell Priory. Permission of Lord St. Oswald*)

Elizabeth of York, mother of Henry VIII. Artist unknown. (*Nostell Priory. Permission of Lord St. Oswald*)

View of London Bridge in 1616, but much as it was in the early 16th century. (*The Folger Shakespeare Library, Washington, D.C.*)

Thought to be Prince Arthur, first husband of Katharine, older brother of Henry VIII. Artist unknown. (*Queen's Collection. Copyright reserved*)

Sixteenth century sports and pastimes. (*The Folger Shakespeare Library, Washington, D.C.*)

Margaret Tudor, Queen of Scotland and sister of Henry VIII.
Late copy by Daniel Mytens. (*Queen's Collection, Holyrood
House. Copyright reserved*)

Mary Tudor, Dowager Queen of France, sister of Henry VIII, with her second husband, Charles Brandon, Duke of Suffolk. Possibly by Mabuse. (*Earl of Yarborough Collection*)

Three days later, Katharine sent a long letter full of filial sentiments in which she said:

> As to the King, my lord, amongst the reasons that oblige me to love him much more than myself, the one most strong, although he is my husband, is his being the so true son of your Highness, with desire of greater obedience and love to serve you than ever son had to his father. . . . And your Highness may believe me that *he is such in keeping obedience to your Highness as could never have been thought.* . . . The news from here is that *these kingdoms of your Highness* are in great peace, and entertain much love toward the King, my Lord and to me . . . our time is ever passed in continual feasts. . . .* [14]

The feasts were to continue, with the guests staying at table as long as seven hours, eating every imaginable meat and fish known in the kingdom down to prawn pastries; but the jellies of some twenty sorts made in the shapes of castles, surpassed everything.

Ferdinand replied somewhat sententiously that he was exceedingly glad to hear that they loved each other so much; he hoped their happiness would last as long as they lived; that to be well married was the greatest blessing in the world; and that a good marriage was not only a good thing in itself, but the source of all other kinds of happiness. He also wrote that God showed his favor to good husbands and wives.[15] Ferdinand believed that Henry would be like wax in his hands, and the italicized sentences in Katharine's letter above show that she was encouraging this belief. The following year Katharine was still writing, "I thank God and your Highness for such a husband as I have." [16]

The history of the next three years shows England more

* Author's italics.

under the influence of Spain than she had ever been before, or was to be again under Henry's reign. Despite her frequent pregnancies, Katharine found time to be her father's successful agent. Her sense of duty at this time both to Ferdinand and her native land was strong even though she had not seen either since 1501. She had indicated even before her marriage that she had no desire to return to Spain; she recognized that her future lay in England. The greatest joy for her would be not only that the two countries should be passively at peace but also actively friendly toward each other. Her efforts were now directed toward this aim. Fortunately for her aspirations, Wolsey, the King's Almoner, was also of the same mind.

While Katharine's influence over Henry was strong at the beginning of their married life, she was nearer to happiness than at any other time in her life, except possibly when she was a child. Yet, her health, her ill-fated pregnancies, and perhaps Henry's dalliance with the ladies of the court were always a worry to her, though she generally gave the appearance of imperturbability. It is difficult today to appreciate fully what constituted happiness in the strange environment of some four hundred and fifty years ago, with its different attitudes toward life and death, hygiene and health, religion, treatment of children, behavior of husbands and wives. But there is no doubt that Katharine's religion was a very real thing to her. She drew spiritual strength from her devotions, and her steadfast belief in God and a world to come helped her bear the daily irritations and her long years of trouble.

Katharine had never been robust. Now she started on one pregnancy after another. Even if she had wanted to, she could not therefore have kept pace with Henry's active social life. The first child was stillborn in May 1510. Katharine was naturally very upset, but Henry was kind and sympathetic. Katharine wrote to apologize to her father that she had not been successful in producing a living child. She asked him not to be angry with her—as if it had been her fault!

On New Year's Day of the following year, a son was born, prematurely, but living. The whole of England rejoiced with the King and Queen:

> *Vive le Katerine et noble Henry*
> *Vive le prince le infant rosary.*

The baby was named Henry with all the pomp and circumstance possible in Tudor times. The christening was followed by jousts and tournaments which were recorded for posterity in the illustrations of the Great Tournament Roll of Westminster.[17] Two months later, the new Prince of Wales was dead. "The King, the more to comfort the Queen, dissimulated the matter, and made no great mourning outwardly: but the Queen like a natural woman made much lamentation, how be it, by the King's good persuasion, and behavior, her sorrow was mitigated, but not shortly."[18]

During the first nine years of her marriage, Katharine bore at least seven children, four of whom were boys. Most of them were stillborn; only one lived more than a few weeks. This was Mary, who was born in 1516. For two more years, she tried for a son; afterward there is no more mention of the Queen's pregnancies.

Meanwhile Henry was young and surrounded by a young and gay court. He delighted in dressing up and in wearing jewelry; at one time he owned 234 rings for fingers and thumbs. He exercised himself "daily in shooting, singing, dancing, wrestling, casting of the bar, playing at the recorders, flute, virginals, and in setting of songs, making of ballets, and did set 2 goodly masses . . . which were sung oftentimes in his chapel and afterwards in divers other places." [19] The masses have not come down to us, but several of Henry's songs have survived, including:

> Pastime with good company
> I love and shall until I die.
> Grudge who lust but none deny.
> So God be pleased and leave will I.
> For my pastance hunt sing and dance
> My heart is set
> All goodly sport for my comfort
> Who shall me let.[20]

Even at the beginning of his reign when he admired and cared for Katharine as his wife, Henry still sought the company of other women. This was the custom of the day and Katharine may not have taken Henry's behavior as much amiss as we might expect. After all, Ferdinand had not always been faithful to Isabella and had at least four other children than those that she had borne him. As far as is known, Henry had only one other child during the time that he considered himself to be married to Katharine.

Katharine generally acquiesced in Henry's behavior, as Isabella had with Ferdinand, knowing that she was his wife and Queen. Other girls could come and go in his life, but she would always be there. In public Henry showed every sign of devotion and esteem. When he dressed up and played elaborate games with the court, it was to amuse her and surprise her. Once he sent her six dozen silk roses after a joust. When he took part in tournaments he wore her favors. He acted the part of the gallant knight of medieval days. His court was a make-believe court of King Arthur, inspired by his father's ancestry.

But, as early as 1510, only one year after their marriage,

there were signs that Katharine could be upset when Henry was flirting with the ladies at court. The Spanish ambassador reported that there had been a quarrel between them probably caused by Henry's attentions to a sister of the Duke of Buckingham. He also said that the King was furious because he believed that several women in the palace were spying on him in order to tell tales to the Queen.

4. Katharine, Regent of England

Henry VII had kept England out of entanglements in Europe. Henry VIII on his accession was put under pressure from the other reigning monarchs to become involved. He was encouraged to help the Venetians against the French, support the French against Ferdinand, help Ferdinand by attacking the Moorish infidels in North Africa, send military aid and money to Maximilian and so on. Many treaties of alliance were drafted and some of them signed, but most of them turned out to be of no lasting value.

It has often been assumed that it was Ferdinand, aided by Katharine and his Spanish ambassador Caroz, who first persuaded Henry to take up arms against France. Ferdinand wrote to Caroz to say that if Henry was disinclined to help him, then he should get Katharine to persuade the King of England. If Katharine refused, preferring "to see the world go to pieces," [21] he was to enlist the help of her confessor, the Friar. In fact, Wolsey, now becoming important as an adviser to Henry VIII, also exerted some influence in this direction.

Henry was encouraged by Ferdinand to try to regain the French territories in Guyenne which had formerly belonged to England. In 1512, after several other small and inconclusive attacks had been made in France, an English army was sent to the Pyrenees to attack France from the south. Nothing came of the attempt. The soldiers sat around waiting for Ferdinand to send them the supplies and armaments he had promised. But he was taking advantage of their presence to attack Navarre. The English drank too much wine. Many were taken ill and died. They became bored and impatient. They behaved badly. Then, disillusioned with the Spaniards, they went home.

Many Spaniards believed that the English did not fight because they had a secret understanding with the French. Ferdinand said that another time help from England would be more useful in the form of money than soldiers. The story spread around Europe that the English, unaccustomed as they were to warfare, showed a marked dislike to performing duties usually performed by soldiers. Margaret of Savoy said, "Englishmen have so long abstained from war, they lack experience from disuse." [22]

After this fiasco, Henry felt duty-bound to wipe out England's dishonor. In spite of criticism at home from the pro-French party, Henry, still encouraged by Wolsey, continued his alliance with Ferdinand. In 1513, he himself crossed into France and led an army against Louis XII. It was not a big step for Henry to take from playing in tournaments at home to taking an active part in a real war abroad. With the same youthful zest he entered into the spirit of both. Safe in the knowledge that England was unified behind him, the civil war a thing of the past, he started on his warlike activities. A special tax was levied to help raise an army. But Henry took a special delight in the navy, which he enlarged out of all recognition. He built the *Henry Grace de Dieu,* or the *Grand Harry* as it was popularly known, his most famous ship. Once, as he was going through the list of new ships being built, he came across the name of *Kateryn*

Pomegranat. He crossed it out and inserted the new name *Swepstaak* (Sweepstake). It is not known why. Perhaps he was feeling annoyed with Katharine that day.

On June 15, Henry, accompanied by his courtiers now gaily dressed as soldiers and followed by 600 archers of his guard dressed in long white tunics and caps, set off from the royal palace at Greenwich. Katharine, who was pregnant again, went with him and they made the journey to the coast by easy stages. In Dover Castle, just before he sailed, Henry made Katharine Regent of England and Captain of Forces. The Archbishop of Canterbury and Sir Thomas Lovell were asked to stay and help her. The Earl of Surrey was also left behind, to his annoyance, to protect the northern borders. There was reason to fear that the Scots might take advantage of Henry's absence to attack—a fear that was justified.

On June 30, "the king took leave of the Queen and of the ladies which made such sorrow for the departing of their lords and husbands, that it was great dolor to behold." [23] He apparently had a calm crossing. Gorgeously appareled, wearing the red cross of St. George on a garment of white cloth of gold and on his head a crown lined with crimson satin, Henry landed in Calais.

Katharine realized that Henry would be occupied with the business of war, but she was very anxious to have news of him. So a few weeks after his departure, she wrote to Wolsey to arrange for a weekly interchange of letters:

Master Almoner, thinking that the King's departing from Calais shall cause that I shall not so often hear from his Grace for the great business in his journey that every day he shall have, I send now my servant to bring me . . . word of the King . . . and so I pray you to take the [pains] with every one of my messengers to write to me of the king's health.[24]

A month later, she was thanking Wolsey for the comfort he gave her. "Master Almoner, for the pain you take remembering to write to me so often, I thank you for it with all my heart." [25]

During her regency, Katharine showed not only a wifely concern for Henry's well-being, but also a strong sense of duty regarding her own activities which she fulfilled more than efficiently. After Henry had left, James IV of Scotland, husband of Henry's sister Margaret, invaded England as expected. Encouraged by the French to divert England's attention from the war in France, he advanced at the head of an army of 60,000 men. The Earl of Surrey rallied an army of 30,000 and set out to meet him.[26] Katharine raised further troops in the south and was ready, as her mother Isabella would have been, to lead them against the enemy. The fact that she was pregnant did not interfere with her activities, though these may have helped cause the ensuing miscarriage.

On August 13, Katharine wrote to Wolsey with almost girlish enthusiasm:

> From hence I have nothing to write to you, but that you be not so busy [with] the war as we be here encumbered with it. I mean that touching mine own [self] for going farther where I shall not so often hear from the King; and all his subjects be very glad, I thank God, to be busy with the Scots, for they take it for a pastime. My heart is very good to it, and I am horribly busy with making standards, banners and badges.[27]

As it happened, Katharine herself did not have to join forces with the Scots. The armies of James IV and the Earl of Surrey met at Flodden. They fought for three hours, by which time the English were undoubted victors. Of the fifteen thousand dead reputed to have been left on the field of battle, only one third were English. James IV was killed and Margaret was left a widow with a one-year-old son. Not long afterward, however, Margaret married the Earl of Douglas and was able to stay in Scotland.

On September 16, Katharine wrote to tell Henry the news of her victory. She sent him a piece of James's coat which had been given to her by the Earl of Surrey:

> . . . In this your grace shall see how I can keep my promise, sending you for your banners a king's coat. I thought to send himself to you, but our English-men's hearts would not suffer it. It should have been better for him to have been in peace, than to have this reward. . . .[28]

It is difficult to tell from her letter whether Katharine was more upset that James had been killed or proud that the victory had been won while she was Regent. She certainly boasted of her achievements against the Scots as compared with Henry's against the French:

> But to my thinking, this battle hath been to your Grace and to all your realm the greatest honor that could be, and more than if ye should win all the crown of France.[29]

Henry, however, showed some regret at the death of his brother-in-law when he wrote that James had paid a heavier penalty for his perfidy than he would have wished.

Meanwhile, the English army under Henry was making good its damaged reputation by winning battles which perhaps Katharine was right in thinking not very important. They took the two French fortresses of Tournai and Therouenne. They also won the Battle of the Spurs, said to have been called that by the French themselves for the way they had spurred their horses into flight. Henry took captive the Duc de Longueville, whom he sent home into Katharine's care. She, however, was embarrassed to have him at court. Besides, she was then occupied with the war with Scotland. She had him sent instead to the Tower where he was well lodged and courteously treated, more a guest than a prisoner. He turned out to be influential and useful later on when Henry began negotiations with France.

After the battles in France, there was much rejoicing. Henry and his companions, including Charles Brandon, stayed on to disport themselves in the company of their allies Maximilian and Margaret of Savoy, then a handsome widow about thirty years old. Henry was reported to have danced with Margaret from suppertime until dawn in his shirtsleeves and without shoes. He impressed everybody with his energy and was said never to have been still or quiet but always vivacious and pleasant.[30] Henry, about this time, also met a French girl who the following year wrote to ask him for 10,000 crowns which she said Henry had promised her when she should marry.[31]

This year marked the peak of Katharine's power and influence over Henry. With insight, it is possible to detect a gradual cooling-off in his attitude toward her after his return from France, even though when they met "there was such a loving meeting that every creature rejoiced." [32] However, for many years more, he continued to treat Katharine with every outward sign of respect and occasionally with genuine affection. She continued to run his household and to advise him, sometimes still with good effect. Ambassadors continued to call upon her and she was present when Henry entertained visiting heads of state—the Emperor Charles when he visited England in 1522; her niece, the Queen of Denmark, who came with the King in 1523; the French ambassadors who came to negotiate a treaty in 1526. The final break between Henry and Katharine was not to come until 1531.

A combination of circumstances led to their gradual estrangement: Henry's disillusionment first with Ferdinand and his policies and later with Charles; Katharine's inability to produce an heir; the disparity in their ages which became more obvious as they grew older and Katharine's health and figure deteriorated. As time went on, Henry, too, became more experienced in statecraft and less dependent on his wife's advice.

5. Rise of Wolsey

Katharine's decline from favor coincided with Wolsey's rise but was not necessarily caused by it. The first rumors of a divorce came at this time, when Wolsey was in Rome seeking to be made a cardinal. In a report supposed to have been written in 1514, the Venetians had said, "the King of England wishes to leave his present wife, who was his brother's wife, because with her he cannot have an issue." [33] The date of this entry has been queried by some historians who think it belonged to a later period. But such a rumor could have been spread even though Katharine was actually pregnant at the time. With her history of miscarriages and stillbirths, it is possible that no one believed the child she was carrying would live.

At first Katharine and Wolsey were on good terms. Both had pro-Spanish policies. Wolsey was an ambitious man. Perhaps he thought that the swiftest road for his own personal advancement lay through her as she was influential with the King. If so, it did not take long for him to reach the point where he could work directly on Henry. Wolsey had begun his successful career during the reign of Henry VII. He is first on record as being a junior bursar at Magdalen College, Oxford. After that he held a number of posts which combined the political, diplomatic and ecclesiastical. He has been called the last of England's great ecclesiastical statesmen. At one time he was chaplain to Sir Richard Nanfan, Deputy of Calais, who had been one of the ambassadors sent to Ferdinand and Isabella in 1488 to negotiate the marriage of Katharine and Arthur. Nanfan is thought to have recommended him to Henry VII, who made him his chaplain.

Although Wolsey's name was not on the list of the King's Council appointed by Henry VII and his mother, Margaret Beaufort, to advise the new King, he joined it shortly afterward when Henry VIII appointed him his Almoner. In 1511, when he was about thirty-six years old, he was made a Privy Councillor and was then well on his way to the top. By 1513, it was reported that all things passed at the will of two obstinate men, Wolsey and Brandon. Brandon's power, however, did not become as great as Wolsey's, whose ambition was insatiable. He wanted to be pope and, on the ladder to that position, had first to be made a cardinal. He was made Archbishop of York in 1514, cardinal the following year, and then became chancellor. He was, however, never elected pope in spite of his intrigues and bribery. The Venetian ambassador referred to him as the *other King* and, in 1519, wrote that the King "devotes himself to accomplishments and amusements day and night, is intent on nothing else, and leaves business to Wolsey, who rules everything." [34]

Wolsey became very rich, partly by virtue of the many offices he held and partly by the bribes which were paid to him both in England and Europe. He lived in a style as regal and sumptuous as the King's in the noble palaces (such as Hampton Court) which he built for himself. He was also the recipient of some of the hatred that might otherwise have been focused on Henry.

Both Katharine and Wolsey had encouraged Henry's expedition to France in 1513. After his triumphant return, Henry's attitude to Spain changed. He began to be as suspicious of Ferdinand as Henry VII had been, and with reason. Ferdinand gloried in his double-dealings. When he heard that someone had complained that he had cheated him twice, he replied, "He lies; I cheated him three times." [35] Henry realized he had been used as a dupe to distract the French while the Spaniards recaptured Navarre. When he found out that Ferdinand had made peace with the French regardless of his English alliance, he was furious. It must have been at such a time as this that Henry wrote a hymn with music, still sung today:

> O Lord, the maker of all things,
> We pray thee now in this evening
> Us to defend through thy mercy
> From all deceit of our enemies.
>
> Let neither us deluded be
> Good Lord with dream of fantasy
> Our waking in Thee Thou keep
> We in sin shall not on sleep.
>
> Father through thy blessed Son
> Grant us this our petition
> To when's will the Holy Ghost always
> In Heaven and Earth be laud and praise.[36]

Henry vented his anger on Katharine and on the Spaniards in England. His mood was not helped by his having smallpox which ravaged the country that spring. Katharine, however, met the situation with courage and dignity. She may have been both ashamed of her father's perfidy and embarrassed since it made her own situation so difficult. Or, perhaps by this time she was used to Henry's fits of temper and knew that he would get over them.

6.   *Marriage of Mary Tudor*

Henry decided that he too would make peace with France. Aided by Wolsey, who had now become strongly pro-French, and by the Duc de Longueville, who had come to live at court, he negotiated a treaty which was to be sealed by the marriage of his eighteen-year-old sister Mary to Louis XII, an "old" man of fifty-two. Mary had been betrothed by her father to Charles, son of Philip and Juana, in 1509 when they were both children. Now that the time was approaching for the real marriage to take place, for Charles had reached the age of fourteen, various delaying tactics were employed on both sides.

Ferdinand was openly against the marriage which he thought would make both Henry and Charles potentially too strong; he had other plans for Louis' allies. Nobody seemed actively to favor the marriage, neither Charles and his guardian Margaret of Savoy, nor Henry and his advisers, though it would be difficult to assign blame for its lapse. Mary was made to renounce the contract. Shortly afterward, on July 30, 1514, she was betrothed instead to Louis XII of France, whose wife Anne had died early the same year.

Charles was about four years younger than Mary, a sickly boy, sedate and melancholy. One of his petulant remarks before their betrothal was broken had been that he wanted a wife, not a mother. But when he heard of Mary's betrothal to someone else, he became angry. He called for a hawk to be brought to him and started to pluck it. When his courtiers asked him what he was doing, he continued his task, then replied, "Thou askest me why I plucked this hawk; he is young, you see, and has not yet been trained, and because he is young he is held in small, and because he is young he squeaked not when I plucked him. Thus you have done by me: I am young, you have plucked me at your good pleasure; and because I was young I knew not how to complain; but bear in mind that for the future I shall pluck you." [37] Charles also used other very strong language.

Katharine was in a dilemma as to whether she should support her husband or her father. She was fond of Mary and did not want her to go away. She also knew that Ferdinand wanted his niece Eleanor, Charles's sister, to marry Louis. But Katharine's life was now in England. If she wanted Henry's affection, she must support him. Her confessor saw this perhaps more clearly than she did. At any rate, it was he who received all the blame from the Spanish ambassador.

Caroz wrote in great anger to Spain saying that the Queen needed some discreet and intelligent person to take care of her soul and to give her advice on how to behave toward both the English and the Spanish. The Friar had told her to forget Spain and all things Spanish in order to gain the love of the King of England and of the English. (Because Caroz said *in order to gain the love of Henry,* it sounds as though Katharine had been in danger of losing it.) Katharine, he continued, had been won over completely by this idea and needed someone who would tell her how to be more useful to her father. Caroz blamed not only the Friar, but also the Spanish members of her household who preferred to be friends of the English and neglected their duties as subjects of Spain. He singled out Maria de Salinas as being the worst influence. She had certainly cast her lot with England and was just on the point of marrying an Englishman.[38]

Henry VIII in his anger behaved so badly toward the Spanish ambassador during this year that Caroz said he was treated by the English not as an ambassador, but as a "bull, at whom everyone throws darts." [39] But within a few months these troubles were over. Both he and the Friar were back in Spain. Katharine had never trusted any of her father's ambassadors and Caroz had been no exception. But, for the Friar, whom she had always liked, she sent a letter of commendation to her father. Others reported that he had left England in disgrace.

In September 1514, both Henry and Katharine, who was again pregnant, went to Dover to see Mary off to France. The equinoctial gales were again at their height and the seas were at their roughest. The superstitious took the terrible storm as an ill omen, but Mary nevertheless was able to leave after some considerable delay. She was accompanied by thirty-four ladies, chief of whom was Lady Guildford, who was to act as her chaperone. Among the company that sailed with her was Sir Thomas Boleyn and one of his daughters, usually thought to have been Anne. The convoy of ships was dispersed by the wind and Mary just managed to reach Calais alive. She had to be carried ashore.

Mary was said to be pretty, smart and gay. "I saw the Princess Mary dressed in the Italian fashion; and I think never man saw a more beautiful creature, nor one having so much grace and sweetness," wrote one contemporary.[40] Margaret of Savoy's representative wrote that he had never seen so beautiful a young woman in the world. "Her deportment in dancing and conversation is as pleasing as you could desire. There is nothing gloomy or melancholy about her. . . . I assure you she has been well-educated." [41]

In spite of her charm and good looks, and loved as she was by Henry and Katharine, Mary was another pawn in the diplomatic marriage game. She had been betrothed to Charles for the position he would hold in Europe, not because he would make her a good husband. She was switched to Louis when a French alliance suited England better. Louis, at the time of his second marriage, was already as old as Henry VII had been when he died. It was of no use for Mary to protest so she made the best of the situation. Louis seemed to love her. He could not praise her enough and she was kind to him when he was ill immediately after their marriage. He rewarded her with valuable jewels which she appreciated at the time and later struggled to retain. But Louis cut down the number of Mary's English retainers as Henry VII had cut down Katharine's Spanish household when she married Arthur. Nineteen people were allowed to stay in France. The rest were abandoned to get back home as best they could.

Within three months of Mary's arrival in France, Louis died. Not yet nineteen, the widowed Queen stayed on at the court of the new French King, Francis I, who did not disguise his own liking for her. Henry VIII thereupon dispatched Charles Brandon to negotiate with Francis and bring Mary home. Mary is reputed always to have been in love with Brandon although he was much older than she and had already had a complicated love-life. He was one of Henry's favorites and had been made Duke of Suffolk as a reward for his friendship and service. Mary persuaded Francis to encourage Brandon to marry her secretly in France. The marriage took place in the Palace of Cluny in Paris. Then she wrote to her brother to remind him that he had promised before she left England that next time she could marry whom she pleased. According to Wolsey, when Henry was told that the marriage had taken place without his consent he was as angry as they feared he might be. Wolsey claimed that he interceded with the King for them. But it is also possible that he exaggerated their misdeeds because he was jealous of Brandon. It is certain that if it was necessary to pacify Henry, Katharine would have spoken on their behalf too.

Henry, however, eventually forgave them. After their return to England, Mary and her husband were married again with great public ceremony in Greenwich on May 13. For two years they seem to have been out of favor but in 1517 they were again to be found at court. Mary had, nevertheless, to give up her jewels and plate to her brother and pay him back her dowry in yearly installments. As the French King continued to pay her an allowance until the time of her death, this was not as much an imposition as it sounds. She retained the title of Dowager Queen of France as well as becoming Duchess of Suffolk. She had four children, but the two sons died. She then not only looked after her own two daughters and two daughters of her husband's by a former marriage, but also the daughter of her sister Margaret and Maria de Salinas' daughter Katharine as well—a houseful of Tudor girls without a single boy!

7. *The New Rulers in Europe*

Louis's death led to further confusion in England's foreign policy. Ferdinand, encouraged by Katharine, took advantage of Henry's displeasure with Francis to try and win back his friendship. He sent expensive gifts which Katharine reported were received with great pleasure by her husband. Henry magnanimously agreed to forget all the disagreeable things which had passed between them. A new treaty with Spain was signed, but Ferdinand was not destined to benefit from it. He was now old and all that winter was ill. He died, generally unlamented, in January 1516, one year after the death of Louis XII.

Charles succeeded his grandfather as King of Spain but did not visit the country for several months. In the interval, a rebellion broke out and Katharine's native land, which had been united by the marriage of her parents, was in danger of breaking up again. Charles arrived in time to suppress the rebellion before it got out of hand and was accepted by the people of Spain as joint ruler with his mother. Juana, however, continued to live in Tordesillas, treated as she had been during the life of her father. Her subjects would have been glad if she could have been cured of her melancholy which some believed had been caused by witchcraft.

In January 1519, when Charles's other grandfather, Maximilian, died, the government of Europe passed into the hands of young men. Henry VIII was twenty-seven, Francis I was twenty-five and Charles V was eighteen. Henry and Francis were both swaggering and hearty men, fond of clothes, of food and drink, of girls and sport; both were also patrons of the arts. Charles was by comparison a weakling, pale and thin with a long protruding jaw. His liking for jousting and sport was only moderate and he did not care particularly for cultural pursuits. He nevertheless was to become the most powerful of them all.

The new rulers had youthful ideas about politics and diplomacy and childish attitudes of rivalry. Henry was curious about the French King he had never seen. The Bishop of Worcester described him as "tall in stature, broad-shouldered, oval and handsome in face, very slender in the legs and much inclined to corpulence." [42] Francis was equally curious about Henry and catechised his ambassador item by item.[43] When the Venetian ambassador came to visit the English King in Greenwich on May Day, 1515, Henry had many questions to ask. " 'The King of France, is he as tall as I am?' I told him there was but little difference. He continued, 'Is he as stout?' I said he was not; and he then inquired, 'What sort of legs has he?' I replied 'spare'. Then Henry was delighted. He undid his doublet to show what a fine calf he possessed." [44]

The ambassador breakfasted in a green bower and the

King was also clad in green from top to toe. Katharine, he said, was dressed in the Spanish fashion. "The Queen is rather ugly than otherwise; and is supposed to be pregnant. The damsels of her court are very handsome." The ambassador added that he had spoken to the Queen in Spanish "which pleased her more than I can tell you; and she commenced talking to me about Spanish affairs and about her mother, making me all possible civil speeches." [45]

When Henry heard that Francis had a beard, he grew one too. Katharine did not like it, so he shaved it off again. Later, however, he let it grow, whether against her will or not we do not know. The rumor was that when Francis and Henry were considering a meeting, Francis doubted Henry's good faith. Henry swore that he would not shave until the meeting had taken place. The state of Henry's beard was therefore watched as a barometer of his inclinations. A meeting did in fact take place and Henry continued to wear a beard the rest of his life. So did Francis.

Henry wanted to be stronger, richer, better looking than Francis, who was said to be extremely handsome, though he was also said to look like the devil. Henry knew he was no longer the youngest king in Europe but the oldest, and his wife was even older; Francis unkindly said that while Henry himself was very young and handsome, he had "an old deformed wife." [46]

The Venetians gave a glowing description of Henry's appearance about this time. They said that he was extremely handsome, very fair and admirably proportioned. He had a beard which looked like gold. He was very accomplished, a good musician and composed well. He was a capital horseman and jousted well. He spoke good French, Latin and Spanish and could understand Italian. The Venetians also said that he was very fond of hunting and tennis, which "it is the prettiest thing in the world to see him play, his fair skin gleaming through a shirt of the finest texture." They also described the English court:

> In short, the wealth and civilization of the world are here: and those who call the English barbarians appear to me to render themselves such. I here perceive very elegant manners, extreme decorum, and very great politeness.[47]

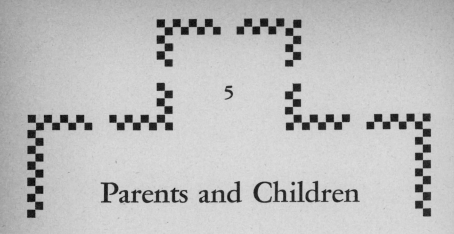

5

Parents and Children

1. *Princess Mary*

In Greenwich Palace at four o'clock on the morning of February 18, 1516, a daughter was born to Katharine. She survived; all Katharine's other children—with the exception of Prince Henry, who had lived for only two months—either had been stillborn or had died immediately after birth. Henry and Katharine were naturally delighted, although they and the rest of England would have preferred a son. Everybody rejoiced with the royal family:

> Pray Christ, save Father and Mother
> And this young lady fair
> And send her shortly a brother
> To be England's right heir.
>
> *Anon.*[1]

And Henry said hopefully to the Venetian ambassador, "We are both young; if it be a girl this time, by the Grace of God, boys will follow." [2]

A living child brought Katharine closer to Henry again, even if only temporarily. It also helped to console her for the loss of her father and sister: Queen Maria of Portugal died shortly after the birth. Ferdinand's death had taken place just before, but the news had been kept from Katharine in order not to upset her at such a crucial time. Katharine and Juana were now the only surviving children of Ferdinand and Isabella—and Juana was as remote from Katharine as if she no longer lived.

When the Princess was only three days old, she was taken to the monastery of the Observant Friars near Greenwich Palace to be both christened and confirmed. The Countess of Surrey carried the child in her arms and was accompanied by the Duke of Norfolk and the Duke of Suffolk, Charles Brandon. A silver font generally used for royal baptisms had been brought specially from Canterbury for the occasion. The child was named Mary after Henry VIII's sister. Wolsey was made her godfather and she had three godmothers, including Margaret Pole, who had now become Countess of Salisbury.

Mary survived the ice-cold ceremony, which is more than many other babies of that period had managed to do. Another Katharine, was appointed her wet-nurse and Lady Margaret Bryan was made Lady Mistress, or Governess.

Henry was a very proud father. He carried his daughter about in his arms and showed her off to the ambassadors at court. He even boasted that she never cried. A story was also told of Henry's devotion by the Venetian ambassador. An Italian friar, Dionysius Memo, had been brought to the English court as it was thought that his musical gifts would please Henry:

> His Majesty caused the Princess, his daughter, who is
> two years old, to be brought into the apartment where

we were; whereupon the right reverend Cardinal
[Wolsey] and I, and all the other lords, kissed her
hand, according to custom;—the greatest marks of
honor being paid her universally, more than the
Queen herself. The moment she cast her eyes on the
reverend Dionysius Memo, who was there, she commenced calling out in English, Priest, Priest; and he
was obliged to go and play for her; after which the
King, with the Princess in his arms, highly commended the friar and praised him.[3]

It would seem that Katharine's kindness of heart and sense
of justice could still influence the King. In 1517, on Evil
May Day, as it afterward came to be known, the apprentices
of London revolted against the foreigners who were living
in the city. There was enough unemployment among the
apprentices at that time to cause unrest and there were one
or two ringleaders [4] to organize it. The foreigners were made
the scapegoats. There was a strong upsurge of feeling which
resulted in considerable violence and damage to property.
The authorities dealt very harshly with the rioters. Thirteen
of them were hanged immediately and four hundred more
were condemned to death. Thomas More and Wolsey were
against such drastic recrimination and tried to have the sentences lifted. According to legend, Katharine and the King's
two sisters, Margaret and Mary, reinforced his pleas by kneel-
ing publicly before the King, begging him to spare the lives
of the boys. Although a foreigner herself, Katharine had
great sympathy with the young people and with their parents.
Henry listened to the three Queens and granted their petition. The boys' lives were saved and England's gratitude
to Katharine was celebrated in Churchyard's song:

> What if (she said) by Spanish blood
> Have London's stately streets been wet;

> Yet I will seek this country's good,
>   And pardon for their children get . . . .
> And so disrobed of rich attires,
>   With hair unbound she sadly lies,
> And of her gracious Lord requires
>   A boon which hardly he denies . . . .
> For which, kind Queen, with joyful heart
>   She heard their mothers' thanks and praise;
> And so from them did greatly part,
>   And lived beloved all her days.

In Europe, too, there was unrest and rumbles of the Reformation. This was the year when Martin Luther made a gesture that was to echo through the years. Reacting against the sale of too many indulgences by the Church, he posted his Ninety-five Theses on the church door at Wittenberg. This was the signal for widespread revolt against the Church. Luther's teachings were also said to have inflamed the Peasants' Revolt which followed. His name was by this time becoming well-known throughout Europe, but some people with otherwise advanced ideas, pretended to know no more than this about him. Erasmus at first disclaimed him though later he was to say there were certain truths in Luther's writings. Thomas More, although critical of the evils of his day and a reformer, too—he had written *Utopia* two years earlier—did not support Luther's views.

Henry VIII had been trained in theology. About this time or a little later he was encouraged by Wolsey to write a book [5] attacking Luther. Four years later, Luther's works were publicly burned in St. Paul's Churchyard and Henry sent as a present to the Pope a copy of his own book bound in cloth of gold. Some of his contemporaries, including Luther himself, did not believe that Henry was the sole author. Thomas More was one of those said to have had a hand in it.

Later, when Henry's attitude to the Pope had changed, he
accused More of having provoked him to write a treatise
upholding the Pope's authority. But at this time he was proud
of the work which won for him the title of Defender of the
Faith.[6] Henry now had a title to match that of Francis, the
Christian King.

In 1517, Mary, Duchess of Suffolk, had her second child,
a girl who was named Frances after the King of France.
Katharine and her infant daughter were godparents, though
they were not present at the christening, perhaps because of
the sweating sickness. This terrible disease had again broken
out in England and continued all through the next year. The
royal court broke up and moved away from London in an
effort to avoid it. Wolsey stayed on to run affairs of state,
but is thought to have caught it. He, however, recovered,
which is more than many people did. Henry wrote to him
sending fond messages from Katharine, who had not yet
come to dislike him as much as she did later. Katharine was
also concerned about both Henry and Mary but they were
spared. Thomas More too was worried. In August, he wrote
to Erasmus:

> We are in such grief and danger as never before.
> Many are dying all round us, and almost everybody at
> Oxford, Cambridge, and London, have been laid up
> within the last few days. Many of our best and most
> honored friends have perished.[7]

It was not long before plans were made for the betrothal
of Mary. In 1518, Francis had his first child, a son. When he
was not quite eight months and Mary was only two and a
half years old, the two children were betrothed and a treaty
of alliance was signed between England and France. The ceremony was the occasion for great rejoicings and ostentatious

feasting. The night before, Wolsey gave a tremendous reception at his house in Westminster which equaled, or outdid, anything the King could have done. Henry, incidentally, was staying at Durham House, Katharine's old home, but it is doubtful whether Katharine was with him. She was again in an advanced state of pregnancy and Henry was solicitous for her welfare. He had already shown his concern in a letter written in July:

> Two things there be which be so secret that they cause me at this time to write to you myself; the one, is that I trust the Queen my wife to be with child; the other is chief cause why I am so loth to repair to London ward, because about this time is partly of her dangerous times, and because of that I would remove her as little as I may now.[8]

Katharine's pregnancy was, however, no secret to the ambassadors who had been reporting it for months.

The day of the betrothal was fixed for October 5. The King and Queen were both present in the Church of the Observant Friars at Greenwich. Mary stood in front of her mother. The little Princess was dressed in cloth of gold and on her head was a cap of black velvet blazing with jewels. The King and Queen were asked for their consent which they freely gave, although Katharine probably had secret misgivings. Wolsey, holding a tiny ring with a huge diamond, came forward. The Lord Admiral, the Earl of Surrey, who stood proxy for the French Dauphin, passed the ring over the second joint of her third finger and Mary was Princess of France. Then followed some of the biggest feasting on record. In one day alone, among many other foods and drinks were consumed 3,000 loaves of bread, 3 tuns and 2 pipes of wine, 6 tuns and 7 hogsheads of ale, 10¾ carcasses of beef, 56 of muttons, 17 veals, 3 porkers, 4 fat hogs, 2 doz. fat

capons, 5 doz. and 7 Kentish capons, 7 dozen of a coarser
kind, 27 dozen of chickens, 2½ dozen of pullets, 15 swans,
56 cranes, 32 doz. pigeons, 54 doz. of larks, 5 doz. and 8
geese, 4 peacocks, 18 peachicks, and 50 doz. crayfish.[9] Francis
put on a show equally magnificent in Paris for the Dauphin.

Just over a month later, on November 10, Katharine's last
child was born, a girl who did not live. She may also have
had another stillborn daughter the previous year. In the general consternation and dismay at the continued lack of a son
and heir, the advisability of the French marriage began to be
questioned. The idea that a French King might one day rule
over England was not liked. It was thought that if the still-
birth had taken place earlier, the betrothal would not have
been concluded.

Katharine and Henry were both exceedingly disappointed.
Much as Henry loved Mary, he still wanted a son to succeed
him and it seemed that Katharine could not give him one.
Katharine was now thirty-three. She was not old by our
standards, but looked more than her age. We do not know
when they realized that she would not be able to have any
more children. It cannot have been long after this, though it
was not publicly admitted for some time. To make matters
worse for Katharine, the following year Henry had an illegitimate son who was given the name of Henry Fitzroy. The
mother was Elizabeth Blount, one of Katharine's young maids
of honor.

2. *Elizabeth Blount*

Elizabeth Blount, as the mother of Henry's son, was of
great importance in Katharine's life, and her story has often
been misrepresented.

Early in Henry's reign it was said by the Venetians that

he was fond of girls. No name, however, with the possible exception of that of the Duke of Buckingham's sister, had ever before been linked with his. No contemporary gossip, no scandals, have come down to us, which would suggest that, if the early Venetian report was true, Henry's fancies were fleeting. He was faithful to his wife after the fashion of other sixteenth-century kings and nobles. His greatest desire was to have legitimate sons so that he could expect at least one of them to live to succeed him. If Katharine's sons had survived, it is likely that Katharine would have remained Queen of England until her death, that Henry would not have had to marry five times in his efforts to achieve his aim. Certainly, Henry Fitzroy and his mother would not have been as important to Henry as they were.

As it was, Elizabeth Blount achieved very little notice that has been recorded. Edward Hall, who wrote after her death, could not, for his own sake, report anything detrimental to the King's character, and so only said:

> The king in his fresh youth, was in the chains of love with a fair damsel called E. Blunt . . . which damsel in singing, dancing, and in all goodly pastimes, exceeded all other, by the which goodly pastimes, she won the king's heart . . . by him she bare a goodly man child, of beauty like to the father and mother. This child was well brought up, like a Prince's child. . . .[10]

There are no known portraits of Elizabeth and we have no clear picture of what she looked like at any time of her life. The only assumptions that may justifiably be made are that she was pretty, gay, attractive and, when she first came to court, very young. The Venetians, usually the first to spread rumors, made no mention of her. From the time of the birth of her child until she eventually married someone else, she was referred to respectfully as the "mother of the King's son." In more recent years, various statements have been made about her not all of which are accurate. It is, however, possible to piece together some of her true story.

Elizabeth Blount (or Blunt) is thought to have been born about the year 1500 at Kinlet, not far from Ludlow. She was the second of six daughters. One of Elizabeth's great-grandfathers, Sir Richard Croft, had been steward to Prince Arthur at Ludlow and his wife had been Arthur's governess. Her grandfather, Sir Thomas Blount, was Steward of the Royal Manor at Bewdley. Sir Thomas knew Arthur and Katharine when they lived briefly in his part of the world and had helped to carry Arthur's body on its last journey from Ludlow to Bewdley on its way to Worcester. Elizabeth's father was John Blount, probably a distant relative of Lord Mountjoy.

Elizabeth is first heard of in London in 1513 when, presumably only just thirteen years old, she received one hundred shillings as her wages at court for the preceding year. Her father, as one of the King's spears, was alloted £500 in the same list. Elizabeth had become one of the Queen's maids of honor as was then customary for young girls of good family. Her father and grandfather accompanied Henry VIII to his battles at Tournai and Therouenne in 1513. It is likely that Elizabeth was with the Queen at Dover both on this occasion, when Katharine went to see the men off and was made Regent, and again the following year when Henry's sister Mary left to marry Louis XII. A month or two later, Charles Brandon, on a mission to the French King, sent a personal letter to Henry VIII with an affectionate message for Elizabeth Blount and her recently married friend Elizabeth Carew. The fact that the King was asked to deliver such a message would seem to show that he was on rather more than just friendly terms with the two girls.

Elizabeth Blount was twice heard of at court in 1514, each time as taking part in the revels. In the Christmas mummeries at Greenwich, she and three other young girls appeared in gowns of white satin lined with blue with hoops of the same color. Their mantles and bonnets were of blue velvet piped and decorated with gold. She must have been one of the "sumptuous" maidens entertained by Robin Hood in Henry's elaborate May Day celebrations the following year and one of the "beautiful" girls reported by the Venetians about the same time. Whenever Katharine's maidens are heard of we may assume that Elizabeth was one of them. The Queen and her older ladies-in-waiting might occupy themselves with the more sedate activities of sewing and embroidery, but the picture conjured up of Elizabeth's life is one of lighthearted pleasure and gaiety.

Her last known appearance before the birth of her son was in October 1518. The occasion was the magnificent banquet given by Wolsey before Princess Mary's betrothal at which Katharine was not present since she was in the late stages of pregnancy. Among Wolsey's many guests were the Duke of Suffolk and his wife Mary, Dowager Queen of France; one of Margaret Pole's sons; the Carews; the Guildfords; and Elizabeth Blount, who was seen dancing with Francis Bryan. He was a gifted poet, but was also thought by some to be a dissolute young man. Many years later the story was told that Henry could not believe that his daughter Mary knew no "foul or unclean" speech "until he had caused Francis Bryan to try it" at one of the court masques.[11]

Not long after the banquet Elizabeth left court life behind her for good. She retired to the Priory of St. Laurence at Blackmore in Essex, where, in June 1519, she gave birth to a son. Henry acknowledged that he was the father and the child was given the name of Henry Fitzroy. Wolsey was made his godfather and he continued to take an interest in him for the rest of his own life.

It is not known how long Elizabeth stayed at Blackmore nor whether the King came to visit her there. A later legend, often quoted but quite unverified, said that he used to come to see her at a house nearby called Jericho, reputed to be one of his houses of pleasure. There is a blank of three years in her life which has to be filled in somehow and this has therefore come to be accepted by many. One thing is certain, she did not return to Katharine's service. Henry Fitzroy was allowed to stay with her for a little time before being given a household of his own. Wolsey continued to keep an eye on her welfare and is supposed to have introduced her to Gilbert Tailboys, whom she married in 1522. A mysterious statement was made at the time of Wolsey's downfall in 1529 about this marriage. A list of misdeeds said to have been committed by Wolsey was drawn up in which it was said that he had encouraged the young gentlewomen of the realm to be "concubines by the well marrying of Bessie Blount, whom we would yet by sleight have married much better than she is; and for that purpose changed her name." [12] As Palsgrave, the man who had a hand in the writing of this document, bore Wolsey a personal grudge, the beginning of the sentence may be discounted. But whether there was in fact a plan to change Elizabeth's name before she married so that her prospective husband would not know who she was, whether there were plans to marry her to someone more important than Mr. Tailboys, whether in spite of these plans she chose to marry whom she pleased—these are questions that cannot be answered with certainty.

The newly married Tailboys were granted the manor and town of Rokeby in Warwickshire, which had formerly belonged to the Duke of Buckingham, and were also given a large sum of money. Shortly afterward, lands in Lincolnshire and East Yorkshire, which were in the possession of Gilbert Tailboy's father, were taken away from him and given to Elizabeth for life. Gilbert Tailboys was knighted and shortly afterward made Sheriff of Lincolnshire. A few years later he was further honored by being made a lord. He and Elizabeth had three children, a girl and two boys, and apparently lived a contented life together. He died in 1530 and the only thing of importance recorded on his tombstone was that he was the husband of Elizabeth Blount. At the time of his death she was living at the Castle of Kyme in Lincolnshire and was described as being eloquent, gracious and beautiful. Three years later, when she was thirty-five, Elizabeth married Lord Clinton, a neighbor of hers in Lincolnshire. He was twelve years younger than she was, so it would seem that she was still attractive. Henry Fitzroy died the following year at the age of seventeen. Here two sons by Gilbert Tailboys were to die about the same age. By Lord Clinton she had three more children who were still very young at the time of her own death, which is thought to have taken place about 1540.

3. *The Field of Cloth of Gold*

The year 1519, which saw Katharine's discomfiture at the birth of Henry Fitzroy, was also the year that her nephew achieved a great victory in Europe. On June 28—Henry VIII's twenty-ninth birthday—Charles V, having already inherited the titles of King of Spain and King of the Romans from his grandfathers, was elected Holy Roman Emperor. Henry VIII and Francis I had both been candidates but had stood no chance against Charles. It was not only a question of who bribed the electors most; Charles was the favorite for hereditary reasons. Henry received no votes at all. The real struggle in Europe then became a struggle between Charles and Francis, with Henry aiding one or the other as he, supported by Wolsey, thought most advantageous. Henry was rich and had money to lend. His friendship was therefore sought by both protagonists, as well as by the Pope—a wordly rather than a holy prince—and by the Venetians. His intervention, however, was to no great purpose except to exhaust his treasury and impoverish his people.

Public opinion in England was divided and not necessarily behind him. On the whole, the English middle class supported Charles, for the bulk of its foreign trade was the woolen trade with Flanders. Generally speaking, Wolsey was on the side of the French, though he supported Charles when Henry demanded it. Katharine's sympathies were naturally with Spain and her nephew. But instead of conflict she would have liked to see a united European front against what she considered to be the real enemy: the Turkish infidel army which was pushing its way into Europe from the East. In 1518, the Treaty of London had been drawn up with just this purpose in view. But immediate jealousies between the great powers were more pressing and the peace did not last four years. Even Katharine herself was sometimes made to feel that maybe the real enemy they had to fight was Francis. The Turks took advantage of the European internal struggles to advance further and further into the continent, even as far as Hungary, before their force subsided.

Katharine now rarely took part in the gayer activities of Henry's court though she still attended diplomatic functions as his Queen. Most outstanding among these was the expensive and fantastic display put on when Henry and Francis met at the Field of Cloth of Gold. Outwardly, it was a ceremonial, friendly gesture but behind the scenes there was considerable mistrust. Katharine was against the meeting from the start as she thought it would result in an alliance with France. When, in 1520, Henry arranged that he should go to see his daughter's future father-in-law in France, Katharine and the Emperor's ambassador, Bernardino de Mesa, immediately got in touch with Charles. With some difficulty, they persuaded him to pay a state visit to England before Henry left for France. On her knees, Katharine begged Henry to grant her the favor of seeing her nephew for the first time, but she did not rely on sentiment alone. Shortly afterward Henry came unexpectedly to a meeting of the Queen's Council where he found Katharine successfully haranguing its members against an alliance with France. He was embarrassed, but also impressed, by her performance. He also saw, though he must have known before, that many members of her council were still anti-French. The result was that Henry and Charles met twice, once in England before the meeting with Francis and once afterward in France.

Charles arrived at Dover at the end of May. He was first met by Wolsey and entertained in Dover Castle. Shortly afterward Henry arrived and together they rode to Canterbury so that Charles could see the Queen of England, his aunt, for the first time. They all spent Whitsuntide together and it is not impossible that the idea first cropped up then that Mary might be married to Charles instead of to the Dauphin. Henry probably hoped by such a match to be able to influence Charles, now twenty years old, as Ferdinand had hoped to influence Henry when he was a young king of eighteen years.

Charles departed from Dover on May 31. The same day, Henry, Katharine, Mary, the Dowager Queen of France, and Wolsey set off to meet Francis. They were accompanied by a magnificent array of courtiers, soldiers and horses. In Henry's retinue there were said to be 3,997 people and 2,087 rses and in Katharine's, 1,175 people and 775 horses. The Cardinal's retinue was also impressive, with Wolsey and two hundred of his followers clad in crimson velvet at their head. A whole town was built in Guisnes to house the English company with state apartments, lodgings and chapels all decorated with the Tudor rose. The King and Queen were lodged in a magnificent palace adorned inside with every kind of rich and sumptuous hanging.

Francis and his court were housed with equal splendor in Ardres, a short distance away. The Field of Cloth of Gold [13] was an apt description of the extravagance which was found at this meeting. The festivities lasted twenty days. During the jousts, Francis had the misfortune to unhorse Henry, who was furious. There was nearly a nasty incident and Henry had to be prevented forcibly from retaliating. Katharine and the French Queen Claude, however, understood each other better and saw the humor in the situation. They became friends and wept when they parted. For some time they kept up a friendly correspondence. It is possible that Anne Boleyn was one of the young girls attending Queen Claude, and, if so, Henry may have caught a glimpse of her.

No sooner was the meeting with Francis over than Henry again met Charles. On their way home Henry and Katharine stayed in Calais. Charles was a short distance away in Gravelines, just over the Flemish border. Henry crossed into Flanders to see him and returned the next day, accompanied by Charles and his aunt Lady Margaret of Savoy. Dressed in black velvet, with her ladies similarly attired, she arrived in a litter covered with black velvet. This was the first time she and Katharine had met since the days in Spain, over twenty years earlier, when Margaret had been a bride and it had been suggested that she should teach Katharine French. When they had embraced and kissed, Margaret went away to her lodging, but they afterward spent the evening together while Charles and Henry discussed business. What they talked about and how they liked each other after all this time is not recorded. Age and experience had changed them both considerably and though they never met again, they continued to exchange letters. In Katharine's later tribulations, Margaret of Savoy was always on her side.

The meeting between Henry and Charles was friendly. "The Emperor made such semblant of love to the English court that he won the love of the Englishmen." [14] They stayed together three days and then all of them went home.

4. *The Endless Circle*

Although Wolsey was more in favor of a French alliance, he carried out Henry's policies in support of Charles. He also helped Henry in another matter: The impeachment of the Duke of Buckingham, the only Duke who had been left alive by Henry VII after the Wars of the Roses. In 1521, a case of high treason was brought against Buckingham. It did not help him that he had been a good and loyal friend of both the King and Queen. His real crime was that he was descended from both Edward III and the Beauforts. Now that it was clear that Katharine was not going to have any more children, he became dangerous. If anything happened to Mary, or if she married out of the country, he was the next in line of succession. He was reported to have said that he intended to claim the throne in the event of Henry's death, though this he denied. He was accused of having consulted a monk before the birth of Mary who had foretold that he "should have all." He was tried, convicted and sentenced to a horrible death by hanging, drawing and quartering. According to Shakespeare,[15] Katharine begged that his life be

spared. If she made this plea, she pleaded in vain. Henry let
Buckingham die. His sentence was changed to a less cruel
one, however. He was executed on Tower Hill but it still
took three strokes of the executioner's axe to sever his head
from his body.

After a great deal of negotiation with Wolsey, Charles
again came to England in 1522. He came to Greenwich
where "he asked the Queen's blessing (for that is the fashion
of Spain between the Aunt and Nephew). The Emperor had
great joy to see the Queen his Aunt, and in especial his young
cousin the Lady Mary." [16] The usual entertainment was provided. Henry took part in the jousting but Charles watched
from a balcony with Katharine at his side. More serious matters concerning an alliance were discussed too. As a result,
Charles and Mary were officially betrothed and the English
alliance with France was forgotten. Details were fixed and a
clause included that if they had a son he would inherit the
throne of England. Henry's sister Mary had been four years
older than Charles when betrothed to him; Henry's daughter
Mary was sixteen years younger. Her father and mother
showed no signs of thinking this odd. Katharine seemed only
to be glad that new ties were being formed between her old
family and her new, between her nephew and her daughter.

Charles charmed everyone and Mary did too. When he
came to London, he was received wtih great pageantry. The
streets were decorated with verses written in gold wishing
prosperity to Charles and Henry as Defenders of the Church
and of the Faith. The citizens of London were not, however,
sufficiently enamored of him to want to pay for his entertainment. Immediately after he left they demanded £20,000 to
cover the cost of the pageants they had put on in his honor.[17]

War with France was now a certainty. Although Wolsey
was intriguing with the French, he raised an army and

English soldiers again went to fight in Europe on the side of the Emperor. By now England was becoming impoverished. Henry had spent his father's money on extravagant living and expensive invasions. He had also lent money to Maximilian and Charles. Wolsey imposed heavy taxes on the citizens in order to meet the costs of the war but only earned their hatred as a result. In the end they rebelled and refused to pay, so no more soldiers were sent abroad and England backed out of the war. Charles, however, had better luck against the French. His army captured the French King and defeated Francis's forces at the battle of Pavia in February 1525. Both Henry and Katharine wrote to congratulate Charles, though at the same time Henry's diplomatic negotiations began to be directed toward an attempt to free Francis. It did not suit the English King that Charles should be so powerful. But Charles held all the trumps. He had won the war while England had withdrawn from it.

In the meantime Katharine had let no chance slip by of praising Mary to Charles. His own representatives transmitted the messages:

> [The Queen said] I should not leave without seeing the Princess dance. Princess Mary did not have to be asked twice; she performed a slow dance, and twirled so prettily that no woman in the world could do better; afterwards . . . she danced a *gaillarde* . . . then she played two or three songs on the spinet . . . she is pretty and very tall for her age, just turned seven and a very fine young cousin indeed.[18]

She had benefited from her father's teaching. Henry boasted that she played better on the spinet than he did and that she was beginning to play the lute.

Before long, however, Mary's betrothal to Charles began

to be in doubt. Charles was being urged to marry his Portuguese cousin Isabella, one of Maria's daughters. She was old enough to give him children right away and also brought with her a large dowry. Mary would bring him nothing as Charles had already borrowed the equivalent of her dowry from Henry and had spent it. Katharine, aware that the relationship with her nephew was strained, still hoped for the marriage. She believed that if he kept his promise to marry her daughter, the alliance would remain unbroken. Wolsey was openly in the opposite camp now. He did everything he could to prevent Katharine from talking to Charles's ambassador or sending any messages to her nephew.

The delays came from both sides. Not only was Charles hesitant to commit himself, but Henry at one moment was pressing Mary on to Francis, at another he was urging Charles to marry her. The ambassadors likened their negotiations to an "endless circle." Charles forced the issue to a conclusion by demanding that Mary should come over at once with her dowry. He said that it was his wish that she should be brought up by his other aunt Margaret of Savoy at whose court he had himself been educated. If, however, Henry would not agree to this, Charles asked that he would free him from his engagement. He would then marry another cousin, who was of a more suitable age. The message was held up and arrived in a garbled form. Henry got the implication of it and was furious. He was also annoyed that Charles made no move to repay his debts in spite of promises to the contrary and Katharine's letters urging him to keep his promises.

Henry felt that Charles's treachery was as great as Ferdinand's had been in 1513. In reply to the request that Mary should be brought up by Margaret of Savoy he instructed his ambassadors to tell the Emperor that if he "should seek a mistress for her to frame her after the manner of Spain . . .

he should not find in all Christendom a more meet than she now hath, that is to say, the Queen's grace, her mother, who is come of this house of Spain . . ." [19] But, at the same time, Henry vented his anger on Katharine and the Spaniards in her suite. Mary did not go to Spain or Flanders. Her betrothal to Charles was broken off on July 6, 1525. The following March, Charles married his cousin Isabella of Portugal.

The rest of the year 1525 was not a happy one for Katharine. Not only had her plans for Mary come to nothing, but all communication with her nephew was at a standstill as the Emperor no longer had an ambassador in London. Bernardino de Mesa, Ferdinand's last ambassador and his only representative to maintain a friendly and useful relationship with Katharine, had stayed on until 1522. He had been particularly helpful in negotiating the alliance with the new Emperor and Charles's betrothal to Mary. His successor, Luis de Praet of Flanders, got nowhere. Prevented by Wolsey from seeing either King or Queen, he went home in frustration at the end of 1524. He was not replaced until the end of 1526, by which time Katharine was lamenting that she had not heard from Charles for two years. Even when the next ambassador, Inigo Mendoza, belatedly reached London, he was not able to be of much help to her. Wolsey still did everything in his power to prevent them from talking privately.

Other things also conspired to make Katharine miserable. Her falling out of favor with Henry again coincided with illness. Her health had been even worse than usual for some time, and she had therefore lived in semi-retirement. We do not know exactly what was the matter with her. It could have been a recurrence of the fevers thought to have been malaria which she had had twenty years earlier. It could have been bronchial trouble as she always seems to have suffered from coughs and colds. Her many pregnancies and miscarriages, without benefit of the medical care and knowledge she would have received today, had left her weak and tired, if nothing else. At one time, she felt so ill and depressed that she thought she was not long for this world. She wrote to Wolsey of "when God calls me" and there were rumors abroad that she was dying.

Henry, too, is believed to have had malaria in 1521, and it recurred from time to time during the rest of his life. He also injured himself in a fall from a horse in the same year and afterward is known to have suffered from headaches and catarrh. The fall could have accounted for the change for the worse in his character which began about this time.[20] Henry also suffered from painful varicose veins in his legs which helped to make him irritable. Although he mixed soothing ointments for himself, he did not stop overeating, lose weight or change any other habits in order to effect a cure.

Annoyed with Charles, Henry began to consider new plans for Mary's future. At the age of nine, she had already been officially betrothed twice. Now an earlier suggestion that she might marry her cousin James V of Scotland was revived. As could be expected, there were also attempts to use her to cement a new French alliance. Francis I, since the death of Queen Claude in 1524, was again in the market. True, he was nineteen years older than Mary and known to be considering marriage to Charles's sister Eleanor, who was nearer his own age. He did not, however, turn down the proposition immediately when it was made to him. And there were also his two sons, the Dauphin and the Duke of Orleans, one of whom might be a suitable match for Mary. They were still prisoners in Spain, but negotiations were under way to free them. Henry also had the thought, especially repugnant to Katharine, of marrying Mary to Henry Fitzroy, his natural son whom he had made legitimate.

Some of Henry's other actions at this time, either by acci-

dent or intent—and it is hard not to believe they were inten-
tional—also caused great distress to Katharine. Henry Fitzroy, six years old in 1525, was brought at nine o'clock one
morning to the new Palace of Bridewell in London and
honors were heaped upon him. He was appointed Keeper of
the City and Castle of Carlisle. He was made Earl of Somer-
set and Duke of Richmond and Nottingham, titles which
had formerly belonged to his grandfather, Henry VII. Shortly
afterward, he also became Lord High Admiral of England,
Wales, Ireland, Normandy, Gascony and Acquitaine; Warden General of the Marches of Scotland; Knight of the
Garter; and first peer of England. He became second in rank
to the King who had a special coat of arms made for his
beloved son.

Katharine was outraged, but this was not all she had to
suffer. According to a Venetian report, "it seems that the
Queen resents the Earldom and Dukedom conferred on the
King's natural son and remains dissatisfied, at the instigation,
it is said, of three of her Spanish ladies, her chief counsellors;
so the King has dismissed them from the court,—a strong
measure, but the Queen was obliged to submit and to have
patience." [21] Katharine begged Henry to reinstate her ladies,
but he refused. Her pride was hurt, but she was helpless.

In the summer came yet another blow. On the advice of
Wolsey and his Council, the King decided to set up two new
royal establishments. First, Henry Fitzroy was sent to the
north of England. Two months later Mary was sent to the
Welsh marches. Katharine and Mary were to be separated.

5. *The Education of Henry Fitzroy*

Henry Fitzroy was staying with his household in Durham
Place, presumably the same as Katharine's Durham House,
at the time he received his many honors from the King. Be-

fore he was sent with a large establishment to the north of England he went to say good-bye to his father at Hampton Court. He then set out on his journey in a horse litter garnished with cloth of silver which had been given to him by Wolsey, his godfather. His footmen were resplendent in blue and yellow and his retinue was large as befitted his new rank as Duke of Richmond. The young Duke did not like being treated as a child, however, and did not want to ride in the litter. He preferred to ride on horseback like the men and his temper improved when he was allowed to do so. The journey was made in easy stages with stops at various places including Huntingdon, Stamford and York. He was given time to practice his skill with the bow and arrow and he also slew a buck while staying near Stamford, no mean feat for a six year old boy.

On August 29, the party reached the castle of Sheriff Hutton, where his grandmother Elizabeth of York and the young Earl of Warwick are thought to have been confined during the Wars of the Roses. This was to be Henry Fitzroy's principal home in Yorkshire, though he is also known to have stayed in York, Pontefract and Newcastle, where courts of justice were held. There were sixteen principal officers in his establishment and 245 servants on the payroll. Sir William Parr was put in charge of the household and Richard Page was made Vice-Chamberlain. The King had appointed Dr. Butts, his own physician, to attend his son. The education of his "worldly jewel" [22] he first entrusted to John Palsgrave, who had also been schoolmaster to Mary Tudor before she went to France. For companions, the boy was given his two young uncles, brothers of Elizabeth Tailboys. Palsgrave obtained permission from the King to teach him Latin. In a letter he wrote to Henry VIII, he said:

> . . . according to my saying to you in the gallery at
> Hampton Court I do my uttermost best to cause him
> to love learning and to be merry at it, in so much
> that without any manner of fear or compulsion he
> hath already a great furtherance in the principles
> grammatical both Greek and Latin.[23]

Henry Fitzroy was said to be of an amiable disposition, good at learning, sports, and music.

Palsgrave, however, was not pleased with Henry Fitzroy's pronunciation of Latin, which he blamed on the clerk who had first taught him his Matins. But, he said, "whereas he is something inclined to lisp, I now trust at the changing of his teeth to amend the default." [24]

Palsgrave found many difficulties put in his way by other members of the household who still believed that learning was more of a hindrance than a help to a nobleman. He aired his grievances to Thomas More, Wolsey, and Elizabeth Tailboys. He said the mother should come and see for herself how her child, who was virtuous and honorable by inclination, was being corrupted by people who taught him to tell lies. Perhaps because of his complaints, he was replaced by Dr. Croke, who ran into the same difficulties. He found particularly annoying two young men in the household who interrupted his lessons and prevented any discipline. They were rude to him in front of his pupils and they taught the boys bawdy songs. They took them out hunting when they should have been working so that they were too tired to do any lessons when they came home. They also prevented Dr. Croke from punishing his pupils.

The King and Wolsey do not seem to have exercised much discretion in their choice of staff to attend the young Duke. After having received constant complaints about theft, vice and the mismanagement of funds, Wolsey tried to cut down on the expenses of the establishment. Some of the offenders ran away to Scotland. Some were told that their services were no longer needed, but when they complained to the King, they were reinstated. Soon afterward the household was broken up and dispersed. In 1529, Henry Fitzroy was living at Windsor, where he stayed for almost three years. Henry Howard, Earl of Surrey, son of the Duke of Norfolk, grandson of the Duke of Buckingham through his mother, was ordered by the King to be his companion. Many dynastic marriages were planned for Henry Fitzroy and there was talk of Surrey's marrying Princess Mary, but nothing came of any of the suggestions. Henry was by this time ten years old and his friend not quite two years older. Eventually, in 1533, Henry Fitzroy married Surrey's sister Mary Howard, and Surrey married a daughter of the Earl of Oxford. As both couples were still considered too young to live together, it is thought that the two boys continued their companionship. Henry and Mary were never husband and wife in anything more than name. Henry died in the summer of 1536.

Surrey was to become a considerable poet. In later years, when he had fallen into disfavor with the King and had been confined to Windsor Castle as a punishment, and when Henry Fitzroy was already dead, he wrote a poem remembering nostalgically the happy carefree days the boys had spent there together:

> *So cruel prison! How could betide, alas!*
> *As proud Windsor, where I in lust and joy,*
> *With a King's son my childish years did pass.*[25]

6. *The Education of Princess Mary*

In August 1525, about the time Henry Fitzroy arrived in Sheriff Hutton, Henry sent "our dearest, best beloved, and only daughter, the Princess, accompanied and established with an honorable, sad [serious], discreet, and expert Council, to reside and remain in the Marches of Wales." [26] Unlike Henry Fitzroy, Mary was given both a household which was a model of virtue and teachers renowned for their learning. Even though Katharine was not to be allowed to exercise direct control over her daughter's upbringing, she had a hand in the choice of those who would. Mary's staff numbered 303. They were dressed, furnished and equipped in a manner befitting the retinue of the Princess of Wales. Mary had no settled place of residence. She is known to have lived in Ludlow Castle, which had been repaired for her; Tickenhill, which had also recently been put into good condition again; and Thornbury, one of the former homes of the Duke of Buckingham.

Margaret Pole, Countess of Salisbury, was Lady Mistress and governess. She looked after the household of Katharine's child as she had formerly helped to look after Katharine when she had been Princess of Wales twenty-four years earlier. The King was at this time well-disposed to Margaret and showed his confidence by entrusting the care of his daughter to his wife's good friend. She was carefully instructed in the way Mary should be brought up: to serve God at due times; to take moderate exercise in the open air for the good of her health; to practice on her musical instruments and to dance, as long as these pastimes did not interfere with her Latin and French; to pay attention to her diet and to see that everything about her was pure, sweet, clean, and wholesome.

The separation from her daughter was hard for Katharine to bear, although she had always known that sooner or later they would have to part. In any case, it had not been customary for Mary to live with her parents. She had spent most Christmas and Easter holidays with them and often paid other visits to court, but most of the time she had resided in separate royal houses. She had, however, never been far from her mother. Now, it was almost as if she were in a foreign country. Katharine was no longer able to teach her or supervise directly her studies, though she continued to take the same interest in them she had always had. Katharine herself had received a broad education at the court of Ferdinand and Isabella. Her daughter might be called upon to rule England as her mother had ruled Spain. Katharine, therefore, thought that Mary should be trained for this purpose and receive as many educational advantages as if she had been a son. She was fortunate in being able to enlist the help of the Humanist scholars then teaching in England.

Linacre had been appointed Mary's first tutor and doctor. As he felt too old to fulfill either duty, he had written a Latin grammar book for her instead. This he was able to finish and present to her before he died in 1524. Thomas More, who in 1521 had been knighted for his services to the King, had also given his advice. He was often invited to supper alone with the King and Queen when they would have had plenty of opportunity to discuss his theories of education. He would rather have been at home with his wife and children, but could not refuse an invitation from the King.

Sir Thomas More's own household was famous for its erudition and learning. His three daughters and several other young people of both sexes were all taught together, a thing unheard of in those days. Special emphasis was laid on their learning to read the Latin classics and Greek. Theology, mathematics, astronomy, rhetoric and grammar, logic and philosophy were all part of their curriculum. More took a keen interest in their progress and expected them to keep him informed of what they were reading and writing when he was away. What was expected of them was probably also expected of Mary.

It was still rare for girls to be taught academic subjects, though the education of boys was beginning to make rapid strides. The Humanist scholars were teaching at new schools such as St. Paul's, which had been started by Dean Colet in St. Paul's Churchyard in 1510. Over two hundred grammar schools for boys were to be founded during the first half of the sixteenth century. Girls, however, continued to be taught the domestic arts at home and, as a rule, learned little or nothing else.

There were exceptions, however, and there were some scholars who believed in the education of girls. Katharine was one of the first to encourage them. Henry VII's mother, Margaret Beaufort, had also been a patron of education, but only for boys and men. Katharine's own interest had been aroused early in life at home in Spain. As early as 1492 Isabella had commissioned Antonio de Lebrija, an Italian scholar at her court, to write a Castilian grammar for the instruction of her ladies. Thomas More had advocated the teaching of girls in his *Utopia* in 1516. In 1523, Juan Luis Vives,[27] a great Spanish Humanist who had been influenced by Erasmus' Latin treatise on the *Instruction of a Christian Prince,* wrote, also in Latin, his *Instruction of a Christian Woman.* Richard Hyrde, a member of Sir Thomas More's household, translated this book into English in 1524 and More corrected it. Two years later in *On Christian Marriage*, Erasmus, influenced by More, also recommended that girls should be educated. He dedicated his treatise to Katharine, "a miracle of her sex, nor is she less to be reverenced for her piety than her education."

Katharine also took a great interest in one of the first

women's colleges. There was at Syon, across the Thames from Richmond, a religious house for girls of good family. Sixty nuns lived there and at this time the prioress was one of Lord Mountjoy's relatives. As it was a religious establishment, the teaching of the Scriptures naturally took up a great deal of time. But the girls were taught by scholar-priests and the monastery had academic connections with the University of Cambridge.

When Mary went to the Welsh border, Dr. Richard Fetherston was sent with her as her tutor. Katharine was happy with this appointment as we know from a letter she sent to her daughter:

> As for your writing in Lattine, I am glad that ye shall chaunge frome me to Maister Federston, for that shall doo you moche good, to lerne by him to write ryght. But yet some tymes I wolde be glad when ye doo write to Maister Federston of your owne editing, when he hathe rede it that I may se it. For it shalbe a grete comfort to me to see you kepe your Latten and fayer writing and all. And soo I pray you to recommaunde me to my Lady Salisbury.*

Katharine's only reference to her own loneliness and troubles was to say that "the long absence of the King and you troublethe me" and that her health was only "metely good." [28]

Dr. Fetherston's appointment was approved by Luis Vives, whom Katharine had also consulted about Mary's education. Vives had first come to teach at Oxford in 1523, at Wolsey's invitation, when he was thirty-one years old. He admired Katharine for her learning, as did his friends Erasmus and More, and dedicated his book *Instructions of a Christian Woman* to Katharine:

* Reproduced here in Katharine's own spelling.

I have been moved partly by the holiness and goodness of your living, partly by the favour, love and
zeal that your Grace beareth toward holy study and
learning, to write something unto your good Grace of
the information and bringing up of a Christian
woman. So in these books shall you see the resemblance of your mind and goodness, because that you
have been maid, wife and widow, and so you have
been handled yourself in all the order and course of
your life, that whatsoever you did might be an example unto other to live after.

Also your dearest daughter Mary shall read these
instructions of mine and follow in living.

His treatise was of a general nature, inspired not only by
Katharine's example but also by a desire to counteract the
evil influence of court life. Vives believed that girls were
frail vessels who should be sheltered from, not taught to
withstand, the temptations of the world, the flesh and the
devil. He also thought they should be kept fully occupied.
This was part of his general philosophy that idleness was
corrupting. "Amongst all good women it is a shame to be
idle. Therefore Queen Isabella taught her daughters to spin,
sew and paint."

To modern ears, some of his ideas seem crude and restric-
tive but generally speaking they were a great advance on
those of the Middle Ages. Some, in fact, are still topics of
discussion today. It had been customary to treat children
harshly and show them few signs of love. Although Vives
seems to have approved the saying, "Never have the rod off
the boy's back; specially the daughter should be handled
without any cherishing," his own advice was kinder. Mothers
should love their children, but hide their love; give them a
kiss as a reward for things well done, but punish them for
their vices.

Vives recommended that girls be brought up with other girls of their own age in the home. It was not good for them to be taught alone, or to be taught in the company of boys. He did not advise that they receive the same education as boys, even though some of them might have minds as good as the best to be found among boys. However bright or dull they were, they should be given a chance to learn; but their upbringing should take note of the different functions they were called upon to perform. A girl was to be brought up to be obedient to her husband as well as to her parents. She should learn how to perform all household tasks, not scorning even the lowliest. She should pay particular attention both to the "innocent" old crafts of spinning and weaving and to invalid cookery, in case her husband or children should be in need of it.

Vives also advised that her reading matter should be of the kind that would teach her good manners. In particular, he recommended among modern books More's *Utopia* and Erasmus' secular works. As a girl was naturally pious, he recommended that when she should learn to write, "let not her example be void verses, nor wanton or trifling songs, but some sad [serious] sentences prudent and chaste, taken out of holy Scriptures." She was to be modest in her food and dress and was not to use make-up. She was not to "paint nor anoint her face, but wash it and make it clean; nor dye her hair, but comb it cleanly, nor suffer her head to be full of scurf."

At Katharine's request, Vives later added a plan of studies and a textbook of maxims for Mary's special use under Dr. Fetherston's guidance. All of Vives's works are of interest as they reflect the change in attitude toward women's education during the Renaissance. Again, it is curious to note that some of the methods recommended by him are still in use in schools today.

All the books Mary was to read were to be of high moral standards. It was important that in Latin she should first learn to speak and write the language. The grammar was to come second; she should make the rules from observation of the authors she had read. She should make her own vocabulary, writing words that were new to her in a book. She should learn how to pronounce words properly, starting with the letters of the alphabet. When she read, she should jot down the points she found interesting. She should cultivate her memory by learning a passage each night. She should use words with their proper, or etymological, meaning and avoid slang. She should have her own dictionary.

As advised by Vives, Mary learned languages, grammar, rhetoric, philosophy and history. In later years it was said that she could speak Latin, French and Spanish and that she had some knowledge of Italian and Greek as well. She had been taught by her father to play on musical instruments and how to dance, though Vives frowned upon such frivolities. From her mother, who by now had given up the dancing she had loved as a girl, she had acquired her deeply religious habits.

Katharine, as Isabella had done before her, now wore under her dress the habit of St. Francis. She no longer desired the beautiful clothes she had craved when she was young. She attended at least two religious services a day. It was said that for the early morning one she dressed herself hastily as she considered the time lost which was spent in adorning herself. Her outlook was sad but philosophical. Vives, in the preface to his book of maxims for Mary, wrote of Katharine:

> I remember your Mother, a most wise woman, said to me as we came back by boat from Syon to Richmond, that she preferred moderate and steady fortune to great alterations of rough and smooth. But if she had to choose, she would elect the *saddest,* rather than

the most flattering fortune, because in the former consolation can be found, whilst in the latter, often even sound judgment disappears.

Perhaps when she said this, Katharine already had some idea that her fortune was going to be a sad one, though she was still not aware of the form it would take.

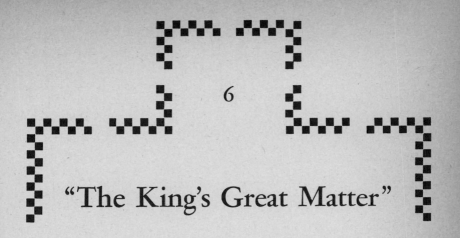

6

"The King's Great Matter"

1. Prelude to Divorce

Although distressed by Mary's absence, Katharine had not much time to mope. There were plenty of tasks to occupy her. She applied herself conscientiously, as was her habit, to the management of her own estates; she visited the sick and gave alms to the poor, of whom there were many; she sewed and she embroidered; and of course she prayed and did not neglect her religious duties.

A few months after her quarrel with Henry, Katharine's life apparently returned to normal. Henry's anger abated as it had always done before. He had long been renowned for his fiery temper. They again lived in the same house. We learn that Katharine was back at court from an order of the King's council dated January, 1526,[1] in which lodgings in the "King's House" were assigned by Wolsey to the Queen's attendants. Among those named were the French Queen Mary and her husband, the Duke of Suffolk; the old Duchess of Norfolk; the Queen's Lord Chamberlain and Vice-Chamberlain and their wives; Lady Lucy; Lady Guildford the elder; Lady Willoughby (Maria de Salinas); Lady Parr, as well as various maidens and gentlemen ushers, Katharine's secretary, physician and apothecary.

Apart from showing who were Katharine's personal attendants, this list is also of interest in that it formed part of a great reorganization and clean-up at court. The plan was to cut down on expenses, keep out undesirable elements, and try to prevent the spreading of the plague which had been particularly bad in 1525. The rules and regulations were tightened as to the number and quality of servants "considering the great confusion, annoyance, infection, trouble and dishonour arising from sickly and unmeet persons and also other rogues and vagabonds being about the court." [2] No substitution or delegation of duties was to be allowed. Fifteen servants designated by name were the only ones permitted to keep the King's chamber "pure and clean." They were also told to keep secret all that happened in the King's chamber and not to enquire where he was going or talk about his pastimes—though this instruction was later crossed out.

The King's pages were to rise at seven in the morning, make the fire and call the King's guard by eight o'clock. The Gentlemen of the Privy Chamber were to be ready to dress the King by seven, or earlier if the King so desired. His room was to be kept warm by the fire which was to be built up the night before. No dogs were to be allowed at court except a few spaniels for the ladies by special license of the King. Hours of meals were regulated for the court. On working days, dinner, the main meal of the day, was to be eaten at ten in the morning, supper at four in the afternoon. Hours for the royal meals were not fixed. Economies were also to be made in fuel, light, bread, ale and wine. Supplies were to be kept locked up to prevent stealing. From all of this it would seem that the court was badly in need of reorganization.

It was not long before Katharine also had the pleasure of seeing her daughter again. Negotiations were now going ahead for Mary's betrothal to the French King or one of his sons. In 1527, Mary visited her parents at least twice when they were entertaining the French ambassadors. She may indeed have been with them all the early part of that year. In February and March they were staying together in London. In April they were all in the royal palace at Greenwich, where the device of the pomegranate was plentifully used in the decorations—perhaps for the last time. Henry encouraged the ambassadors to speak to Mary in French, Latin and Italian, in all of which she answered them. They were suitably impressed, for she was only eleven years old.

Katharine had reluctantly consented in principle to Mary's betrothal to a French prince, though she was not very happy at the idea. She made one attempt to prevent the ambassadors from seeing Mary, but she was powerless to hinder the negotiations. In fact most details were deliberately kept from her on Henry's instructions. Katharine did not like the way foreign affairs were being shaped. She still would have liked to see Europe united against the common enemy, the Emperor Soliman the Magnificent. In May she wrote to Charles, with whom she was again in touch, to say, "There is urgent need that peace between Christian Princes be concluded before God sends down his scourge." [3] Henry's flirtation with the French seemed to her likely to help bring about the downfall of the whole of Europe, but she was helpless to prevent it. The personal relationship between her and Henry had deteriorated too far; she could no longer influence his decisions.

* Suleiman

Katharine spent her days in a state of uneasy quiet, with terrible rumors circulating around her. Charles's new ambassador, Inigo de Mendoza, had fortunately arrived in time to be at her side when the storm eventually broke, when Katharine first learned that Henry wanted to leave her forever. There was never any question of divorce as we understand it today, though it is the word generally used to describe the events of the next few years. All the efforts of Henry and his advisers were directed toward having his marriage to Katharine annulled, as if it had never been. At the time, the proceedings were referred to as the "King's Great Matter."

2.   *The Bull and the Brief*

Henry's first known step toward permanent separation from Katharine took place in London on May 17, 1527. The King caused himself to be summoned before a secret court held in Wolsey's palace, York House, where the two archbishops, Warham and Wolsey, charged him with having lived in sin with his brother's widow. They said that the Bull of dispensation sent to England by Pope Julius II after the death of Arthur was inadequate and therefore the marriage between Henry and Katharine not legal. Wolsey's devious mind had been able to pick many holes in the Bull. In fact, he said, it was so loosely drafted that whoever had done it must have been asleep. Some of the learned English bishops were also asked to give an opinion. To Wolsey's surprise, there was a dissenting voice: John Fisher, Bishop of Rochester, declared the marriage to be valid. As no unanimous decision could be reached, the court which had met three times in all was abandoned. It was decided that the matter be referred to the reigning Pope, Clement VII.

But this was not a propitious moment. Rome had just been overrun by the soldiers of Charles and the Pope was virtually a prisoner in the castle of St. Angelo. Much as he wanted to be saved from the Emperor, he was not yet ready to throw in his lot with the Kings of France and England. His mind was apparently as agile and certainly as well-versed in Church laws as Wolsey's. He and his legal advisers were well able to cope with the technical points raised. But a decision either way in regard to the adequacy of the Bull, and therefore the validity of the marriage, could only bring more disaster upon himself and the Church; so he settled on procrastination as the best strategy.

News of the secret court was not long in reaching the ears of both the Queen and Mendoza, who relayed it immediately to the Emperor. Not until June 22, however, did Henry come to speak to Katharine privately in her chamber, to tell her himself of the doubts he said had been troubling his conscience. He told her that much as he esteemed her he feared that their marriage was not, and never had been, valid in the eyes of God. As they were not husband and wife, they should therefore part. Although Katharine had not been unaware of the kind of thing he was going to say, her behavior showed how shocked and horrified she was to hear it from his own lips. She burst into tears. Henry himself was agitated and embarrassed. He clumsily tried to comfort her before he left by saying all would be done for the best, but this did not mean he had changed his mind.[4]

It was not only that Katharine's pride was hurt or that she thought she was to be succeeded by another woman— this knowledge came later. What worried her was that if Henry had his way, not only would she be considered as having lived in sin for eighteen years, but also that their daughter Mary would be considered illegitimate. Henry had told her he was speaking to her in secret. He was afraid of what the public might do by way of demonstration if they heard his plans. But the rumors had already been flying around London and were now spreading to the rest of England and to the Continent. The "King's Great Matter" was public gossip, "as notorious as if it had been proclaimed by the public crier." [5] Katharine, however, was content that no decision could be taken against her behind closed doors. More important still, she believed that now that the Emperor knew Henry's intentions he would take steps on her behalf in Rome.

This was not the first time the legality of the marriage had been questioned. It had been suggested that one of the reasons why Charles had hesitated about his betrothal to the Princess Mary was because her mother had been the wife of Henry's brother and there was, therefore, some doubt as to Mary's legitimacy. Even earlier, in 1509, Archbishop Warham had had some scruples but had nevertheless himself performed the marriage ceremony between Henry and Katharine. After the death of Arthur, at the time when the second marriage was being discussed, it had been realized by both Ferdinand and Isabella, as well as by Henry VII, that a special dispensation would be required from the Pope in order to allow Prince Henry to marry his brother's widow. This dispensation had been requested and, after much delay, had been sent to both Spain and England. Henry VII had received a Papal Bull, that is a legal document from the Pope, authorizing the marriage in 1505. It was the adequacy of this document that Henry now disputed.

In the light of later knowledge it would seem that Ferdinand had anticipated trouble. He had rightly assumed that other monarchs could be as devious in their ways as he was himself. He had taken the further precaution of covering

the possibility that the first marriage had been consummated
although he himself said that he did not believe this to be
true.* If it had, as Katharine's tutor Geraldini had asserted,
the dispensation was necessary; if it had not, as Donna Elvira
claimed, it was still important that the dispensation should
cover the possibility of consummation as nobody would
believe the contrary. As a result, the document received in
Spain shortly before Isabella's death in 1504 was apparently
different from the one sent to England. It was a Brief, or
formal Papal letter, which, in giving the required dispensation, covered the possibility that the marriage had been consummated. If a copy of this Brief had ever been sent to
England it was no longer to be found and Henry VIII had
never heard of it.

Henry's case was based only on the Bull which his advisers, after all these years, had suddenly discovered to be
faulty. During the course of 1528 what is thought to have
been Isabella's copy of the Brief conveniently, but none the
less credibly, was found among the papers of the late Dr.
de Puebla. It is thought that Ferdinand had sent it to him
so that he could show it to Henry VII. When the Emperor
saw the Brief, he sent a copy of it to Katharine, who produced it in England late in the autumn of the same year.
When asked why she had not produced it earlier, she said
that she had not thought it would be required. According to
Mendoza she said that it had been in her possession for six
months and that he had given it to her. He supported her in
this claim although apparently not altogether believing her.
"When I am questioned," he wrote to Charles, "I shall so
shape my answer that it may not disagree with the Queen's
declaration, nor make it appear as if she had stated an un-
truth." [6]

* See Chapter 3: *Marriage Negotiations Again.*

Henry VIII on hearing of the existence of the Brief
refused to believe it was genuine. It seemed to him a strange
coincidence that a papal document bearing the same date as
the Bull, December 26, 1503, but containing none of its
errors should be found so opportunely. It cut the ground from
under his feet. He demanded to see the actual Brief which
was being held in Spain. He put pressure on Katharine to
obtain it from her nephew, who, he said, had no right to it.*
Charles was suspicious of Henry's motives. He had also been
secretly warned by Mendoza not to accede to Katharine's
request to send the Brief to England as she had been coerced
by Henry into asking for it. Charles therefore refused to send
it to England though he did send an attested copy. Henry
then said that the Brief was a forgery as there was no record
of it in Rome—which was true. Papal authorities, however,
came to the conclusion that it was none the less authentic.

Legal experts have found very little difference between the
Bull and the Brief except that the latter contained none of
the loopholes of the former. Discussion has raged through
the centuries as to whether Katharine and Arthur were
husband and wife in more than name. It has been asserted
that the Bull did not give enough dispensation to cover this
possibility but that the Brief did. In fact Henry's council
did not query the Bull in this context. They rested their case
on legal technicalities such as that Henry was under age at
the time of the dispensation and therefore ignorant of what
was being arranged, and that the Pope had the right to
dispense in such matters only when the security of nations
was at stake (which had not been so in regard to England and
Spain at the time). It has been argued that, strictly speaking,

* Henry also had no right to the Emperor's copy. If it was a
forgery, as he claimed, it had obviously not been addressed to him,
nor had it been paid for by the English.

under canon law the fact that Arthur and Katharine had even been betrothed, regardless of whether they had been married or had consummated the marriage, provided the necessary obstacle to the second marriage. But there must have been some doubt or ignorance of this in people's minds at the time. Otherwise, Katharine would have made the question of her virginity an issue and the Black Friars court would not have had reason to debate it.

After the recognition of the Brief, Henry shifted the grounds of his case to deny the Pope's power to dispense in such a matter. He chose to regard a passage in Leviticus, "If a man shall take his brother's wife . . . they shall be childless," [7] as the law of God. This passage is, however, open to a different interpretation as it says nothing about a brother's *widow*. It is also contradicted by a passage in Deuteronomy where it is explicitly stated, "If brethren dwell together, and one of them die, and have no child, the wife of the dead shall not marry without unto a stranger . . . her husband's brother shall take her to him to wife." [8] There is, however, some question as to whether the degrees of relationship forbidden in marriage under canon law were in fact founded on the Old Testament. Canon law was not codified and absolute. It was based on cases that had come up for jurisdiction. As dispensation for similar marriages had been granted in the past, notably to Charles Brandon and to King Manuel of Portugal, precedent alone should have been enough to have validated this particular dispensation.

Katharine herself confused the issue by denying firmly and repeatedly that she had ever been Arthur's wife in anything but name. Although it was she who produced the Brief in England, she always avowed that she could not make use of it in her defense because it falsely said that she had consummated her marriage to Arthur. Her case would

have been easier to uphold if it had been based only on the
adequacy of the Bull, which was the course advised by
Vives, Fisher and Mendoza. In the end it did not matter
whether the marriage had been consummated or not, if
indeed it had ever mattered to anyone but Katharine. Clement VII's final and belated decision, announced in March
1534, six months before his death, was that the original
Bull was adequate. The College of Cardinals had also
ruled that the Pope was qualified to dispense. The marriage
of Henry and Katharine was therefore declared valid without reference to Katharine's virginity at the time of their
marriage.

By the time the decision came, however, it was too late to
be of use to Katharine. Henry had already taken matters
into his own hands and had secretly married Anne Boleyn
four months earlier. But this is looking far ahead. When
the "King's Great Matter" was first broached in May 1527,
there was no mention of Anne as a possible successor to
Katharine. Not till August of that year did Mendoza write
to tell the Emperor that Henry intended to marry Anne
Boleyn as soon as his marriage to Katharine was annulled.

3.   *Catholics and Protestants*

When Katharine first heard the news from Henry that he
intended to leave her, she did not blame him for the decision.
She held Wolsey responsible, perhaps justifiably in part.
Wolsey certainly aided and abetted Henry in his efforts
to have the marriage annulled. He thought that Henry
would then marry a French princess who would bear him
sons and so cement the alliance Wolsey had always favored.
It is doubtful, however, whether Wolsey actually instigated
the King's action. Both Wolsey and Henry later claimed

that the Bishop of Tarbes had raised the subject when he was negotiating the betrothal of a French prince to the Princess Mary early in 1527. This he may have done, but he cannot have been the first to raise the issue if the report of earlier rumors is true.

Henry's confessor, Longland, Bishop of Lincoln, was also thought by many to have helped prod Henry's conscience. It was said that Longland had suggested the "divorce" ten years earlier, perhaps at the time of the Italian report that Henry was going to leave Katharine as she could not bear him children who were able to live. Some people have blamed Anne Boleyn, saying that when Henry became infatuated with her, she refused to become his mistress as her greatest desire was to become Queen of England. From the evidence it is more likely that, in spite of his undoubted infatuation, Henry refused to make Anne his mistress because he wanted her to be the mother of his legitimate heirs. As an ambitious woman, Anne was not averse to the prospect of succeeding Katharine and played her cards accordingly.

Today it is not possible to be sure who first encouraged Henry to make the momentous decision which was to lead to both the separation of the English Church from Rome and the establishment of Protestantism in England. We do not know on whom to lay the blame or praise. In the succeeding centuries, Protestants and Catholics have taken sides according to their religious beliefs. The legitimacy of two future Queens of England, Katharine's daughter Mary and Anne's daughter Elizabeth was to depend upon whether it was the authority of the Pope or of the Archbishop of Canterbury that was accepted.

Henry himself, however, was not a Protestant and his private affairs were not the sole cause of the Reformation in

England. It is likely that the Reformation of the Church would in any case have spread to England sooner or later. The same seeds which had produced Luther's rebellious doctrines in Germany had also found fertile soil on the other side of the Channel. Henry only took advantage of the way things were going to shape them to his own ends, but in so doing he himself became a tool of the reformers. He who had once gained the title of *Defender of the Faith* never ceased to be a Catholic although he came to deny the authority of the Pope. Many otherwise good Catholics who had long been angered by the greed of the priests and envious of the riches piled up by the Church were willing to support him. They were, however, concerned more with the abuses as practiced by the clergy than in attacking religious belief itself.

But there also were in England reformists who were extremely critical of the form and content of the Catholic religion: scholars, clerics and laymen, who had read Luther's books and believed in his so-called heretical doctrines. By supporting the King in the matter of his divorce, their party gained strength. Henry's desire for an heir and the machinations of the Boleyn family speeded up their victory. The Boleyns became identified with the movement. The success of their careers depended on it. It is open to question whether Anne herself was aware of the wider implications of her becoming Queen in spite of the fact that she and her father were said to be more Lutheran than Luther himself. Luther, however, it is interesting to note, declared against the divorce.

Henry longed to have sons to succeed him. For some time Katharine had been known to be "past that age in which women most commonly are wont to be fruitful and have children." [9] She had been ill for several years and was no longer attractive in appearance. All her children had died except for the one girl. In the course of English history no woman had ever been crowned Queen of England in her own right. Henry genuinely feared that England would again be plunged into civil war at his death if Mary remained his only heir. Although he had legitimized Henry Fitzroy, it was not at all certain that others would accept him as heir to the throne. There would be other distant male claimants who could be expected to fight, however tenuous their claims. In spite of the executions of Warwick and Suffolk there were still living descendants of Edward IV and his brother, as well as the children of Margaret and Mary, Henry's sisters. Even if Henry's daughter was allowed to succeed him, her choice of husband could present England with two disagreeable alternatives: a foreign prince or an Englishman who was not of royal blood on the throne at her side. The solution that seems obvious to us now was thought of then but not pursued as it might also have led to bloodshed. If Mary had married her cousin James, the union between England and Scotland might have been brought about some seventy years earlier than it was. Even marriage to Reginald Pole, son of the Countess of Salisbury, would seem to have been a possibility, uniting again the offspring of the red rose and the white. As it turned out, Mary was to marry none of the many suitors selected by her father. She made her own disastrous choice to marry the son of her cousin Charles V many years later when she had succeeded to the English throne.

By chance, the time when it became known that Katharine was unable to bear more children seems to have coincided with the time when Henry was first attracted to Anne Boleyn. This was a superstitious age and Henry was as superstitious as the rest. Perhaps he genuinely believed or persuaded himself into believing that his so-called childlessness was a punishment for having married his brother's widow. Katharine too was superstitious and came to think that perhaps her marriage had been doomed from the start for a different reason. She had never forgotten that the execution of the Earl of Warwick had preceded her coming to England so that her parents could be assured of the stability of the English throne. Now, it seemed to her that she was being punished for this bloodshed, although she herself had had nothing to do with it. She remembered too her terrible journey across the Bay of Biscay in 1501, "by reason whereof she mistrusted ever and feared some unlucky and unhappy chance impending on her." [10]

4.   *"The King's Gorgeous Lady"*

To thread one's way to the whole truth about Anne Boleyn through the labyrinth of fable and fantasy which has grown up around her is impossible. Some things are certain; others a matter of conjecture, especially where dates are concerned. The time of her birth is not established; details of her dramatic end are widely known, though the allegations against her were never proved. She brought tragedy to other lives besides those of Katharine and Mary, yet herself died perhaps the most tragic figure of all.

The noble pedigree which the heralds traced for the Boleyn family in 1530 was a fabrication. Her father, Sir Thomas Boleyn, was a rich man of middle-class origins with only vague noble connections. His family became intimately connected with the court at the time of the accession of Henry VIII. He had two daughters, Mary and Anne, each of whom became in turn the King's mistress. It has been suggested that it was on their account that many honors and important offices were bestowed upon him. Sir Thomas had, however, given good service to the King, was much in favor with him, and had been rewarded for his loyalty before either of his daughters caught Henry's wandering eye. His first post was that of knight of the King's household. He was made Viscount Rochford in 1525 on the same occasion that Henry Fitzroy was made Duke of Richmond, after Henry's affair with Mary and before Anne had become what Wolsey's biographer George Cavendish was to call "the King's gorgeous lady." [11] Anne received the title of Lady Anne Rochford at the same time. In 1529, Viscount Rochford was created Earl of Wiltshire and Ormond. In spite of gossip to the contrary, there is perhaps no real reason to doubt that these titles were as much a reward for his services to the Crown as for his being the father of Anne. By that time the two issues were confused.

Anne's mother, Elizabeth, was one of the Howards, a family that had been famous though it was momentarily in decline at the time of the marriage and was to become famous again. Elizabeth Boleyn's claim to noble ancestry was stronger than her husband's. Through her mother, Anne was descended from Edward I and was related to, among others, the Duke of Norfolk, Sir Francis Bryan and the two poets Sir Thomas Wyatt and the Earl of Surrey. The name of Elizabeth Boleyn is found in the records of the masques and revels which took place at court in the early years of Henry VIII. Much later, it was said that she too had been one of Henry's mistresses, but this cannot be proved and Henry himself denied it. More likely, this was just another scandalous rumor circulating among the many people who hated the Boleyns. Anne also had a brother George, whose name was to be linked incestuously with hers. He shared in the family's favor at court and later suffered the same fate as his sister.

Mary Boleyn is reputed with some justification to have been the King's mistress before Anne, but it is not known exactly when. Staunch Protestants have since denied the truth of any such report. Henry, however, asked the Pope for dispensation to marry Anne. After he had married her he saw that an Act of Parliament was passed to permit marriage to the sister of a mistress. When Anne fell into disfavor and was executed Henry had the Act repealed. None of these things would have been necessary if there had been no relationship with Mary.

It is not known when Mary was born and the conflicting dates of 1503 and 1507 have been suggested for Anne. It is, therefore, not certain which was the elder sister. It was thought for a long time to have been Mary if only because she married first and knew Henry first. Persuasive arguments have been produced by serious scholars to prove the case for either one.

According to Camden, the antiquarian who wrote about fifty years after Anne's death, Anne was born in 1507. In this case, she would have been about nineteen when Henry first thought of divorcing Katharine. But there is a portrait said to have been of Anne by Holbein, painted in 1530, on which the age of the sitter is given as twenty-seven. If this is correct, Anne would have been born in 1502 or 1503 and would have been about twenty-three when Henry is thought first to have fallen in love with her. Art experts, however, say that although Holbein was actually in England at that time he did not paint this particular picture. They go further and say that it does not represent Anne Boleyn but Anne of Bohemia, who is known to have been twenty-seven in 1530. This is typical of the kind of problem one runs into when trying to discover the truth about Anne Boleyn.

Both Boleyn sisters are thought to have stayed in France

at some time in their lives. One of them, recorded only as "M. [Mademoiselle] Boleyn," [12] accompanied Mary Tudor when she went to France in 1514 to marry Louis XII. This sister was one of the few attendants allowed to stay with the new French Queen when the rest of her retinue was sent home. She remained in France when, the following year, the newly-widowed Queen went home to England as Charles Brandon's wife. One sister, perhaps the same one, was brought up at the court of the French Queen Claude, the first wife of Francis I, in a way somewhat similar to that in which Elizabeth Blount had been brought up at Katharine's court. She was one of three hundred girls who, together with a large number of young pages, waited on the Queen and attended her on her public appearances, forming a kind of aristocratic finishing school. She may have taken part in the pageantry of the Field of Cloth of Gold, though there is no mention of her name. She may have seen something of her father just before this as he was in France preparing the meeting between Henry and Francis. Sir Thomas Boleyn himself was not present at the pageant as he had moved on to prepare the ensuing meeting between Henry and Charles.

There is a certain amount of evidence to show that Anne spent much of her youth in France. One of the Boleyn girls also achieved a certain amount of notoriety for her *amours* while living in France, but it is not known which girl or at what period. Cavendish said of her, "Anne Boleyn being very young was sent into the realm of France, and there made one of the French queen's women." [13] A contemporary Spanish history [14] of Henry VIII tells how she was brought up in France and there are French accounts of her life which assert that she accompanied Mary Tudor and stayed on with Queen Claude until the time of the Queen's death. All these accounts, however, were published ten to twenty years after her own death, though one of the French ones [15] written in verse claims to have been written two weeks after her execution. There is no strictly contemporary evidence, but it is difficult to understand why such a legend should have been current if it had no basis in fact.

Mary was probably the first sister to come home, for early in February 1521, she is known to have married Mr. William Carey, one of the King's bodyguard. They had three children before Mary was left a widow in 1528. It is not known whether Henry's affair with her took place before or after she was married, but it seems more likely to have been after. Slanderous tongues were to say that Henry was the father of her son born in 1525. Even if it were so, Henry must have had doubts for he never acknowledged him as he had Henry Fitzroy. Her son was given the name of Henry, but so were many boys at this time as a compliment to the King. (The two daughters which followed were called Katharine and Mary.) The name alone, whatever it may suggest, proves nothing. In 1534 Mary was dismissed from court for "gross misconduct." [16] In spite of her sister's advancement, Mary's social position deteriorated partly as a result of her second marriage which was frowned upon by both Henry and Anne.

Anne is known to have been living permanently in England by 1526 but is reported by Francis I to have left France in 1522 when the relationship between France and England had declined to the point of war. On her return, she became one of Katharine's maidens. She was an instant success at court. Several people became enamoured of her, including her cousin Sir Thomas Wyatt, who was already married. When she was very young, she had been betrothed by her family to a distant kinsman. At court, she met a young man in Wolsey's household, Sir Henry Percy, son of the Earl of Northumberland, and they fell in love with each other. Although he was already betrothed to Mary Talbot, daughter of the Earl of Shrewsbury, Anne and Percy decided to ignore the arrangements made by their families and go against the convention of the day. Their plan, however, was foiled by Wolsey, some said later, at the King's suggestion. Percy was married to Mary Talbot and Anne was sent away from court, either back to France or to her father's home.

It is not known exactly when Henry first became captivated by Anne Boleyn nor when she became his mistress. It is open to question whether she refused Henry's advances because she hoped that by so doing she might become his wife, or whether Henry refused to make her his mistress because he wanted her to become the legitimate mother of his children. The motives were probably mixed. It is clear that they met at court sometime between 1522 and 1526, but their names were not openly linked, as far as we know, until August 1527. In this context, however, we should not forget that nothing was recorded about Henry's affair with Elizabeth Blount until after their son was born. In regard to Anne, however, there had been pointers which, with hindsight, we can recognize. For instance, one of Henry's ships was listed in 1526 as the *Anne Boleyn*. At the Mardi Gras revels of the same year Henry had changed his chivalric motto from the "Noble Loyal Heart" he had chosen for Katharine in 1511 to "Declare I Dare Not."

It is evident both from the love-letters[17] Henry wrote to Anne and from some of his poems probably written about the same time that in the early stages of their friendship she had quite definitely not become his mistress. It is obvious too that Henry was very much infatuated with her. The letters, unfortunately, are not dated, though from internal evidence they are generally assumed to have been written between 1527 and 1528. There was, apparently, nothing remarkable in Anne's appearance to explain the hold she obtained over Henry. A Venetian report said, "Madame Anne is not one of the handsomest women in the world. She is of midding stature, swarthy complexion, long neck, wide mouth, bosom not much raised, and in fact has nothing but the King's great appetite, and her eyes which are black and beautiful." [18]

5. *The Pope's Procrastination*

In the spring of 1527, when Henry first tried to have his marriage annulled, neither Katharine nor Wolsey were aware of the threat inherent in Henry's relations with Anne. Wolsey, therefore, departed with no misgivings on a state visit to France in July. Officially, he had a double aim. He was to negotiate a French marriage for Henry when he was free of Katharine and encourage Francis to undertake an expedition to Italy to rescue the Pope from the Emperor's clutches. Privately, he also hoped he might persuade them to make him Vicar-General, or Deputy Pope, while the real Pope continued in captivity. In this way he would have been able both to help Henry dissolve his marriage and to consolidate his own position. He assumed that Katharine would agree to retire gracefully from the scene.

When he returned to England at the end of September, Wolsey had a rude shock. Katharine was stubbornly refusing to be coerced. Anne Boleyn was publicly the King's favorite and it was generally known that the King wished to marry her. She and her friends had taken over control during Wolsey's three-month absence. They were present when he came to give his report to the King, whereas formerly he had been accustomed to having a private audience. Anne let him know that she was now somebody to be reckoned with and she did not conceal her dislike. Mendoza reported that Anne "seemed to entertain no great affection for the Cardinal."[19] She reputedly bore him a grudge for having broken off her engagement to Percy and she was not pleased that he had tried to find a French bride for Henry. Even worse for Wolsey was the fact that her family and supporters were those who most hated him and what he stood for. Only by bringing about the "divorce" could Wolsey hope to remain in favor, so he set to work to aid the woman who was his enemy. Anne was affable as long as it served her purpose, but she was instrumental in bringing about Wolsey's downfall when he was unsuccessful.

During Wolsey's absence Henry had started on his own plan. He had sent ambassadors to the Pope to ask for a dispensation to marry Anne while he was still married to Katharine; he had also wished to have his marriage to Katharine annulled and yet keep Mary legitimate. A dispensation to marry Anne was necessary as she stood in a similar sort of prohibited relationship to him as Katharine. Her sister Mary had been Henry's mistress and the Church did not discriminate between licit and illicit associations. But, by making these requests, Henry implicitly recognized the power of the Pope to dispense, a power he was afterward to deny. The Pope granted the dispensation but made it valueless by not permitting it to take effect until after Henry's marriage to Katharine had been annulled. When Wolsey came home and grasped the situation, he decided to work in the opposite way. He persuaded Henry to wait to marry Anne until he had received the Pope's verdict on his marriage to Katharine, which he assured Henry would be in his favor. Another delegation was then sent to Rome to urge the Pope to have the case tried in England, where Wolsey knew the climate would be more propitious.

Henry had been encouraged by Wolsey from the beginning

to believe that his "Matter" would be quickly decided.
Perhaps if Wolsey had stayed at home in charge of the
proceedings Henry might not have been disappointed, Wolsey himself might not have fallen into disgrace and the
Boleyns might never have gained the ascendancy. But Wolsey's desire for the French alliance led him to France at
the crucial moment. Henry's case dragged on for years,
delayed by the discovery of the brief, by opposition from un-
expected quarters, by Katharine's own obstinacy and by the
hesitation of the Pope to make a decision. Henry became
more and more bad-tempered and Anne more impatient.

Katharine at first did not believe that Henry would carry
through his plan. Once her tears were dried, she became
her usual cheerful self. But this time Henry meant what he
said and tried every means within his power to achieve his
aim. Rebuffs only made him angry and more obstinate. But
Katharine could be obstinate too, especially when she
believed she was in the right. She was fighting for her own
good name and for the legitimacy of her child. She was a
sensible pious woman with immense reserves of courage
behind her ready tears. She put her trust in God and hoped
that Charles would persuade the Pope to help her too. But
Charles and the Pope were far away. They did not always
agree with her methods and were sometimes dilatory in
their support.

Katharine was occasionally hurt by her nephew's apparent
neglect. However much Charles sympathized with his aunt
he did not want to provoke war with England on her account; nor did Katharine wish it herself. The Pope was in a
dilemma, not daring to offend either the Emperor or the King
of England. Even though he had been set free by Charles in
December 1527, he was still very much in the power of the
Emperor. He hoped that time might settle the question, that

Henry might forget his quarrel with Katharine when he tired of Anne; alternatively, Katharine might conveniently die as she had for a long time been known to be far from well. The struggle, however, seemed to give her a new lease on life or, at any rate, coincided with a period of better health.

Throughout the years that followed, Katharine was often to say that she had no friends in England. Strictly speaking this was not true. She long continued to be kept in touch with events by her friends and was often better informed than the Emperor's ambassador. Katharine was always loved by the people of England, especially by the Londoners who demonstrated for her and against Anne on several occasions —to Henry's great annoyance. She was not only respected morally for her uprightness of character and for her piety; she was also the symbol of the people's material well-being in so far as trade with Spain and the Low Countries was concerned. She had friends in influential circles too, but dared not make open use of their support. The King was all-powerful and it was dangerous to be on the Queen's side. Henry considered any one who was not openly for him as being against him. As a result, many were to lose their lives in Katharine's cause or in the cause of the Catholic Church which became bound up with hers. As Erasmus later said, in England either everyone had been snatched away by death or fear had shrunk them up.

Katharine was surrounded by spies, and members of her household were pressed to give information detrimental to her. Her old friend Vives was one of those interrogated to see what he could tell. But as he wrote, "Not that it would injure any one to relate it, even if it were published on church doors." [20] Katharine had poured out her troubles to him the year before when, as he said in the same letter, "she began to unfold to me this her calamity, since I was her compatriot and spoke the same language; thinking too, that I might have read something which might be a consolation to her grief. Then she wept over her own fate that the man whom she loved more than herself should be so alienated from her as to think of marrying another, which was a grief the more intense as her love was the greater." He then added, "Who does not admire and respect the moderation of the Queen? Other women would have aroused heaven and earth, and filled all with clamour and tumult. She merely seeks from her sister's son that she may not be condemned unheard." [21]

Vives could speak kindly of her even though she did not treat him very well. He had refused an invitation from Henry to become her advocate as he did not think he could be helpful. Henry and Katharine were then both angry with him and his salary was withdrawn. For a time he lived in dire poverty in London, where he complained of his boredom. He was cold and sometimes hungry in his little room near the Tower. Once he was permitted to leave the country he understandably refused any further invitation to return. He bore Katharine no grudge for her treatment of him, however, and continued to write in her support.

During the summer of 1528 the sweating sickness again ravaged England and the royal court split up. There was a pause in the divorce proceedings. Henry traveled around from place to place in his efforts to avoid infection as all those around him sickened. Mary Boleyn's husband and several of Henry's close friends died. Anne was sent back to her father to Hever Castle in Kent. She also succumbed to the epidemic but had only a mild attack. Henry wrote her loving letters and sent one of his doctors to attend her. By the autumn the infection had died down and the court reassembled. The King and Queen were again seen together at

Greenwich, where Anne also joined them. At this time, in spite of Katharine's objections, the Pope at last consented to have Henry's case tried by a Vatican court in England.

6. Attempts at Conciliation

Two cardinals, Thomas Wolsey and Lorenzo Campeggio, were chosen to act as judges. Wolsey was already there on the spot. Campeggio was to be sent specially from Rome. He had been selected because he had previous knowledge of England and English ways; he was a cardinal in England, though he did not live there. With pressure being put upon him from all sides, the Pope delayed Campeggio's departure as long as he dared. Once he had set off, Campeggio also lingered over the journey. He left in June but did not arrive in England until October. Even allowing for slowness of travel in those days, four months was a long time. Partly because he was tired and partly because he suffered greatly from gout he also rested awhile before presenting his credentials to Henry. But at last, one pouring wet autumn day, he rode in a sedan chair with Wolsey on horseback by his side to Bridewell where the King and Queen were in residence.

Before he left Rome, Campeggio had been given two documents by the Pope to bring to England. One was an open commission empowering the two cardinals to try the King's case. The other was a secret letter, or decretal, from the Pope which Campeggio was instructed to show only to the King and to Wolsey and never to let out of his sight. It is thought to have authorized the two cardinals to decide in the King's favor without further reference to Rome. But the Pope later regretted having put his name to such an instruction. In his fear of offending the Emperor, he ordered

Campeggio to burn the decretal. This Campeggio must have done as it was never found in spite of all the searches instigated by Henry. A secret letter which could not be shown to anyone else was useless to Henry, so he naturally tried to get it into his possession.

Campeggio's first aim was to try and bring the King and Queen together again and, if that should prove difficult to achieve, to delay the sitting of the court as long as he could. Wolsey did not oppose him in this as he had no incentive to force a speedy conclusion. Wolsey knew that once the case was over Anne would have no further use for him and would see to it that he was removed from office. He was in an uneasy position, hated by both Katharine and Anne. Charles tried unsuccessfully to bribe him, but in the end Wolsey was driven into reluctant support of Katharine, not through any good motives but solely on account of his own fear and dislike of her rival.

Campeggio did not find the climate in England favorable toward his conciliatory efforts. Both Katharine and Henry were immovable. Of Henry he wrote that an angel from heaven would not be able to persuade the King that his marriage was not invalid. He and Wolsey went to see Katharine. They tried to persuade her to submit to Henry's wishes and offered her the face-saving choice of either returning to Spain or retiring into a convent. She firmly turned down both alternatives. She spoke in anger to Wolsey:

> But of this trouble I may only thank you my Lord of York, because I ever wondered at your pride and vainglory and abhorred your voluptuous life, and little cared for your presumption and tyranny, therefore of malice have you kindled this fire, especially for the great grudge you bear to my nephew the emperor, whom you hate worse than a scorpion, because he

would not grant your ambition by making you Pope
by force.[22]

This last sentence was a reference to the year 1522 when
Wolsey had hoped to be elected Pope but Charles had not
supported him. All attempts to make Katharine change
her mind were useless. She insisted that she was the legitimate wife of the King of England and nothing would make
her say anything to the contrary. She held her husband's conscience and honor in more esteem than anything else in this
world, but she had no scruple at all about the legitimacy of
her marriage. She would die as she had lived, a wife as
God had made her.

A short time afterward, with Henry's permission, Katharine went to see Campeggio to confess to him in his capacity as a priest. She swore that she had never been married
to Arthur in anything but name; she had not slept with
him more than seven nights and had remained a virgin. Even
if she were torn limb from limb she would not say anything different.[23] Campeggio was inclined to believe her
but, as a lawyer, did not think her case would hold up in a
court of law. Mendoza wished she would speak less about the
nonconsummation of her marriage and rest her case on the
dispensation. It was in this same month of November that
Katharine produced the brief, which had the effect of delaying proceedings still further.

In order to counteract any sympathy for Katharine, Henry
decided to address a public assembly at Bridewell Palace. He
spoke in rhetorical terms which would have been more
moving if they had been less hypocritical:

> If it be adjudged that the Queen is my lawful wife,
> nothing will be more pleasant or more acceptable to
> me, both for the clearness of my conscience, and also

for the good qualities and conditions I know her to
be in. For I assure you all, that besides her noble par-
entage, she is a woman of most gentleness, humility,
and buxomness; yes, and of all good qualities pertain-
ing to nobility she is without comparison. So that if I
were to marry again, I would choose her above all
women. But if it is determined in judgment that our
marriage is against God's law, then shall I sorrow,
parting from so good a lady and loving a companion.
These be the sores that vex my mind! These be the
pangs that trouble my conscience, for the declaration
of which I have assembled you together, and now
you may depart.[24]

Some of his audience "sighed and said nothing, others were
sorry to hear the king so troubled in his conscience." [25]

But two days afterward, Henry saw Katharine in private
and was both angry and unkind. He told her that the Pope
had already condemned her; she was no longer his wife
and Campeggio had come to execute sentence. Katharine was
not intimidated and showed spirit in her reactions. She
asked, "How can the Pope condemn me without a hearing?"
Henry replied, "The Emperor has answered for you and
consequently the Pope has decided against you." He then
threatened her, saying that if she did not retire willingly
into a convent she would be compelled to do so. Undaunted,
but now with tears in her eyes, Katharine answered him,
"May God forbid my being the cause of that being done
which is so much against my soul, my conscience, and
my honor." [26] She ended by begging to be allowed to plead
her own case, to which the King assented.

A Queen's Council was thereupon appointed to help Kath-
arine. Among its members were to be found Warham,
Archbishop of Canterbury; Tunstall, Bishop of London;
Fisher, Bishop of Rochester; Richard Fetherston, Mary's

Sir Thomas More, by Hans Holbein. (*Frick Collection, New York*)

Coronation of King Henry VIII
and Queen Katharine. Artist unknown. (*University Library, Cambridge*)

Thomas Cranmer, archbishop of
Canterbury, by Gerhard Flicke.
(*National Portrait Gallery, London*)

Mary Tudor, daughter of Henry VIII and Katharine of Aragon, later Queen of England. Artist unknown. (*National Portrait Gallery, London*)

Henry VIII, in his early forties. Artist unknown. (*Queen's Collection. Copyright reserved*)

Charles V, Hapsburg Emperor, nephew of Katharine, by Lucas Cranach. (*Thyssen-Bornemisza, Lugano*)

Francis I, King of France, by Joos van Cleve. (*The Metropolitan Museum of Art, The Michael Friedsam Collection, 1931*)

Katharine of Aragon. Johannes Corvus [?] (*John Guinness Collection*)

Katharine of Aragon. Artist unknown. (*National Portrait Gallery, London*)

Extract from Katharine's letter to Wolsey. (*Facsimile of Crown copyright document SPI /5/219 in The Public Record Office. Appears by
permission of the Controller of Her Majesty's Stationery Office.*)

Cardinal Wolsey. Artist unknown. (*National Portrait Gallery, London*)

Anne Boleyn, second wife of Henry VIII. Artist unknown. (*National Portrait Gallery, London*)

Thomas Cromwell, by Hans Holbein. (*Frick Collection, New York*)

The Field of Cloth of Gold. Artist unknown. (*Queen's Collection.*
Copyright reserved)

schoolmaster; Thomas Abell, the Queen's Chaplain; and Dr. Powell, a court preacher. Katharine doubted the impartiality of her advisers. Some had indeed been briefed by Wolsey, but some were loyal to her cause. The last four mentioned later paid the penalty for their devotion with their lives. Warham was too afraid of the King. Not till he was dying, in 1532, did he dare to speak out against him. The legal help Katharine sought from abroad from her old friend Margaret of Savoy did not materialize. Margaret herself died in 1530, leaving Katharine with one friend less among an ever-diminishing circle. Henry was undisturbed by Margaret's death, but she was mourned by the merchants of London and very much missed by Katharine.

A few days after it had been appointed, the council came to ask Katharine if it was true she had tried to poison the King so that she could marry her daughter where she wanted. This accusation Katharine vehemently denied and it was probably never believed by anybody. But there were genuine fears, on the other hand, that she and Mary might be poisoned. It was thought that the Boleyns were not beyond using this method of getting rid of their enemies, though in England it was not a favored method and Henry himself was against it. The crime was high treason and the punishment to be boiled alive.

Henry still maintained that it was lack of an heir that made him wish to dissolve his marriage. No official mention was made of Anne, even though by now most people believed she was his mistress. In his attempt to settle things out of court, Campeggio took Henry at his word. He now suggested that a marriage between Henry's daughter, the Princess Mary, and her half-brother, Henry Fitzroy, Duke of Richmond, might settle the matter of the succession. The Pope was willing to grant a dispensation permitting such a

marriage. But this did not satisfy Henry. Whatever his initial motive had been in seeking the annulment of his marriage, his heart was now set on marrying Anne. The suggestion was dropped, presumably to Katharine's relief, but her
heart was heavy. That Christmas, Henry and Katharine were
together at Greenwich, but the "Queen made no great joy of
nothing, her mind was so troubled." [27]

The Pope was agitated. He now wished Henry had never
consulted Rome. He would have preferred Henry to have
acted on his own initiative, to have divorced Katharine and
married Anne. Katharine would have been left to complain
to Rome after the event, by which time it would have been
too late. This course of action would have saved the Pope
much worry and trouble.

The Pope himself was a sick man and subject to fits. On
Easter Sunday, 1529, he had a rather worse fit than usual and
was afterward very ill. For some weeks his life was despaired
of and at one time he was reported dead. Wolsey's hopes
again soared. At last he would be able to satisfy his greatest
ambition and at the same time escape from the trap in which
he was now caught. He would be able to declare the marriage
invalid and thereby satisfy Henry as well as his enemies, the
Boleyns; Katharine would be powerless to gainsay him. But
the Pope recovered and the situation was unchanged.

Mendoza felt frustrated and useless. He too fell ill and
said he would die if he was left any longer in England. He
pleaded to be recalled, asking that someone better versed in
the intricacies of Church law and more knowledgeable about
English and French politics be sent in his place. He managed
to persuade both the Emperor and the King to let him leave
England. By June, when Katharine had real need of an ambassador to advise her, she had no one. Mendoza was writing
from Calais, thankful to have arrived there. Though techni-

cally still in English territory, he was a stage nearer home. He was not replaced for another three months, but he continued to report to the Emperor on Katharine's behalf. He again asked that someone should be sent quickly in his place as the Queen was "very perplexed."

Campeggio too had had enough of the case. His conciliatory efforts were getting nowhere. He began to regret that he had ever come to England, but he was unable to leave until his task was completed. His compassion was aroused by Katharine's courage though he realized what complications her obstinacy made for the Church and indeed for Europe. Much more was involved than the vindication of Katharine's cause. Even if all moral right was on her side, no one could afford to quarrel with the King of England at this moment when Europe was in turmoil. There was enough religious ferment and political unrest already and it could only be increased by a decision in her favor. Katharine either did not see or did not want to see this point of view. She, therefore, continued to fight on stubbornly for her own good name and that of her daughter. Her immortal soul was at stake.

7. *The Court at Black Friars*

After almost eight months in England Campeggio could find no further excuse for delay. It was arranged that the King's case should be heard at Black Friars, a religious house by the Thames, where a special courtroom was prepared. Henry firmly believed that at last a judgment was to be made in his favor. It was now two years since his "Great Matter" had first been made public and he was tired of waiting for a decision. Katharine distrusted everybody connected with the court and was still determined to have the case referred to

Rome. When the court opened on May 31, 1529, Henry was residing in his palace down the river at Greenwich; Katharine stayed separately at Bridewell Palace in London. A day or two later, Katharine appeared before the court without Henry in order to deny the competence of the court to sit. Both Vatican legates, she claimed, were biased in favor of the King. She first asserted that she had never been married to Arthur in anything but name and then asked that the case be heard in Rome where she would get a fair hearing. For three days the court debated its own impartiality before coming to the decision that it was competent to judge. The King and Queen were both summoned to appear before it. There was then enacted one of the most memorable and moving scenes in history. There are several contemporary accounts which differ only in small details. Cavendish, who at this time was one of Wolsey's gentlemen ushers and probably an eyewitness, described the scene:

> At one end of the courtroom the two judges sat, side by side, with the legal officers at their feet. Near them sat the King in state and, some way below him, Katharine. The opposing counsellors faced each other across the bar. When all the people had taken their places, the crier called for silence. The open commission given by the Pope to Campeggio was read aloud. This ended, the crier called, "King Henry of England, come into the court." Henry answered, "Here my Lord." Then the crier called, "Katharine, Queen of England, come into the court." At this summons, Katharine arose, crossed the room and knelt at Henry's feet, where she made an impassioned speech in broken English.
> "Sir," quoth she, "I beseech you for all the loves that hath been between us, and for the love of God, let me have justice and right, take of me some pity and compassion, for I am a poor woman and a stranger

born out of your dominion, I have here no assured
friend, and much less indifferent counsel; I flee to you
as to the head of justice within this realm. Alas! Sir,
wherein have I offended you, or what occasion of
displeasure have I designed against your will and
pleasure? Intending as I perceive to put me from you
I take God and all the world to witness, that I have
been to you a true humble and obedient wife, ever
conformable to your will and pleasure, that never said
or did any thing to the contrary thereof, being always
well pleased and contented with all things wherein
you had any delight or dalliance, whether it were in
little or much, I never grudged in word or countenance, or showed a visage or spark of discontenta-
tion. I loved all those whom ye loved only for your
sake, whether I had cause or no; and whether they
were my friends or my enemies. This twenty years I
have been your true wife or more, and by me ye
have had divers children, although it hath pleased
God to call them out of this world, which hath been
no default in me.

"And when ye had me at the first, I take God to be
my judge, I was a true maid without touch of man;
and whether it be true or no, I put it to your conscience. If there be any just cause by the law that ye
can allege against me, either of dishonesty or any
other impediment to banish and put me from you,
I am well content to depart to my great shame and
dishonor; and if there be none, then here I most lowly
beseech you let me remain in my former estate, and
to receive justice at your princely hands.

"Therefore I most humbly require you, in the way of
charity, and for the love of God, who is the just
judge, to spare me the extremity of this new court,
until I may be advertised what way and order my
friends in Spain will advise me to take. And if ye
will not extend to me so much indifferent favor, your
pleasure then be fulfilled, and to God I commit my
cause!" [28]

But Henry made no reply, though some said he was in tears. Seeing that nothing was to be gained by waiting, Katharine stood up, made a low curtsey to the King and walked out of the court, leaning as was her custom on the arm of Griffiths, one of her advisers. As she left, the crier called out, at the King's command, "Katharine, Queen of England, come again into court," but Katharine ignored the summons and continued on her way. Three times she was called. When Griffiths would have stayed, Katharine said, "On, on, it makes no matter for it is no indifferent court to me, therefore, I will not tarry." [29] Outside, a crowd of women had gathered to cheer her, which they did so enthusiastically the French ambassador reported that if the women had had to decide Katharine would have won the case.

Inside, however, there was great consternation. Katharine was declared *contumacious,* wilfully disobedient to the court, which continued to sit without her. Witnesses were called to prove that she had in fact been a real wife to Arthur, but most of the evidence was worthless gossip, based on hearsay. It was known that, according to the custom of the day, she and Arthur had been put to bed together in front of witnesses on their wedding night.* Some of the witnesses now claimed to remember, twenty years afterward, what Arthur had said the next morning. Only Katharine could now give a true account of what happened that night, but it was impossible to prove her statement in a court of law. John Fisher, Bishop of Rochester, alone spoke in her defense and declared her marriage to Henry valid. He earned Henry's disapprobation

---

* See page 5. The part of the account in italics has been altered twice. First the passage was erased and then reinstated. It is not known at what date either change was made, but presumably both were connected with proving or disproving Katharine's statement.

by publishing pamphlets to support her case. His continued advocacy of her cause was later to cost him his life. But his dissent meant that no unanimous decision could be reached —to Wolsey's great consternation. Campeggio disagreed with his fellow judge and spoke in favor of referring the case to Rome. On July 23, the court met for the last time. It was first adjourned for the summer recess and then a short time afterwards "advoked" to Rome. Katharine had gained her point, but it was a hollow victory. The King of England was not likely to leave his own country to be judged in a foreign court.

When it became obvious that the case was not going to be decided in his favor, Henry made one more effort to persuade Katharine to submit. The task was entrusted to Wolsey and Campeggio. They arrived unexpectedly at Bridewell and demanded to see the Queen. According to Cavendish, who was in attendance on Wolsey at the time, Katharine came out of the room where she had been sewing with her ladies, with a skein of white thread still around her neck. Wolsey first asked to speak with her privately, to which she replied that there was nothing he could say to her that could not be said openly before her maidens. He next began to speak to her in Latin, but she stopped him: "Nay, good my lord, speak to me in English I beseech you, although I understand Latin." [30] Wolsey then told her his errand, in English, that he and Campeggio had both come to advise her in regard to the matter between her and the King. Katharine with more modesty than accuracy, or perhaps even with sarcasm, replied: "Alas, I am a poor woman, lacking both wit and understanding sufficiently to answer such approved wise men as ye be both, in so weighty a matter." [31] She continued in the same vein, but then led them into an inner room where they argued privately for some time. The two cardinals, however, failed to move her. For years Katharine took the line in argument that she was a helpless woman beset by astute enemies. On one occasion it was pointed out to her that she had her own learned councillors to advise her. In fact, she did not trust many of them. Some, however, were reliable and she herself was a better advocate of her own cause than she would admit.

8. *The Fall of Wolsey*

Before the court broke up it had become obvious that Wolsey's authority was much diminished. His enemies spoke openly against him in a way they would not have dared earlier. According to Cavendish, Suffolk, encouraged by the King, turned upon him during the last session and said, "It was never merry in England whilst we had cardinals among us." [32] Wolsey answered him soberly, reminding him that he owed his own life to Wolsey's intervention at the time when he had secretly married the King's sister Mary in France.

Once the case was referred to Rome, Wolsey's career was over. Katharine, who had at one time blamed him for all her woes, then found it in her heart to pity him. But Anne and her friends were ruthless in their persecution. They prevented Wolsey from meeting the King again although Henry himself seems to have retained some affection for his old Chancellor. At times the King missed him but he was too weak to let his former friendship influence his actions to any great extent. He was as much in the power of the Boleyn faction as he had formerly been in Wolsey's. His most influential advisers became Anne's uncle—the Duke of Norfolk—and the Duke of Suffolk, formerly a member of Katharine's household. There was considerable rivalry between the two. They were both forced to take action against Katharine, though their hearts did not always seem to be in it. It was said that the Duke and Duchess of Suffolk would, if they dared, oppose the King with all their force. Suffolk's wife, Mary, found it difficult to maintain her friendship with Katharine, but was courageous enough to do so. At one time the whole court was in an uproar because Mary had used "opprobrious" language against Anne.[33] When, a few months after Mary's death in 1533, Suffolk married the fourteen-year-old daughter of Maria de Salinas, his new wife was equally loyal to the Queen's cause.

In order to trap Wolsey, the ancient statute of *Praemunire* (so-called as that was the first word in the Latin script) was revived. It forbade any interference by the Pope in English affairs. Wolsey was accused of having received office from the Pope and of having introduced papal bulls into England. In using this law, however, Henry was not consistent. He ignored the fact that he himself had constantly accepted the authority of the Pope, in particular when he asked for the legatine court to try his case at Black Friars. Wolsey was found guilty and deprived of all state office. His money and possessions, which were considerable, passed to the King. He left London and set out for York where, he said, he would devote himself to his flock. In 1530, before he had reached York, he was summoned back to London to be tried on a charge of high treason. He died on the way, at Leicester. He was fifty-seven years old. Cavendish was with him till the end and reported the much-quoted speech he is reputed to have made on his deathbed: "If I had served God as diligently as I have done the King, he would not have given me over in my grey hairs." [34]

Wolsey was succeeded as Chancellor by a layman, Sir Thomas More, and the office never again passed back into the hands of the Church. On his appointment, More made a speech violently attacking the actions and character of his predecessor, a speech which accords ill with the noble and generous nature usually attributed to More.

9. *Arrival of Eustace Chapuys*

In August, just too late to be of any assistance to Katharine during the Black Friars sessions, the Emperor's new ambassador, Eustace Chapuys, arrived in London. He was not a Spaniard, as previous ambassadors had been; he came from Savoy. But Katharine trusted him from the start and he was devoted to her. To his long-winded copious despatches we owe much of our knowledge of Katharine's last days and the events surrounding them. From his reports to the Emperor, however, it is clear that Katharine was often better-informed than he was. This was partly due to the fact that he neither spoke nor understood English. At court, he always spoke in French. He admitted that he was always at a loss when the others spoke in English and had to rely upon someone to translate for him. If, therefore, he was to be kept in ignorance of what was being discussed, it was easy enough to achieve. Some allowance must also be made for his natural bias in Katharine's favor. Not everybody in England found him as honest and trustworthy as she did. One of Henry's Gentlemen of the Chamber, Lord Paget, said that Chapuys was a great "practicer," with which term he covered tale-telling, lying, dissimulating and flattering.

It was not always easy for the Queen and Chapuys to communicate as a close watch was kept on both of them by Anne's spies. They nevertheless found ways of exchanging information, often through Katharine's physician at that time, Fernando Vittoria. On his arrival Chapuys reported that he found Katharine comparatively cheerful. She was still hopeful that Henry would drop all proceedings against her. She still believed in his intrinsic goodness and blamed his recent peculiar actions on his evil counsellors. She gave Chapuys advice on how to handle him, saying that Henry's nature was more accessible to persuasion than to threat. She was just as confident that the Pope would decide for her if the case reached Rome as she had formerly been sure that an English court would be prejudiced against her. This point of view was shared by Campeggio, but he was anxious to get away and leave the case behind him. On October 8, not long after Chapuys's arrival, Campeggio left England for good. Chapuys stayed on and was there to see Katharine's confidence sapped as events turned against her. By the end of the same year, Katharine admitted that she had lost all hope of regaining Henry's affections.

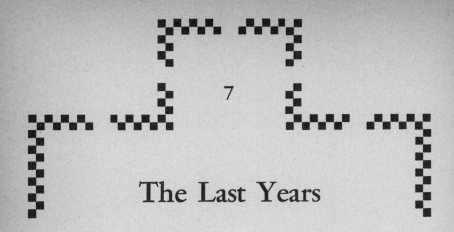

7

The Last Years

1. Parliamentary Background

After the fiasco at the court of Black Friars Henry was momentarily at a loss. He had to find other ways of bringing about the dissolution of his marriage, preferably outside Rome. For centuries England had acknowledged two authorities: that of the State and that of the Church. Each had its own governing and legislative body; Parliament for the laymen and the two Convocations of Canterbury and York for the clerics. Each also had its own law courts and tax systems. But, though no layman could be a member of Convocation, many clerics sat in the House of Lords; laymen could be tried in either court of justice, but no cleric could be tried in a lay court. The clerics, therefore, exercised considerable power over the laymen, a power they sometimes abused. Through the years the Church had amassed great riches and had become more influential than the State, especially after Wolsey had concentrated several offices with their considerable revenues into his own hands.

Although the clerics were generally Englishmen, their first allegiance was to the Pope as head of Christendom, their second to the King. Normally the two allegiances ran smoothly side by side. But the moment there was a clash Henry was not prepared to take second place. The fall of Wolsey and the necessity of procuring his divorce spurred Henry on to action. He was himself subservient to the Pope in spiritual matters. As long as the old system held he must wait for the Pope's decision on the legality of his marriage. He therefore set about changing the system. His first step was to recall Parliament. At first, Parliament did not show itself as much in favor of Henry's divorce as he had hoped, but in the end it was the instrument he used to achieve his object. Within two years the rule of the State with the King as its head had been substituted for that of the Church.

On November 3, 1529, Parliament met for the first time since 1523 when it had been dissolved by Wolsey after his failure to persuade them to vote money for the war against France. It sat only for a few weeks and most of its work was directed against the clergy. Although it was not convened regularly after that, there were very few years during the rest of Henry's reign when it did not meet. The revival of government by the two Houses of Parliament, the Commons and the Lords, proved to be a popular move throughout the country, for the greed of clerics in general and of Wolsey in particular had long been a source of discontent. It has been said that Henry's Parliament was packed with his own men committed to support his measures. It was, however, elected according to the system of the day and showed its independence on occasions by throwing out a bill which the King would have liked to see passed. This does not mean that there were no King's men in Parliament. One of them was the member for Taunton, Thomas Cromwell, who had been quick to realize that here lay for himself the most promising road to power.

Chapuys gave a thumbnail sketch of Cromwell's early life in one of his letters. If he was right in his information, Cromwell had had a checkered career. He was the son of a poor blacksmith who lived just outside London. One of his close relatives was cook to Archbishop Warham. In his youth he was rather wild and was sent to prison. When he came out, he traveled in Europe, staying in Flanders, Rome and other places in Italy. On his return to England he married the daughter of a clothworker and set up in the same business himself. Later he became a solicitor, at which time he first met Wolsey.

Thomas Cromwell had also been a member of the short-lived Parliament of 1523. As this held out no hope of a career to an ambitious man, he had next attached himself to Wolsey, the most influential statesman he could find. One of his duties had been to help in the dissolution of the smaller monasteries in order to raise money for the new colleges Wolsey was building at Oxford and Ipswich. When his master fell from favor, he was full of sorrow, but only for himself. He was then between forty and fifty years of age. He felt his career so far had been a waste of time and effort. Cromwell, therefore, looked around again to see in whose hands the real power lay. He hastened to court to declare his allegiances to both the King and Anne Boleyn, who eventually were to find him of great service in removing the obstacles to their marriage; his past experience was to prove most useful in finding further ways of plundering the monasteries.

He first approached one of Wolsey's greatest enemies, the Duke of Norfolk, who willingly lent him a helping hand, expecting to profit from his disloyalty to the disgraced

Cardinal. The Duke's reward was to be superseded as the power behind the throne by his protégé, who quickly rose to a position of authority. Later, however, Norfolk had his revenge. He accused Cromwell of treason and was thus instrumental in sending him to his death.

It is a matter of dispute whether it was Cromwell or the King who instigated the measures which were now to be taken against the Church, but there is no doubt that Cromwell drafted the statutes presented to Parliament. Chapuys first mentioned Cromwell as a man of power in February 1533. By April he referred to him as the man with perhaps the most influence. As far as the Church itself was concerned, both the King and Cromwell were helped by the new Archbishop of Canterbury, Thomas Cranmer. Parliament gave him the power to act, and he made the decision that Henry's marriage to Katharine was null and void. He was able to act in regard to the King's Matter as Wolsey had formerly hoped to act had he been elected Pope.

In 1529, however, Cranmer, who was then about forty years old, had rarely been heard of outside Cambridge, where he was a lecturer in Divinity. He was known to have associated with the Church reformists in the university—men like Tyndale and Latimer, who were translating the New Testament—and to be sympathetic toward them. In August, to escape an epidemic of the ever-recurrent sweating sickness, he moved with two boys he was tutoring to their father's house in Waltham, Essex. Here, by chance, were also staying Stephen Gardiner, who was the King's Secretary, and Richard Fox, the King's Almoner. In conversation with them, he suggested a new move for the King to make. The learned doctors and Church lawyers of the different universities of England and Europe, he said, should be asked to give their considered opinion on the legitimacy of a man's marriage to his brother's widow. If they all were to find such a marriage invalid, then the Church courts would be able to decide the King's case without reference to Rome. Henry, who was ready to clutch at any straw that might help him, approved of both the scheme and its author. He at once ordered Cranmer to give up his teaching and to devote himself to working on the King's Matter.

In November, Cranmer was sent to live for a time with the Boleyn family at Durham House in London. Here he met Anne, to whose cause he was always to remain devoted. In January, he accompanied her father on a mission to Bologna where he saw the Emperor and the Pope. He also took an active part in canvasing university opinion. In December, one year after Cromwell had been chosen to represent Taunton in Parliament, Cranmer was created Archdeacon of the same place. He was appointed Henry's ambassador to the Emperor in 1531 and it was from this post that he was recalled to become Archbishop of Canterbury on Warham's death, an appointment which surprised him, Chapuys and many others beside. While on the continent, Cranmer had taken part in many theological discussions and had shown that his sympathies lay with Lutheran doctrine. He had also married for a second time (his first wife had died in childbirth), proof that he was not expecting an ecclesiastical office reserved for celibates. However, when summoned, he obeyed. He carried out the King's will, even when it meant contradicting himself. When the time came he was as ready to declare Henry's marriage to Anne Boleyn invalid as he had formerly declared it valid or as he had pronounced judgment against Katharine. He believed in the divine right of kings. But Cranmer also carried out many reforms concerning the dogma and practices of the Church during his many years in office. Notably, he encouraged the translation of the Bible into English and saw that a copy was placed in every church in England.

One of Wolsey's last acts of friendship toward France had been to persuade Henry, in 1528, to declare war on the Emperor. But the people of England were too strongly against such a war for any troops to be sent over and a few months later a truce was signed. In 1529, the Emperor and the King of France came to terms at the Peace of Cambrai, the "Ladies' Peace," which was negotiated by Charles's aunt Margaret and Francis's mother, Louise. The Emperor and the Pope also came to an agreement. They arranged to meet in Bologna early in 1530 when the Pope should crown Charles as Holy Roman Emperor. Henry thought to take advantage of this meeting by sending a delegation to try and bribe Charles away from support of Katharine. But his choice of Anne's father as ambassador was unfortunate. Charles was annoyed and the Earl of Wiltshire came home discomfited with a summons for Henry to appear before a court in Rome to answer Katharine's appeal. Pressure from Charles, more than Katharine's many urgent letters, had at last had some effect on the Pope. Henry was naturally loth to appear before a court he knew would be biased against him. If he had to go outside England, he would have preferred a neutral meeting-ground such as Cambrai, but neither Katharine nor her supporters would agree to this.

So far, Henry's attempts to win over Parliament, the universities and the Emperor had failed to advance his case. Any efforts on Katharine's behalf had been no more successful. Threat and counter-threat were used but with no result. Sometimes it almost seemed as though Henry had lost his initial enthusiasm. But it was too late for him to turn back and Anne was behind him to needle him into further activity if he flagged. The Emperor felt obliged to support his aunt but his support was lukewarm and he was clearly embarrassed by the situation. The Pope was said by the Duke of Norfolk not to want a conclusion of the question or peace between the Christian Princes for fear they would then unite and turn their minds to reforming the Church.[1]

The King's next move was a realization of the Pope's fear. Wolsey had died at the end of 1530. In 1531, Parliament and a convocation were summoned to hear the clergy charged under the same statute of *Praemunire,* which had been used against him. According to Chapuys, no one in England knew anything about the law as its whole basis was in the imagination of the King. But he was not quite accurate; *Praemunire* had been used earlier in Henry's reign. The clergy was intimidated and easily gave in. Hoping to appease the King's anger, it paid a colossal fine into his depleted exchequer, ostensibly to provide funds in case of war. Much more important, they were also made to deny the power of the Pope in England. Archbishop Warham proposed that Henry be recognized as the singular protector, and supreme lord, and, "so far as the law of Christ allows," also supreme head of the English Church and clergy.[2] The motion was not put to the vote. The silence of Convocation was taken to mean consent.

Although in general Parliament was jealous of Convocation and glad to see its powers curtailed, there was much criticism of the way in which this particular measure had been carried out. In the House of Lords Fisher spoke out strongly against the capitulation of the clergy. Sir Thomas More was horrified and talked of resigning as soon as possible. Henry, unperturbed, took the opportunity while Parliament was still sitting to have one of his men raise the question of his divorce. There was, however, stronger opposition to this and the matter was allowed to drop for the moment. It was feared that the Archbishop of Canterbury might be persuaded to hear the King's case in England but, when he was approached, he refused to act. Katharine and Chapuys were naturally distressed and justifiably afraid of what might follow.

Parliament met again in 1532. It opened with a petition to the King by the House of Commons against the clergy, known as the *Supplication of the Commons against the Ordinaries.* This was a direct threat to the power of the clergy to pass its own laws in Convocation and to pass judgment in its courts. It was accompanied by the *Act of Annates,* which gave the King power to abolish certain payments by the bishops to the Pope. Henry, however, only intended at this time to use this act as a threat to the Pope. When Convocation met to discuss these measures, the clergy gave in completely and put itself in the hands of the King. Its surrender is known as the "Submission of the Clergy."

Sir Thomas More thereupon resigned. Archbishop Warham, who had supported the King during the whole of his reign in matters he sometimes felt to be dubious, could not support the King in measures directed openly against the Pope. An old man now in his eighties, he at last found the courage to write the objections he had not been able to voice. He died in August 1532, before the King's wrath which he had feared for so long could fall upon him.

2. Final Parting

Against this background of Machiavellian scheming it is surprising that any sort of domestic life had been possible for Katharine and Henry. Habit, Katharine's tenacity and a certain respect for public opinion held King and Queen together for a time. They kept up appearances by dining for-

mally together at Church festivals and Katharine sometimes
accompanied Henry on his hunting expeditions. Anne, however, had her occasional petty victories even before she
achieved her final great one. At the end of 1529, there was
a banquet at court, followed by a ball, to celebrate the titles
which had just been bestowed upon the Boleyn family. The
newly created Lady Anne Rochford was given the place of
honor at table, taking precedence over the King's sister and
the King's daughter. The King's wife was not present. She
was staying in a house about seven miles away. Her absence
was noticed and Anne's presence adversely commented upon
by many. Perhaps as a result of this criticism, Katharine was
back at court at Christmas, presiding over the revels as usual.
But Anne was never far away. Even if Henry could still show
signs of domestic habit by sending Katharine a length of
cloth to make him shirts—to Anne's great annoyance when
she heard about it—it was Anne who shared his social activities. She went with him to London; she more and more
became his companion on his hunting expeditions, sometimes
even sharing the same horse, while Katharine was more
often left alone.

On the last day of November 1529, the King and Queen
dined together. Katharine commented that this was now a
rare pleasure. Henry replied that he had been busy and that
in any case there was no reason why he should visit her as
she was not his wife. This provoked Katharine to argument.
She expressed herself so forcibly that Henry went away discomfited and downcast. When he afterward told Anne, she
said, "Did I not tell you that when you disputed with the
Queen she was sure to have the upper hand? I see that some
fine morning you will succumb to her reasoning, and will cast
me off. I have been waiting too long, and might in the
meantime have contracted some advantageous marriage, out

of which I might have had issue, which is the greatest consolation in the world; but alas! farewell to my time and
youth spent to no purpose at all." [3] She knew the sure way
to retain Henry's attention.

Anne grew more spiteful and bad-tempered as time went
on with no progress in their plans. She was heard to say that
she wished all Spaniards at the bottom of the sea. She nagged
at Henry, who at times was led into quarreling with her too.
He was driven on one occasion to say that she was not
like Katharine, who had never used bad language (*mauvaise
parolle*) to him. Within a few years Anne was to alienate
even her own kinsfolk. She was positively hated by the people, who hissed and booed and called rude names after her
when she appeared in public with the King.

Sometimes, when Henry was angry with Katharine, he
refused to speak to her and ordered her not to write or communicate with him in any way. Sometimes, she was kept
away from court altogether. Anne also contrived to make
life as difficult as she could for her. Katharine was ill in the
fall of 1530 and ran a high fever, for which she was purged
and bled. Anne took advantage of the occasion to forbid her
her usual visitors so that the Queen could not find out what
was going on. Anne had already introduced her own spies
among Katharine's ladies so that she could be fully informed
of her activities.

Anne tried to prevent Henry from seeing his daughter, of
whom she seemed to be more jealous and afraid than she was
of Katharine. She was not always successful. Henry occasionally visited Mary and, when he did, showed himself an affectionate father. Once, when she had been ill, he saw her twice
a day for a week. He was hunting in the neighborhood and
made a point of calling on her. It is not recorded where
Anne was at the time. On Whitsunday 1531, Henry and

Katharine were again dining together.[4] Henry was in a good mood so Katharine summoned up courage to ask if Mary could come and visit them. Henry, however, was too much under Anne's influence to agree. He told Katharine roughly that there was nothing to prevent her from visiting Mary and staying with her too. Katharine was faced with a dilemma. She was torn more than most mothers by the choice between husband and child. She refused, however, to be the one to leave. She thought her only chance of survival as Henry's wife and Queen of England was to stay at his side no matter what happened or what insults she had to bear—and insults were plentiful. But occasionally Henry went away without her and once in a while Anne was ill. She and Mary were then able to visit each other.

The divorce proceedings which had lagged for four years were at last, in 1531, to come to a climax. Henry had continued to hope that Katharine might be persuaded or bullied into acquiescing to his plans so that he could again be on good terms with the Pope and the Emperor. In an attempt at conciliation, he had promised the Pope during the autumn of 1530 not to go further with his divorce proceedings until the new year. When he saw that Katharine was not to be won over, he decided to go ahead with the arrangements for the break with the Pope that he had been threatening for some time. In January he took the first step when he had himself declared head of the Church in England and became, according to Chapuys, King, Emperor and Pope all in one as far as England was concerned. He still hesitated, however, to take advantage of his new position. There were still many people who, though they had in fright voted him to be the head of the Church, balked at the mention of his divorce.

Henry had been angered by Katharine's direct representations to Rome and by the bulls and briefs issued by the Pope ordering him to put Anne away, to take Katharine back and, under pain of excommunication, not to proceed to a second marriage. He nevertheless made another attempt to make Katharine see what he called reason. On May 31, a large delegation headed by Norfolk and Suffolk and including the Bishops of Lincoln and London and Stephen Gardiner, the King's First Secretary, went to see her at nine o'clock in the evening—a late hour for an official call, though Katharine had been forewarned. Their aim was to make her withdraw her appeal to the Pope to have the King summoned to appear in Rome. They told her that the King was angry because of the way the Pope had treated him, the Pope having just issued a brief forbidding him to proceed with the divorce. They were, however, unable to make any impression upon her. She had herself long been impatient with the Pope, she said, whose dallying "keeps my Lord, the King, bound hand and foot by his enemies." But she refused to recognize any other authority than his even though up to the present time he had "shown himself so much inclined and so partial to the King." She continued, "I myself, and no one else, have reason to complain of his Holiness." Katharine stated her case so clearly that even the King's men sent to intimidate her were impressed. They "secretly nudged one another when any point touched the quick." In any case, many of them were sympathetically disposed toward her and had only come on the deputation because they dared not refuse the King. They went back to report their failure to Henry, who was scarcely surprised. He thought for a while and after a few moments said, "It is now necessary to provide for the affair by other means." [5] The other means were already prepared.

Henry was further angered in June when he heard that the court which was to hear Katharine's appeal in Rome had at last been summoned. He actually had no cause for alarm. When it met it was immediately adjourned till autumn. But the following month Henry made the decisive step he had so far resisted and left Katharine forever.

The King, the Queen and Lady Anne Rochford had all come to Windsor Castle from Hampton Court. One morning, Henry and Anne, accompanied by a large retinue, rose early to go out hunting as they had often done before. This time, they did not come back. Katharine was not altogether unprepared. The break had been threatened for some time. News of the preparations involved must have been leaked to her by her friends in spite of all efforts to keep her in the dark.

Henry and Anne went on to Woodstock, beyond Oxford, and Katharine was told that she was not to follow them. She waited a day or two and then sent a messenger to Henry, as was her usual custom when he was away. She asked after his health and said they ought at least to meet to say good-bye. Henry was furious and replied that he did not want her inquiries after his health since she had caused him so much sorrow and anger by her behavior. Katharine sent back a soft answer but did not succeed in turning away his wrath. A short time afterward an insulting official reply in writing informed her that the King did not wish to see her again, that she was wrong to maintain that she had been a virgin when he married her, and much more in the same vein.

The following month when Henry and Anne wished to return to Windsor, Katharine was told to be gone before they arrived. She was allowed to choose one out of four of the King's houses where she would like to live, but her choice was not accepted. She, therefore, put herself into the King's hands. She was first sent to a house called the More, which had formerly belonged to Wolsey; it was near St. Albans, where she and Henry had often stayed together in the past. She said that she would have preferred the Tower of London, for her sufferings could not be greater than they already were. Not long afterward, when certain apartments in the Tower were being redecorated, many people believed they were intended for Katharine. But this was a fate she escaped.

After Henry had gone away with Anne, Mary went to stay with her mother at Windsor. They passed their time in a seemingly pleasant enough way hunting and visiting other royal houses in the neighborhood. When Henry returned to Windsor and Katharine was sent to the More, Mary was separated from her mother and sent to Richmond. Katharine never saw Henry again and it is almost certain that she and Mary were given no further opportunity of meeting. Mother and daughter were allowed to write to each other for a time, but about two years later even that pleasure was forbidden them.

Both separations were hard for Katharine to bear, but she grew to accept the fact that Henry would not come back. Her one hope, about which she began to write more and more insistently to her nephew and to Rome, was that the Pope would declare that she had been married legally and that her daughter was therefore legitimate. She was more afraid for Mary than she was for herself. Mary was young, vulnerable and possibly in danger of her life. Although it was normal for royal children to live with their own establishments apart from their parents, it was not normal for them to be surrounded by so much hatred and danger. Mary was also not very strong. She seemed either to have inherited her mother's poor constitution or the distress caused by the rift between her parents when she was at a susceptible age (she was ten years old in 1526 when the trouble started) affected her health. Now in 1531, when she was separated from her parents, she was about the same age Katharine had been when she had first come to England. She was to have an even worse time than her mother had had. Katharine was still often ill herself and not in a position to help her daughter. She could not always see that Mary received even such medical attention as was available in those days. She did manage on one occasion to persuade Henry, through intermediaries, to let her doctors visit their sick daughter, even though she herself was not allowed to be at her side. Although to us Mary was very young when her misfortunes began, it should be remembered that in those days girls of her age were considered mature enough to marry and bear children.

In October, Henry tried again to win over Katharine, hoping that she might accept a *fait accompli*. But the two delegations he sent had no more success than the others. Katharine would not budge and loudly proclaimed her case so that all could hear. She could not be persuaded into giving in to Henry whatever means he tried. He, on the other hand, was hesitant to proceed with his threats but was in the end forced to do so by her obstinacy. If Katharine had given in meekly, Henry would still have married Anne but he would not have been driven into breaking with the Pope on her account. Katharine, feeble as she was physically, always had the moral strength to resist. But, as she wrote to the Emperor the following month, "God knows how I can support all I have to suffer. All this put together is enough to put an end to the lives of ten people, how much more so to mine which is now so shattered by misfortune that no human creature ever suffered such agony." [6]

Katharine's household had been cut when she was sent away but it was still large as befitted a royal princess. There is a Venetian account of a visit paid to her in November, in which she is said to have been attended by thirty maids of honor, with fifty more to wait upon her, and a court of two hundred around her. Katharine herself was also described:

> The Queen is of low stature, rather stout with a modest countenance; she is virtuous, just, replete with goodness and religion; she speaks Spanish, Flemish, French and English. She is beloved by the islanders more than any Queen that ever reigned; she is about forty-five years old . . .[7]

A picture of Henry was given at the same time:

> . . . His face is angelic rather than handsome; his head imperial and bald, and he wears a beard, contrary to English custom . . . He sits his horse well, and manages him yet better; he jousts and wields his spear, throws the quoit and draws the bow, admirably; plays at tennis most dexterously.
>
> . . . Beside the Latin and his native tongue he learned Spanish, French and Italian. He is kind and affable, full of graciousness and courtesy, and liberal; he took such delight in his own rule that from liberal he became avaricious . . . He appears to be religious.[8]

3.   *Anne's Triumph*

Anne was in her element now that Henry had at last made a positive move to separate from Katharine. She still had some eighteen months to wait, however, before her ultimate wish was fulfilled. Chapuys reported that her own uncle and father claimed to be responsible for the delay as they opposed the marriage. They were annoyed that Anne was unpleasant in her behavior to them. They also thought that she was overreaching herself. Anne prepared herself for the great occasion by taking over Katharine's royal apartments, amassing jewels and fine clothes and generally making her presence felt at court. She boasted openly that she soon would be crowned Queen of England. During the Christmas revels of 1531, Anne presided in Katharine's place but, according to Hall, "all men said there was no mirth in that Christmas because the Queen and her ladies were absent." [9]

It was customary in England at that time to exchange gifts on New Year's Day. Henry gave lavish presents to Anne, including a bed covered with gold and silver and crimson cloth very richly embroidered at great cost. He sent a gold cup to his old girl-friend Elizabeth Blount, now Lady Tailboys, whose husband had recently died. There were rumors that he might marry Elizabeth instead of Anne. (A contemporary reference comes from an English priest in Louvain who, when asked to compare the two favorites, replied that Elizabeth was prettier but Anne more "eloquent and graceful, more really handsome.")[10] To Katharine, Mary and their households, Henry gave no presents. Moreover, he also forbade any member of his council to give them anything. Katharine, however, although not allowed to write to Henry, sent him by messenger a fine gold cup. He was extremely angry but controlled his feelings in front of the court. He examined the cup with apparent appreciation in public, but sent it back privately afterward.

It was said in Rome that Anne had had a miscarriage that Christmas, but there is no evidence to support such a report. It has generally been assumed that about September of the following year, when she was made Marchioness of Pembroke, Anne became in fact what she had long been thought to be—the King's mistress. There was, however, a conflicting French report at the time that Anne had been bought off by the title. Katharine herself half-believed this but was not long left under that delusion. It soon became obvious that

Anne was more firmly entrenched in the King's favor than ever. Henry's behavior did not go unreproved. Both Pope and Emperor protested. Churchmen bravely preached against him. But Henry was undeterred.

Henry was planning to meet the King of France in the fall of 1532. His followers, it was said, would number three to four thousand, all male. Katharine, who was not without her own sources of information, heard the rumor which she passed on to Chapuys that Anne was also preparing to accompany Henry with a big train of female servants. The lords and courtiers were then instructed to keep their wives in readiness to travel with them if necessary. Henry and Anne were apparently both excited at the prospect of the journey, but there was no great enthusiasm on the part of the husbands and wives who were to escort them.

Anne blew hot and cold, and every rumor about her was reported back by Chapuys to the Emperor. She wrote to her best friend at court, he said, to ask her to be prepared for the journey and interview "where what she had so long been wishing for will be accomplished." [11] This was naturally interpreted as meaning that Anne expected to be married to Henry in France. Katharine found little comfort in the contradictory report that Anne had said that "were the King to wish it, she would never consent to the marriage taking place out of England but only on the very spot and with the same ceremonies used by the English Queens at their marriage and coronation." [12]

Katharine wrote to her nephew in alarm:

> There are many signs of the evil meditated here; new books are being printed, full of lies, impurities and blasphemies against our common faith, showing their staunch determination to bring the suit to an end in this Kingdom, all of which, coupled with the contem-

plated interview of the princes, and the infamy
brought upon the whole Kingdom by the lady companion the King takes with him, and the authority he
bestows upon her, has, Your Majesty may be certain,
caused scandal and fear throughout this Kingdom, and
all dread that some calamity is impending.[13]

After many delays and many ill omens, Anne crossed the
Channel with Henry. It took them seven hours on a fine day.
The Venetians thought they would take the opportunity to
marry while they were in France. But, if a marriage had been
contemplated, there is no record that it took place. Anne had
rich new clothes for the occasion. She also took with her
Katharine's jewels which she had asked Henry to obtain for
her. Katharine had lent them reluctantly and after some hesitation only as a sign of obedience to her husband. She said
that she could not give them to him as he would not accept
gifts from her but, "if the King sends expressly for my jewels,
I am ready to obey his commands in that as well as in all
matters." [14] She never saw them again, which seemed to
annoy Chapuys more than it did her.

The two Kings met on October 21. The meeting turned
out to be much less elaborate than originally planned and of
little diplomatic significance. If Anne had been present at the
Field of Cloth of Gold and expected another such glamorous
event with herself as one of the chief participants, she was
to be disappointed. The meeting was postponed several times
and, in the end, very few followers accompanied either King.
Although it was said that Anne had been invited by Francis,
she did not in fact enter French territory. She stayed in Calais,
which was still English, while Henry met Francis quietly
across the border between Calais and Boulogne. Neither
Francis' Spanish wife, Eleanor, one of Juana's daughters and
sister to Charles V, nor his sister the former Duchess of

Alençon, at whose court Anne was said to have spent some time seven or eight years earlier, would meet the King of England's companion. Eleanor came with Francis, but stayed separately a few miles from Boulogne. When the Kings had concluded their business, however, Francis came back with Henry to Calais for a day or two and allowed himself to be entertained by Anne. After his departure, the English party was ready to return home, but they were held up by bad weather in the Channel and did not reach Dover until the middle of November. They spent a few days inspecting the fortifications before they were next heard of at Eltham on November 24.

Both before and after the meeting there was much speculation in England and in Europe as to what the two Kings would talk about. An invasion of Flanders was to be prepared; a peace with Scotland was to be negotiated; concerted action against the Turks, who were invading Europe, was at last to be undertaken; the divorce was to be discussed. The Kings of England and France, however, maintained that their meeting was solely to provide good cheer, for the sake of amusement and enjoyment. This no one believed, least of all Katharine, who naturally suspected that whatever was to be discussed would be directed against her. As she wrote to the Emperor, "The thunders of this land bear no lightning except to strike me." [15]

The purpose of the meeting remained a well-guarded secret in spite of the spies of many nationalities who hovered round to pick up information. No foreign ambassadors were invited, again to Chapuys's annoyance. The only positive piece of information which leaked out, and Katharine was one of the first to hear about it, was that two French cardinals were to be sent to talk to the Pope. The exact nature of their mission could only be guessed at. The meeting fizzled out and was not worth the furor it had created. But a treaty of sorts had been drawn up between the Kings; the Duke of Richmond and the Earl of Surrey were left behind in France as tokens of Henry's good faith. The Emperor and the Pope retaliated by meeting together in Bologna.

Not long after she had come back to England, it became apparent that Anne was pregnant. She made no attempt to hide it. Henry was determined that his child should be legitimate and therefore married Anne secretly. Early in 1533 it was already being rumored that the marriage had taken place on January 25 in Whitehall Palace. It is not known who performed the ceremony. Cranmer denied any knowledge of it. The most likely name suggested was that of George Brown, an Augustinian Friar, who later became Bishop of Dublin. Hall and Holinshed,[16] when writing their histories not many years later, back-dated the marriage to November of the previous year in an attempt to show that the child had been conceived in wedlock. As Henry and Anne had been delayed in Calais and did not get back to London until the end of November, this date is questionable—unless by chance they were married quietly in Calais after all, which was never suggested at the time. Henry's marriage to Katharine, however, had still not been annulled by any court. Further action had to be taken quickly if Anne's child and Henry's heir was to be legitimate beyond any shadow of doubt. As it was unlikely that the Pope would help, it was necessary that someone in England should be given power to annul the previous marriage.

Thomas Cranmer, as Archbishop of Canterbury-elect, was the obvious choice. He was devoted to Anne and loyal to the King. The Pope was asked to speed up the bulls of his appointment, which normally took about a year. The Pope must have been aware of Cranmer's past history and Lutheran associations. He knew that Henry had denied the papal authority. Nevertheless, he willingly and quickly sent the bulls. Such swift action was out of character. Perhaps he wanted the divorce taken out of his hands or perhaps he thought Henry had repented. On March 30, 1533, Thomas Cranmer was consecrated Archbishop and publicly swore his allegiance to the Pope. Secretly, he had already declared that his only allegiance was to the King of England. The Pope's representative stood at Henry's right hand during the ceremony and permitted himself to be feted, thus giving the impression to the public that King and Pope were again on good terms. He had brought with him a brief ordering Henry to separate from Anne and return to Katharine, but he pretended to find no suitable opportunity for handing it over.

Katharine no longer believed that Henry would return to her. She now only begged the Pope to decide for her before it was too late so that "she might live and die comparatively happy, knowing that the Pope had justified her cause. Her conscience would then be satisfied with the thought that Mary had not lost her right to the throne. She had another year to wait before this verbal comfort was to be given to her.

Under Cromwell's guiding hand, several Parliamentary and Church decrees were rushed through to curb still more the power of the clergy. There was opposition, but this was silenced by threats. The *Submission of the Clergy* was reaffirmed. By the *Act of Appeals* all legal power in regard to matters both spiritual and temporal was vested in the hands of the King. No appeal could be made to any court outside the country. The Archbishop of Canterbury, as the King's servant, was to be judge of ecclesiastical cases. In this way, any appeal to Rome by Katharine and any decree in her favor by the Pope were rendered valueless in England. The stage was now set for the final scene. Before the curtain went up, Henry tried once more to win over Katharine.

Yet another deputation, headed by Norfolk and Suffolk, was sent to her at Ampthill in Bedfordshire, where she was staying in April 1533. She was told that if she would renounce the title of Queen and allow her case to be decided in England she would be well provided for for the rest of her life. This offer seems to have been made in good faith. Henry showed many times that he would have liked at any rate to be kind to her, though it is open to question whether Anne would have allowed him to be so. But Katharine refused every overture he made because her conscience would not let her submit. If her conscience had been otherwise, she might have lived out her life in lonely comfort as an English princess. Mary also might have been better treated and as a result her nature might have been less harsh. Henry was furious that he could not bend Katharine's will to his, so he allowed her to be ill-treated and let Anne have her way with Mary.

Katharine refused the conditions offered by the delegation, as they knew she would. They then broke the news to her that all resistance was futile as the King had already married Anne. This, however, was no surprise as she had already been told by Chapuys. Lord Mountjoy was left behnd to act as her guardian as it was feared, unnecessarily, that she might try to leave the country. He had the unenviable task of telling her that in future she would be known as the *Old Princess Dowager;* that the King would no longer be responsible for her personal expenses nor for the wages of her servants; and that she was to retire to a small house of her own and live on a small allowance. Katharine replied with some spirit that she would continue to call herself Queen as long as she lived; she did not care to start housekeeping at her time of life; and, as for her staff, she would be content as long as she was allowed to keep her confessor, physician and apothecary and two maids to look after her chamber.

As Princess Dowager, only those monies would be due to her which had been granted when she married Arthur. These were considerably less than the income she was receiving as Queen. For the time being, however, neither staff nor allowances were cut as it took more than a threat from the King to undo what had been granted by an act of council. But Katharine had been warned and now knew what to expect. She also knew that though many might secretly support her cause few would come to her aid. Henry had already tried, though without notable success, to wipe out support for Katharine by forbidding anyone to speak against his marriage to Anne. Now people were encouraged, by the promise of a reward, to denounce such slanderous talk.

On May 10, the new Archbishop of Canterbury summoned Katharine to a court to be held at Dunstable; it was near Ampthill where she was living but far enough away from London not to attract attention. Katharine, on Chapuys's advice, refused to attend the court on the grounds that she only recognized the authority of the Pope. She was again declared contumacious. On May 23, Cranmer declared at Dunstable that the Pope was not competent to dispense in the case of a man wishing to marry his brother's widow if the first marriage had been consummated. He then asserted that the marriage between Arthur and Katharine had been consummated and therefore the marriage between Henry and Katharine was not valid. A few days later, in London, he declared the marriage between Henry and Anne to be legal, though he did not say when the marriage had taken place.

For her coronation Anne came to London from Greenwich

in Katharine's royal barge. Katharine's coat of arms had been
removed and cut to pieces. Isabella's lion of Castile and
Ferdinand's bundles of arrows, together with Katharine's
emblem of the pomegranate, disappeared from the gate of
the Great Hall at Westminster and other public places; they
were replaced by the crowned falcon standing on a branch
bearing red and white roses which Anne had chosen as her
own device. The people of London turned out to gaze and
the usual pageants were arranged to welcome Anne, though
Chapuys reported that enthusiasm was lacking. On June 1,
Anne was crowned Queen of England in Westminster Abbey
with all the pomp and circumstance she had desired. Katharine, said the Venetians, still looked cheerful and arrayed
her retinue in new uniforms decorated with *H* and *K*.

4.   *Life at Buckden*

The Pope refused to sanction the marriage legalized by
the Archbishop of Canterbury. He threatened to excom-
municate the King of England, his new Queen and Cranmer, though he never put his threat into execution. The
College of Cardinals decided at last that the Pope had the
power to dispense for a man to marry his brother's widow,
though their decision was not immediately made public.
Nevertheless, it is likely that the King heard the news from
his agents but, having put himself and England outside the
Pope's jurisdiction, he gave the impression that he no longer
cared what was decided in Rome. He and Anne waited
confidently for the birth of the son the astrologers were
predicting.

Yet another deputation, composed this time of her own
household officers with Lord Mountjoy reluctantly at their
head, came in July to see Katharine at Ampthill. On the

King's instructions, they tried once again to make her accept the title of Princess Dowager, affirming that only through arrogance, selfishness or vainglory could she still claim to be Queen. Although Katharine was ill in bed with both a cough and a sore foot, she was not too weak to reply with her customary vehemence. She refused to recognize any title other than Queen. Even threats against Mary could not move her. Although, as she admitted, she would be very much affected if Henry ill-treated their daughter, "yet neither for that nor for a thousand deaths would she consent to damn her soul or that of the King, her lord and husband." [17] When Cromwell received the report of the interview, he expressed admiration for the Queen's tenacity, saying that God and nature had done her great injury in not making her a man.

According to Chapuys, England was in a state of chaos. He urged the Emperor to come with an army in support of his aunt as the time was ripe for action. Undoubtedly there was unrest, but not as much as Chapuys would have had the Emperor believe. Katharine, perplexed and distraught as she was and much as she wished for the Emperor's help, did not want war on her account; she would have rather died than provoke one. She would not leave the country nor encourage any plan to remove herself and Mary to a place of greater safety, as that would have meant going against her husband's will. The Emperor was greatly relieved by her attitude. He was already at war with Soliman the Turk and his ally Barbarossa of Tunisia and did not want another war on his hands.

Since leaving Windsor two years earlier, Katharine and her household had been constantly on the move. Before going to Ampthill, she had been heard of at the More, Easthampstead, the More again, Enfield, Bishop's Hatfield and, during Henry's visit to France, Hertford Castle. In most, if not all of these houses, she had formerly stayed with Henry and it was not abnormal for members of the royal family to change residence frequently. But now, in the summer of 1533, after further threats to cut down her allowances and staff, Henry sent her to Buckden on the edge of the fen country in the county of Huntingdon. The day she moved, whales were seen in the Thames which the superstitious regarded as an ill omen. She was housed in the palace of the Bishop of Lincoln, who had always supported Henry against her, so that she could more easily be watched. On her way there from Ampthill she was enthusiastically greeted as Queen by many people who had come to pay her homage as she passed by. (They just as strongly voiced their disapproval of Anne Boleyn.) Mary was also greeted in a similarly friendly way when she changed residence. But, at most, this reception was a hollow pleasure to Katharine. The people could not help her and their behavior was a further source of annoyance to the King and Anne. After such demonstrations Chapuys thought it unlikely that either Katharine or Mary would ever be moved publicly again.

Maria de Salinas wished to join her mistress in her new home, but was not allowed to do so even though she offered to serve at her own expense. Katharine hated Buckden, which she considered more of a prison than a home. But, after Henry left her, she hated every place she had to live in and every change made in her circumstances. In particular, she complained that Buckden was damp and unhealthy, which it may well have been for her.

A picture of Katharine's life at this time has been left by Nicholas Harpsfield, a professor of Greek at Oxford. He praised her in *A Pretended Divorce,* a book written not many years after her death during the reign of her daughter

Mary when such a book was again welcome. He described how her solitary life was spent

> . . . in much prayer, great alms, and abstinence. And when she was not this way occupied, then was she and her gentlewomen working with their own hands something wrought in needlework costly and artificially, which she intended to the honour of God to bestow upon some churches. There was in the said house of Buckden a chamber with a window that had a prospect into the chapel, out of which she might hear divine service. In this chamber she enclosed herself sequestered from all other company a great part of the day and night, and upon her knees used to pray at the said window leaning upon the stones of the same. There was some of her gentlewomen which did curiously mark and observe all her doings, who reported that oftentimes they found the said stones so wet after her departure as though it had rained upon them. It was credibly thought that in the time of her prayer she removed the cushions that ordinarily lay in the same window and that the said stones were imbrued with the tears of her devout eyes. I have credibly also heard that at times when one of her gentlewomen began to curse the Lady Anne Boleyn, she answered: "Hold your peace. Curse her not, but pray for her; for the time will come shortly when you shall have much need to pity and lament her case!" And so it chanced indeed.[18]

Anne, having already taken from Katharine her husband, title and jewels, now coveted a "rich and gorgeous" piece of cloth which Katharine was said to have brought with her from Spain to use as a christening robe. At Anne's request, Henry demanded the cloth for the child they were so eagerly awaiting. Katharine's answer was completely in character: "God forbid that I should ever be so badly advised as to give help, assistance, or favor, directly or indirectly, in a case so horrible and abominable as this." [19] It is not recorded whether Katharine was made to give up the cloth.

On September 7, Anne's child was born. The physicians, astrologers, wizards and witches who had been consulted as to its sex all proved wrong. It was another girl. The disappointment and chagrin of both parents can be imagined. At first it was rumored that she too was to be given the name of Mary, but in fact she was christened Elizabeth. The Dowager Duchess of Norfolk and the Dowager Marchioness of Exeter were called upon to act as godmothers. They may have been afraid to refuse. But Thomas Cranmer had earned the honor of being godfather and was doubtless pleased to accept.

Already before the birth of the child, Henry's attentions were being paid to another girl at court. Anne complained to Henry of his behavior and was told that she should "endure as those better than herself had done." [20] According to Chapuys, the Duke of Norfolk bore out this statement: "Among other virtues of the Queen, the Duke pointed out to me as a most prominent one her great modesty, prudence and forbearance, not only during these last disagreeable differences, but likewise on former occasions the King having been at all times very much inclined to amourous intrigues." [21] Katharine also must have been aware of how things were going, if the account of her charitable remarks about Anne is true.

Anne, however, had by no means lost control of the situation. As Chapuys said, she well knew how to get round the King. Steps were immediately taken to ensure the legitimacy of her child and the illegitimacy of Katharine's. Cromwell claimed to have no wish to declare Mary a bastard as her parents had married in good faith and were not aware at the time of her birth that they were living in sin. But Anne carried the day. Many attempts were made to make Mary acknowledge Elizabeth as the true Princess of Wales but, at the age of seventeen, she proved as resolute as her mother. In December, the three-month-old Elizabeth was set up at Hatfield with her own establishment presided over by Anne's aunt Lady Shelton, the Earl of Wiltshire's sister. In due course they moved to Hunsdon and then to various other houses in the manner of the day. Mary was forced to accompany her, always with Lady Shelton as her governess.

5. Mary Out of Favor

For some time Mary had been living quietly in Beaulieu, though after the birth of Elizabeth there were rumors that her way of life was to be changed. In December 1533, her household and allowances were cut down. Shortly afterward, she was taken away by the Duke of Suffolk to serve in a humble position in her half-sister's house. Her own staff was dismissed. Her governess, the Countess of Salisbury, begged to be allowed to accompany Mary without being paid for her services, but her request was refused. Mary was no longer supposed to write to her mother or to receive letters from her, even if she promised to write only harmless letters about the state of her health. She was, however, suspected of being somehow in touch with Katharine. Neither Henry nor Anne believed she could resist the treatment she received or make the replies she did unless she had been coached. They were right. After Katharine's death Mary gave in; she denied her mother's right to the title of Queen and her own to Princess of Wales. The one chambermaid left to serve Mary was suspected of being the go-between and was dismissed. Chapuys admitted in his report to the Emperor that Mary had used her to send letters to him and he was still in touch with Katharine.

Lady Shelton was encouraged by Anne to treat Mary as one of the servants. She was told to shut her in her room, reputedly the worst in the house, and to slap her if she was rebellious. But she evidently was not strict enough and was later taken to task by other members of Anne's family. Every effort was made to break Mary's spirit. Her confessor was sent away and a Lutheran of Anne's choice was put in his place. Mary, with her upbringing, found this hard to bear. She was also frightened, not knowing from day to day what was going to happen to her or to her mother. The maid who should have tasted her food was also sent away. For reasons which may have nothing to do with this Mary often suffered from an upset stomach. It is not surprising, therefore, that Chapuys suspected she was being poisoned. There were not only fears for Mary's physical condition, but also for her moral well-being. The plans were, so Chapuys affirmed, to bring about her death through grief, neglect, ill-treatment or, possibly, poison; to force her by such measures to renounce her rights; to marry her to some "low fellow" so that she could thereby be made to lose her claim to the throne; or to encourage her "to fall a prey to lust," which would give the excuse for disinheriting her.[22]

Katharine, realizing the dangers that lay in store for Mary, had tried to prepare her to cope with them. Before the privilege of exchanging letters had been denied them, Katharine had written to encourage her daughter. Although her own heart was heavy she gave no sign of it. She wrote firmly and apparently cheerfully, anxious not to make Mary more afraid than she already was. She combined spiritual consolation with practical advice: Believe in God, but lock your door. She wrote:

Daughter,

I heard such tidings today, that I do perceive, if it be true, the time is come that Almighty God will prove you, and I am very glad of it, for I trust He doth handle you with a good love. I beseech you agree to His pleasure with a merry heart, and be sure that, without fail, He will not suffer you to perish if you beware to offend Him.

I pray you, good daughter, to offer yourself to Him. . . . And if this lady do come to you, as it is spoken, if she do bring you a letter from the King, I am sure in the self-same letter you shall be commanded what you shall do. Answer you in few words, obeying the King your father in everything, save only that you will not offend God and lose your own soul; and go no further with learning and disputation in the matter. And wheresoever and in whatsoever company you shall come, obey the King's commandments. Speak you few words and meddle nothing. . . . And sometimes for recreation use your virginals or lute, if you have any. But one thing specially I desire of you for the love that you do owe unto God and unto me, to keep your heart with a chaste mind, and your body from all ill and wanton company, not thinking or desiring any husband, for Christ's passion, neither determine yourself to any manner of living until this troublesome time be past, for I dare make sure that you shall see a very good end, and better than you even desire.

I would, good daughter, that you did know with how good a heart I write this letter unto you. I never did one with a better for I perceive very well that God loveth you. I beseech Him of His goodness to continue it; and if it fortune that you shall have no one to be with you of your acquaintance, I think it

best you keep your keys yourself, for howsoever it is,
so shall be done as shall please them. . . . When they
have done the uttermost they can, then I am sure
of the amendment . . .

your loving mother
Katharine the Queen.[23]

To Katharine it was a matter of religious belief that she
and Mary would lose their souls if they gave in. For this
reason she suffered oppression and encouraged her daughter
to do the same. She explained her position to the Emperor:

Indeed, there is no need for relating Your Majesty
the sufferings that I and my daughter undergo, as
well as the treatment to which we are daily subjected
. . . for our troubles are matters of universal notoriety; and . . . if the All merciful did not help us
throughout, the burden would be insupportable. However, as I do consider that my purgatory, [and] my
daughter's, is in this world, we are both of us doing
what we can in defence of our right. As to me, Your
Highness may be sure I shall not fail [in this task]
till death, as otherwise I should imperil my soul; and
I hope to God the Princess will do the same, as a
good daughter should.[24]

Mary was able to resist the temptations of court life, possibly because they did not really tempt her. She withstood
the pressure put upon her by the Boleyn family. But, she was
never able to be truly merry. The iron entered her soul. Ill-
health tortured her body. The humor and kindliness that
were so much a part of her mother's character were conspicu-
ously lacking in Mary, though perhaps only suppressed by
circumstance. The tight-lipped, suspicious expression to be
seen on her portraits could be explained by the sufferings she
had to endure, and which she only just managed to survive.
She was often ill and, during the last years of her mother's

life, always miserable. Unlike her mother, she would have been only too glad to have been able to escape from England and her persecutors.

For over two years Mary lived in a subordinate position in Elizabeth's household and during this time she was sometimes so ill that her life was despaired of by the physicians who visited her. Henry sent his own physician and even allowed Katharine to send hers. But when Katharine begged that her daughter come to be nursed by her, Henry refused. He was afraid of Katharine's influence. It would seem that Katharine was suspicious of the cause of Mary's illness. She may, however, only have been referring to the general conditions of her life rather than suggesting poison when she wrote that if Mary should die as a result of the treatment to which she was subjected, it would be a twofold crime.

In the same December of 1533 that saw Mary's peace at Beaulieu disturbed, another attempt was made to intimidate Katharine at Buckden.[25] Once again the Duke of Suffolk was the bearer of the King's will. Though his mother-in-law, now Maria de Salinas, claimed he was most unwilling to come, he nevertheless allowed the members of his commission to carry out their duties and behave in the most heartless fashion. Suffolk's task was threefold: to persuade Katharine to withdraw her appeal to Rome; to make all Katharine's followers swear to her as Princess Dowager; and to remove her and her household to a place more remote than Buckden, either Fotheringham or Somersham. Both the suggested houses, Katharine had already been told, were surrounded by water and marshes, the unhealthiest in all England. Her pride, too, suffered at the thought of having to live in an even smaller house. She considered her health bad enough at Buckden without having to move to an even damper place right in the heart of the fens.

It was rumored that Anne's intentions were to have Katharine locked up on an island difficult of access and to declare her insane. It would then only have been a matter of time before the damp climate—or some other, more secret means —either brought about her end or reduced her to real madness. It would have been difficult for the Emperor to complain if his aunt received the same treatment he himself had meted out to his mother.

If the rumor was true, Katharine was able to prevent it from becoming a fact: she refused to withdraw her appeal from Rome; her servants refused to acknowledge her as anything but Queen; she would not leave Buckden. Suffolk and the other members of his commission, having failed to achieve their object by the use of "strong and disrespectful language," then resorted to harsher measures. Katharine's house was dismantled and her possessions packed up ready to be sent away. Her staff, including her chamberlain, chancellor, almoner, groom and ladies-in-waiting, was either dismissed or arrested. They were replaced by rougher men from the northern counties. Thomas Abell,[26] her chaplain, was sent to the Tower for the second time and on this occasion not allowed to come out again.

Katharine still had some fight left in her. She steadfastly refused point by point every argument produced by Suffolk. Her logic, coupled with her usual hyperbolic language, managed to gain some concessions. As she claimed she could only confess in Spanish, three Spaniards were allowed to stay in her service: her confessor, Jorge de Athequa, the Bishop of Llandaff; her physician, de la Sa; and her apothecary, de Soto. As she refused any chambermaids other than those she knew, saying that she would never undress to go to bed and would be responsible for locking her own door, she was allowed to keep only two, though not the two she would have chosen.

The commissioners stayed six days, hoping their conduct might frighten Katharine into consent. On the day they proposed to move her from Buckden she barred herself in her room. When they came to fetch her, she called out, that if they wished to take her away they must first break down the door. Then, their courage failed them. They did not know if they were empowered to use force of this kind. They were also afraid for their own safety as, in the meantime, a crowd had gathered from the neighborhood ready to protect Katharine and attack them. They therefore acted with discretion and went away without her.

For the rest of that winter Katharine was permitted to go on living in Buckden. She was highly suspicious, however, of the new members of her household and refused any meals prepared by them. She ate very sparingly in any case and only such food as was cooked for her by her own women in her own room. Parliament made lawful Henry's threat to take away the lands and income she had enjoyed as Queen. Henry made great show of offering her others of even greater value if she would accept them as Princess Dowager. But Katharine was not to be bribed or bullied. Attempts were also made to bribe Mary into accepting the titles of Princess Dowager for her mother and Madame Mary for herself. When she also refused, Anne was furious and swore she would put down that proud Spanish blood.

In March, Katharine's steward and guardian at Buckden, Sir Edmund Bedingfield, reported with some alarm that Katharine had asked if she could perform publicly in Buckden church the usual Maundy ceremony. It was customary to wash the feet of as many poor people as one had years and then give them money. Bedingfield's instructions came back quickly. Katharine could perform the ceremony privately in her room if she wished but only in her capacity as Princess

Dowager. This was tantamount to a straight refusal. She was forbidden to give money to the poor as it was claimed this was the "real cause of the love and affection all the English bear her." [27]

In the spring, Katharine was moved quietly from Buckden to Kimbolton Castle and there was no public outcry. But, before that happened, important decisions had been reached in both Rome and London which greatly affected the treatment she and Mary were to receive.

6. *Vindication and Defeat*

On March 24, 1534, the Pope in consistory in Rome, after a delay of almost five years, declared the dispensation of Pope Julius II to be sufficient and the marriage of Henry and Katharine therefore valid. Six months later Clement VII died. Perhaps when he felt the approach of death, he feared the wrath of his Maker more than any human recrimination; so, as Archbishop Warham had done before him, he declared in Katharine's favor. Katharine was reported to have received the news from Rome with immense pleasure and satisfaction. Now she could die in comparative peace of mind. The highest authority on earth had confirmed that she had not been living in sin and that her daughter was legitimate. Their souls were saved. The King, though he showed a good front, was inwardly displeased. He had, however, already set in motion certain measures which would undermine the Pope's decision. By coincidence, on practically the same day, the House of Lords ratified Henry's marriage to Anne and settled the succession on their children. Katharine showed that in her heart of hearts she wanted more than for her soul to be saved in order to be able to die in peace; less than a year later, she wrote to the Emperor regretting that no good effect had come from the Pope's decree.

In its first session of 1534 Parliament, prodded by the King and Cromwell, had been pushing forward with further legislation directed against the clergy and the authority of Rome. It decided that in the future the Pope should be known in England only as the Bishop of Rome, thus denying his claim to be the head of Christendom. His power in England was also reduced by the *Second Act of Annates,* which confirmed the first which had been used as a threat and had never been put into action. The submission of the clergy was reaffirmed. By the new *Act of Succession,* the children of Henry and Anne were made heirs to the throne and Mary was declared a bastard. In its second session Parliament passed the *Act of Supremacy,* by which Henry was declared Supreme Head of the Church in England. The *Statute of Treasons* made it high treason to deny the succession law or the King's supremacy by spoken or written word or by deed. A number of people in high places, especially those whose loyalty was suspected, were made to swear to both. Refusal meant death. By this means a reign of limited terror was instituted which removed some of Katharine's strongest supporters and frightened the rest into silence.

The terror could be said to have begun on April 20 when a woman called Elizabeth Barton was beheaded at Tyburn for treason. Her head was set on London Bridge, according to custom, as a warning to others. The crime of which she had been convicted was that she had falsely claimed to see visions and to be able to foretell the future. In particular, she had prophesied that if the King should proceed with his divorce and marry Anne Boleyn, in one month's time he would be King no more. It was said that not only the simple but also the wise had believed in her supernatural powers. Archbishop Warham had been sufficiently impressed to have two monks investigate her case. As a result, she had been made a nun and had become known as the Holy Maid of

Kent. Some of Katharine's supporters had talked to her and were said to have used her in their plots. Katharine herself had very wisely refused to have anything to do with her. The previous November the nun had been arrested and while in prison had been made to implicate several of Katharine's friends including Bishop John Fisher of Rochester and Sir Thomas More. Both went to the Tower, but Sir Thomas More was set free after he affirmed that he had only advised the nun not to meddle in political affairs.

More escaped his enemies only for a short time. Another pretext was found for arresting him and soon he rejoined Fisher in the Tower. Both of them were asked to swear to the Act of Succession and to the Act of Supremacy. Fisher refused. On June 22, 1535, at the age of seventy-four, he was executed. More, as a lawyer, was able to delay his own sentence by legal technicalities. He accepted the Act of Succession but his conscience would not let him repudiate the Pope. He did not deny Henry's supremacy, however; he only refrained from affirming it, saying that "No statute can inflict punishment on a man for his silence." But his respite was short. On July 6 he followed Rochester to the block. As Wolsey's before him, his last words have passed into history: "I die the King's good servant, but God's first." Others executed at this time included the head of the monastery at Syon, to which Katharine had devoted so much time in the past. The order of the Observant Friars, in whose chapel at Greenwich Henry and Katharine had been married, was suppressed. Father Forrest from Greenwich and Mary's teacher Fetherston were imprisoned and executed at a later date.

Meanwhile, Katharine herself was placed under closer supervision. She was staying at Kimbolton Castle which was less accessible than Buckden as it was surrounded by two moats, but it was a more up-to-date building.[28] It was also further from the fens and therefore likely to have been somewhat healthier. The house was smaller but, as Katharine continued to live more or less in one room, this did not really affect her. Her staff was increased, but how many were of her choice and how many were placed under Bedingfield by Henry is difficult to ascertain.

Emissaries from Henry had visited Katharine at Buckden to ask her to swear to the Act of Succession, but they had not pressed her too hard. Now they came to her again and with many rude and uncouth words threatened that refusal could mean death. As could be expected, she refused to do what was demanded of her. She only asked that if she was to be put to death it should not be in the privacy of her room but publicly. The few Spanish servants she had left were put under house arrest and four were sent to prison. Katharine kept to her rooms by her own choice and so could not be sent there. Her food, as at Buckden, was still prepared by her own women; but it was prepared in a little passageway just outside her bedroom. Henry spread the rumor that she was dying of dropsy. Chapuys claimed she had never had such a disease; if she now suffered from it, it was a false dropsy induced by the wine she was drinking. Whether Katharine suspected this too we are not sure, but she complained of the wine she was given and wanted to order some of better quality. She was, however, refused permission and was told she could only eat and drink what was provided by the King.

Her high steward, Sir Edmund Bedingfield; her chamberlain, Sir Edward Chamberlain; their wives, and the rest of the staff rarely saw Katharine, if at all. She voluntarily cut herself off from them and was herself cut off from the outside world by the moat she could see from her windows. Her letters were intercepted and read, though she still was granted the privilege of writing to Chapuys and, occasionally, of sending him verbal messages. He was, however, no longer allowed to visit her. In any case, by fair means or foul, Katharine's friends were fast disappearing from the scene. Margaret of Austria had died in 1530, Henry's sister Mary and Lord Mountjoy in 1534. Fisher and More had been executed. Erasmus and Vives were no longer in England. The Countess of Salisbury's son, Reginald Pole, one of Katharine's fervent supporters, was in Italy; Margaret herself was out of favor with the King and out of touch with Katharine, though not yet in prison. Maria de Salinas was forbidden to go near her mistress; her daughter and the Duke of Suffolk were well on the way to becoming Lutherans. Katharine's friends in the religious orders were either dead or deprived of power.

Chapuys made one brave attempt to see Katharine. He rode out from London with sixty horsemen but was intercepted on the way and told that the King did not wish him to proceed. Obediently, after first finding out Katharine's wishes, he kept at a distance. But some of his suite showed themselves at Kimbolton "to the great consolation, as it seemed, of the ladies of her household, who spoke to the men from the battlements and windows, with as much joy on the part of the peasantry in the neighborhood, as if the Messiah had actually come down." [29] But even though Chapuys had not been able to see Katharine, he had been to Kimbolton. He knew now quite definitely that she was a prisoner and what the situation was. He reported every detail to the Emperor.

7. The End

At the beginning of December 1535, Chapuys heard from Cromwell that Katharine was very ill. He was naturally alarmed. He asked permission to visit her but his request was turned down. As he left Cromwell's room, he was given a letter from Katharine's physician to say that she was already much better and it was not necessary for him to come to see her. Shortly afterward, he was further reassured when he received a letter from Katharine herself, though the contents, as he told the Emperor, would have moved a stone to pity. She begged him to try and have her removed from her present house and to obtain for her in time for Christmas some of the money due to her. Cromwell generally received requests of this kind with apparent favor and then ignored them. So it happened on this occasion. Katharine's material condition remained unaltered.

At the end of the month Katharine had a relapse. Both her physician and her apothecary wrote to inform Chapuys. De la Sa thought it would be a great consolation both for Katharine and for her household if Chapuys could visit her. Her English apothecary, Philip Grenacre, followed this letter up with a more urgent one asking Chapuys to come quickly as Katharine was getting worse every hour; for two days and nights she had been unable to hold down any solid or liquid food and she could not sleep due to the pain in her stomach. Chapuys was already on his way when this message arrived in London. Although he had not taken the physician's letter over-seriously, he had sent one of his secretaries to ask Cromwell for a license to visit Kimbolton. Cromwell replied that it could be arranged but, he added, the King first wished to speak to Chapuys on matters of great importance. An audience with the King was therefore arranged for the following afternoon, Thursday, December 30, at one o'clock.

When they met, the King spoke at great length on many matters concerning the Emperor. Only as the ambassador was about to leave did he mention Katharine. He said that

madame would not live long and once she was dead the
Emperor would no longer have a pretense for interfering in
the affairs of England. Henry had, however, apparently not
yet received the latest report about Katharine. As Chapuys
was about to leave the royal palace, the Duke of Suffolk
overtook him to tell him that the news had just arrived that
Katharine was dying. If he went to Kimbolton it was unlikely
that he would find her alive. Chapuys took this to be a rather
exaggerated statement. Nevertheless, he stopped only to write
out a report to the Emperor of his conversation with the
King, then he rode off to Kimbolton.[30]

Maria de Salinas had also been informed that her former
mistress was dying. On the same Thursday she wrote to
Cromwell to beg him to obtain for her a letter from the King
which she could show to the officers of Katharine's household
in order to gain admittance. Cromwell's reply was too slow
in coming, so she set off without it.

Mary too knew how serious her mother's illness was and
had asked Chapuys to beg her father that she might be allowed to see her. He had passed on her request to the King
when he saw him at Greenwich, but Henry had refused.
When Chapuys pressed him further, he had said that he
must have advice. Presumably he dared not give permission
without first consulting Anne and he knew beforehand what
her reply would be.

Katharine's steward and chamberlain seemed to have been
the last to have been informed of what was happening in the
house they supervised. Cromwell lost no time in reprimand-
ing them for having allowed the King to receive the first
information of Katharine's relapse from Chapuys. Bedingfield received Cromwell's letter between seven and eight p.m.
on Friday, the 31st. He replied at once to excuse himself. He
said that he had written the moment he himself had learned

the news—presumably the message Henry had received just as Chapuys was leaving Greenwich. He added that it showed in what "great trust Master Chamberlain and he are both with her and such as be about her, that the Ambassador should have knowledge before them who daily continue in the house." [31] He described Katharine's symptoms in much the same way as Grenacre had described them. She was very weak and her stomach still gave her great pain. De la Sa had suggested she see another doctor but she refused.

Maria de Salinas is thought to have reached Kimbolton on the evening of New Year's Day. She gained admission by a ruse. She arrived after dark and asked for shelter, saying that she had fallen from her horse. When asked for her permit she made some excuse and said she would show it later. Either Bedingfield was taken in by her story or he was not averse to showing one last kindness to his dying mistress. He allowed Maria de Salinas to go into Katharine's quarters but, in his report to Cromwell of the events of that evening, he wrote that "since that time we never saw her, neither any letters of her license hither to repair." [32]

The following morning, Sunday, January 2, Chapuys arrived before dinner and was immediately admitted into the castle. Not only had he a license but he was accompanied by Stephen Vaughan, a friend of Cromwell's who, Chapuys said, had been sent by the King as a spy. He had his first meeting with Katharine in the afternoon. By arrangement between them it had been decided that Vaughan, Bedingfield, Chamberlain and other officers of the household should be invited to be present. Katharine's officers were seeing her for the first time for over a year. For Chapuys it was even longer. They could not help but notice how thin and wasted she had become, how tired and ill she looked. There was no question of their thinking her illness had been feigned. Chapuys kissed her hands and Katharine greeted him with pleasure, saying that if it pleased God to take her now she could at least die in his arms and "not unprepared, like a beast." [33] As they continued their conversation in Spanish, the observers were not much the wiser as they did not understand the language.

After fifteen minutes they all left, but shortly afterward Katharine sent a message to Chapuys asking him to return. Bedingfield [34] tried to find out what they discussed but again failed in spite of the presence of Vaughan and various ladies because they continued to speak in Spanish. Chapuys had, however, no nefarious plans; his only aim was to console and comfort Katharine as far as he was able; to explain away the dilatoriness of the Pope and the Emperor in coming to her assistance; and to quiet her conscience which was showing some scruple that the heresies being practiced in England had arisen from her affair.

Bedingfield heard from her doctor that Katharine had taken great comfort from the "coming of these folks," [35] Chapuys and Maria de Salinas, and was sleeping better at night. She was again able to eat and was even heard to laugh at the antics of one of the men who had accompanied Chapuys. She felt so much stronger that she and de la Sa persuaded Chapuys it would be better if he went away again so as not to abuse the license given him by the King. Chapuys therefore said good-bye to Katharine on Tuesday night and set off for London the following morning, traveling slowly in case anyone came after him to call him back. Katharine continued to improve for a short while. She was able to sit up in bed and comb her own hair. But in the early hours of Friday morning she took a turn for the worse. She continually asked what time it was but refused to hear mass until daybreak. At ten o'clock the Bishop of Llandaff anointed her and read the last service. Katharine uttered all the responses with great religious fervor. She prayed for God to forgive the King and swore, according to one report, that the statement she had written and signed in her own hand affirming that she was a virgin at the time of her marriage was true. She retained her reason to the end. She died at two o'clock in the afternoon of January 7.

Chapuys heard the news on his arrival in London. He immediately wrote to tell the Emperor.[36] His first fear was for Mary's safety. He believed Katharine had been poisoned and thought the same fate was in store for her daughter. The Emperor, although he did not admit it publicly, also believed that his aunt had been poisoned. De la Sa told Chapuys that Katharine had become worse after drinking some Welsh beer but that only after she was examined would it be possible to tell the cause of her death. Katharine was opened eight hours after her death and enbalmed. The operation was performed by a candlemaker, not a surgeon, and de la Sa was not permitted to be present. Her confessor was told in secret afterward that all the organs were sound except for the heart which was "completely black and of a hideous aspect." [37] The cause of her death, if it was known, was not disclosed and the rumor spread quickly in England and Europe that she had been poisoned.

Katharine left no will in the strict sense of the word as she believed that everything she possessed belonged to Henry. But, shortly before she died, de la Sa wrote out for her the few bequests she wished to make.[38] She left to Mary her furs and the gold collar with a cross she had brought from Spain. She asked that her servants be paid their wages and rewarded for their loyal service. The material from her robes was to be made into church ornaments. As for herself, she wished to be buried in a convent of the Observant Friars.

She either did not know, or had forgotten, that the order had been suppressed. Cromwell was willing to carry out her wishes, but Henry was of a different mind. The Church, he said, had a superabundance of ecclesiastical ornaments and was rich enough without Katharine's bequests. Mary had first to show herself obedient to her father before she could receive her mother's gifts. Later, Mary is known to have had in her possession a cross which it is thought Cromwell allowed her to keep only when he discovered it was of no value except as a religious relic. Katharine's possessions were stored in Baynard's Castle and an inventory of them was made.[39] Henry and Anne looked them over and took whatever oddments they fancied: A coffer covered in crimson velvet and garnished with gilt nails went to Anne; a desk similarly covered in black velvet and two sets of ivory chess men and boards went to Henry. The rest was dispersed.

Katharine had dictated one last letter to Henry,[40] although for many years she had been forbidden to write to him. It was affectionate but not likely to please Henry as she had both addressed him as her husband and called upon him to repent:

> My lord King and ever dearest husband, greetings. The hour of my death now approaches, and at this moment my love compels me to remind you a little of the salvation of your soul. This last you should put before all mortal considerations, abandoning on this account all those concerns of the flesh on account of which you have plunged both me into manifold miseries and yourself into more anxieties. Yet this I forgive you, and I both hope and with holy prayers implore that God will forgive you. For the rest, I commend the daughter of our marriage to your care, whom I beseech you to behave towards entirely in that fatherly fashion which I have on other occasions de-

sired of you. I specially pray you also to take care of
my maids and to see that at the right time they are
given good husbands (which is not much to ask, for
there are only three of them); and out of your grace,
good will and generosity to pay my servants the salaries due to them and also for a further year, lest they
should seem to be forsaken or in want. Lastly I have
only one thing to declare: that my eyes long for you
above all else. Farewell.

One account[41] says that there were tears in Henry's eyes as
he read the letter. Another,[42] not incompatible, says that
when Henry was first told of Katharine's death he exclaimed
fervently, "God be praised that we are free from all suspicion
of war." The next day, "clad all in yellow from top to toe
except the white feather he had in his bonnet,"[43] together
with the "Little Bastard," as Chapuys irreverently called
Elizabeth, Henry and Anne were conducted triumphantly
to mass with the joyous sound of trumpets. Mary was not
told of her mother's death until four days later when her
governess broke the news unceremoniously and without any
warning. Mary, naturally, was very much upset and also
frightened as to what the future might hold in store for her.
The Emperor and his court went into mourning, but they
too were relieved that there was now no question of war
with England.

Katharine lay in state at Kimbolton until January 27.
Meanwhile, Henry decided who should be invited to attend
her funeral[44] and Cromwell and one of his clerks busied
themselves with the details. When everything was ready—
the body embalmed and placed in its coffin of lead, the black
cloth assigned for the mourning clothes cut and sewn, the
company assembled, the order of the procession arranged,
the services selected—the cortege set out for the Benedictine

abbey church of Peterborough, where Henry had decided
Katharine should be buried with all the rites due her as the
Dowager Princess. Her coffin was placed on a wagon drawn
by six horses covered with black cloth down to the ground.
The wagon was covered with black velvet in the middle of
which was a great silver cross. Some of the mourners followed on horseback, some in carts. At dusk they reached
Sawtry, nine miles away from Kimbolton, where they rested
for the night. Katharine was received into the abbey and
her body placed in the choir. The next morning, after mass
had been chanted, the procession set off again for Peterborough.

Chapuys had been invited to attend but had refused, after
having first consulted his superiors at the court of the Emperor, because Katharine was to be buried as Dowager
Princess and not as Queen of England. Mary had not been
allowed to come. Henry himself never even considered put-
ting in an appearance. The man of highest rank present was
the comptroller of the King's household. Anne would not
have been expected to attend but, in any case, she was unable
to as about the same time she lost the child she had been
carrying for over three months, to her own and Henry's
great distress. The chief mourner was Eleanor, daughter of
the King's sister Mary and the Duke of Suffolk. The second
was Katharine, the Duke of Suffolk's latest wife. Her
mother, Maria de Salinas and the wife of Sir Edward Bedingfield were also among the chief mourners.

After the final mass Katharine was lowered into her grave,
watched by hundreds with watery eyes. Her steward and
chamberlain broke their rods of office and dropped them in
after her. The grave was covered with the black cloth from
the wagon and afterward a "hearse of wax wrought curi-
ously" was placed above it. Over and around the hearse were

set banners and pennants among which could be seen Katharine's emblem of the pomegranate, the arms of the Emperor, of Ferdinand, and of Prince Arthur—but not those of Henry VIII.

So ends the story of Katharine of Aragon, who for thirty-five years courageously bore the blows of adversity which fell upon her in the country of her adoption.

Epilogue

As a last gesture to the memory of Katharine, Henry later allowed the abbey of Peterborough to be raised to the status of a cathedral. During the following century, the hearse and a chapel which had been built around it were destroyed by Oliver Cromwell's soldiers. Katharine's grave remained neglected until 1895 when various other Katharines from England, Scotland, Ireland and the United States marked it with a simple slab similar to Isabella's in the Monastery of San Francisco in Granada. Above it were hung two banners: that of a Princess of Spain and, at last, Katharine's banner as Queen of England.

It remains now to look at some of the unresolved problems of her life and try to put them in persepective. In her tragic story, the most dramatic personal feature was undoubtedly her separation from Henry VIII. Historians have ever been concerned with the question whether Katharine's marriage to Arthur was consummated and, arising from that, whether

Henry VIII genuinely believed that his marriage to Katharine was invalid. The evidence is inconclusive.

In support of Katharine, apart from her own word, there is the letter written by the Spanish ambassador Don Pedro de Ayala to her parents shortly after the wedding ceremony, which suggests that Arthur was not well enough to be anything other than a husband in name. There is the letter from Ferdinand to his ambassador in Rome contradicting the statement in the second marriage treaty drawn up between Henry VII and Ferdinand and Isabella that the marriage had been consummated. But although Ferdinand may in fact have received information from his daughter and his agents in England, his character was not such that his word is necessarily to be believed. There is also the statement made by Katharine's governess, Donna Elvira, but this is canceled out by that of her tutor, Geraldini. At the court of Black Friars, Katharine herself called publicly upon Henry to affirm that he had found her a maid. It is difficult to believe that she would have dared to do this unless she knew it to have been the case. Henry did not deny or affirm it; he kept silent, which could be interpreted either way. Prudery had no place in Tudor England. It is unlikely that Katharine felt any sense of modesty, as the Victorians suggested, in discussing the question of her virginity; nor would she have expected Henry to reply as a "gentleman." She asked for and expected a straight answer.

Against Katharine were the witnesses at Black Friars who, after she had left the court, swore to Arthur's boasts the morning after he and Katharine had been publicly bedded in the Bishop of London's Palace. But there is no evidence that such stories were current at the time of the marriage and repetition of a boyish boast made twenty years earlier, especially when the stories were only variations of the evi-

dence of one person, means very little. It is also possible that
the witnesses had been bribed, but there is no evidence to
this effect.

By far the strongest evidence in Katharine's favor is the
undoubted probity of her character, though one sometimes
wonders if such a quality was regarded as being of much
importance in the days of Ferdinand and Isabella, Francis I,
Charles V and Henry VIII. Katharine herself seems on one
occasion to have had a lapse. Mendoza recounted to Charles
V that when Katharine produced the brief in 1528 she said
that she had had it for six months, which he doubted. It
may, however, have been only an error on her part, as she
did not in any case consider the brief to be important.

In every other respect but the question of the legality of
her marriage, Katharine was entirely obedient to her husband,
as she had been taught was proper and as she believed all
wives should be. One reason that might have made her dis-
obey and depart from the truth in this instance was the
legitimacy of her daughter. But more was at stake than mere
bastardy or the loss of Mary's royal heritage, though these
were important. As a good Catholic, Katharine's chief desire
was to save her own soul and that of her daughter and no
lie could have achieved that. For this reason I personally
think that Katharine spoke the truth.

Incidentally, if Katharine was a virgin when she married
Henry, then most of the scandal concerning her and Fray
Diego would be disproved, though her behavior could still
be considered indiscreet. As far as is known, Henry VIII
never referred to the friar in this context. If he had believed
the reports of the Spanish ambassador, he would surely have
sent Fray Diego away the moment he became King, not six
years later. It would be too cynical to think that he did not
care.

It is difficult to know whether Henry really believed that

his marriage to Katharine was invalid after having lived with her for twenty years with apparently no doubts. Belief in his honesty depends on one's point of view. Some people think one motive predominant, some another. I have come to think that a genuine desire for male children first made him question his marriage at a time when Katharine is known to have been unable to bear any more children; this led to a superstitious belief that his lack of heirs was a punishment for having contracted an illegal marriage; this in turn coincided with his passion for Anne Boleyn, who he hoped would produce children. Opposition to his wishes only made him stubborn. In any case, he firmly believed in himself as the embodiment of the divine right of Kings, exemplified on an earlier occasion by his statement, "Nor do I see any faith in the world save in me, and, therefore, God Almighty, who knows this, prospers my affairs."

From a wider historical point of view, the most important event in Katharine's life is that in obtaining the annulment of his marriage, Henry VIII denied the authority of the Pope and in so doing established Protestantism in England. But a full discussion of this change is outside the scope of this book. Here I will content myself by saying that Henry only chose to repudiate the Pope because he was driven to do so by Katharine's stubbornness. It would be wrong to suppose that either he or Katharine were moved by great philosophic conceptions of the relationship between State and Church. Henry's part in bringing about the establishment of a native church in England was a by-product of his own personal and dynastic difficulties. But, even without Henry's quarrel with the Pope, revolt against the established Church was already evident in England as it was throughout Europe. It was only a matter of time.

It is not possible to be dogmatic as to whether Katharine's death was brought about by poison. The symptoms of her last illness were not incompatible with that view and the rumors current at the time were certainly believed by the Spanish ambassador and Charles V. But poison could only have been introduced into Katharine's food if one of her maids had been tempted to betray her. It is hard to believe that this would not have been discovered. In any case, food poisoning and bad health were symptomatic of the day and she died at a normal age for women of her time.

If Anne had had anything to do with bringing about Katharine's death or trying to poison Mary, her enjoyment of the result was short-lived. She too was unable to provide a son. Less than four months after the death of Katharine, Anne was arrested, found guilty of incest and unfaithfulness and within seventeen days was beheaded. The following day Henry was betrothed to Jane Seymour, a small, redheaded young woman, one of Anne's ladies-in-waiting. A year later she gave birth to the much-desired son, but died herself soon afterward. Henry was to marry three more times in his efforts to produce another son, but without success.

Shortly after Jane became Queen, Mary was taken back to court but only on condition that she accepted what Katharine had so determinedly fought against: that her father's marriage to her mother was illegal and that she herself was illegitimate. Cromwell stayed in power until 1540 when he too fell from favor and was executed. The same month, Thomas Abell and Richard Fetherston were hanged, drawn and quartered for maintaining that Henry was still married to Katharine. A year later the Countess of Salisbury was beheaded in the Tower. But Cranmer survived to comfort Henry on his own deathbed on January 28, 1547, when the lion* whose roar had brought down Wolsey, Rochester, More, Cromwell and so many others himself succumbed.

* Erasmus quoted Amos 3: 8: "The lion shall roar, who shall not fear" in reference to Henry VIII in a letter to Bartholomew Latomus.

Jane Seymour's son, who was then only nine years old, succeeded his father as Edward VI. He died of tuberculosis before he was sixteen. Elizabeth Blount's son had already died, shortly after he had witnessed the execution of Anne Boleyn. So, in spite of being a woman, in spite of her father's fears and all his endeavors to prevent such an event, Mary inherited the throne. She tried to put back the clock but without success. An abortive attempt was made to revive the Spanish alliance with her unfortunate marriage to Philip II, son of her cousin Charles V. For a brief spell Catholicism was again the religion of England and Protestants were cruelly suppressed. It was Cranmer's turn to be deprived of office and accused of treason. He was condemned to death and burned at the stake, one of the first Protestant martyrs out of some three hundred who perished while she was Queen. For this reason, she was known as "Bloody Mary." But, if during her reign hundreds were sent to their deaths, it must be remembered that during the reign of her father those who were executed numbered thousands. It is now thought that Mary, unlike her grandmother Isabella, was by nature too merciful to revenge herself in this way for what had been done to her and her mother and friends in the past. But once the laws against the heretics had been passed by Parliament, Mary was too weak to prevent her statesmen from carrying them out.

After five unhappy years Mary died childless, leaving the country in a turmoil. Lady Jane Grey, granddaughter of Mary Tudor and Charles Brandon, reigned for nine days before being executed and replaced by Anne Boleyn's daughter Elizabeth. Protestantism was re-established and welcomed after the holocaust that had accompanied the Catholic revival. During the long reign of Elizabeth, the "Virgin Queen," England's affairs at home and abroad were run so brilliantly and successfully that even Henry VIII would have

been more than satisfied with the achievements of his un-
wanted daughter.

With the death of Elizabeth in 1603, however, the Tudor
line came to an end. Then, one of the dynastic marriages
which had been so carefully arranged by Henry VII at last
had the desired effect—England and Scotland were united
under one Stuart King: James VI of Scotland, a descendant
of Margaret Tudor and James IV of Scotland, became
James I of England.

CHAPTER NOTES

ABBREVIATIONS [Numbers in Brackets refer to Reading List]

Grose [9]
Hall [13]
Ep. Erasmus [11]
Leland [15]
Pol. Vergil [17]
Forrest [12]
Foster Watson [30]
Cavendish [10]
Harpsfield [14]

Wood [20]
Ellis [18]
Halliwell [19]
E. H. R. [38]
Mem. H. VII [4]
L. & P.H. VII [5]
Sp. Cal. [7]
L. & P. [6]
Ven. Cal. [8]

ST. PAUL'S CATHEDRAL: SUNDAY, NOVEMBER 14, 1501

[1] The Gothic Cathedral Katharine knew was burned down in the Great Fire of London. The Renaissance building now standing in its place was built by Sir Christopher Wren in the late seventeenth century.

[2] Grose II, p. 292. Original document is in the College of Heralds, London.

Chapter 1

[1] *Prescott's Histories.* Selected and ed. I. R. Blacker, (London, 1963), p. 90.

[2] *Ibid.,* p. 91.

[3] *Hall,* p. 454.

[4] Katharine's birthplace is still to be seen in Alcalà de Henares, a small town not far from Madrid. Isabella later founded there a

famous university which became the University of Madrid.

5 Isabella's grandmother was a daughter of John of Gaunt by his second wife, Constance of Castile.

6 *Sp. Cal.,* I, p. 11.

7 Roger Machado translated in *Mem. H. VII,* p. 328 sequ.

8 *Ibid.*

9 This relic of Roman Law was not changed in England until 1929.

10 *Sp. Cal.,* I, p. 177.

11 *Ibid.,* p. 187.

12 *Ibid.,* p. 226.

13 Translated in Wood, I, p. 121.

14 *Sp. Cal.,* I, p. 253.

Chapter 2

1 *L. & P. H. VII,* I, p. 113.

2 This was the first time the title of Duke of York had been given to a second son. From that time on it has remained the title of all second sons of British monarchs.

3 The population of England and Wales was then not much more than three million as compared with over fifty-five million today. For a detailed description of England at that time see *Ven. Cal.* II, pp. 51 and 90; Grose, I, p. 271.

4 *Sp. Cal.,* I, p. 262.

5 *Ep. Erasmus,* I, p. 203.

6 *Ibid.,* p. 204.

7 *Hall,* p. 425.

8 *L. & P. H. VII,* I, p. 126. Original letter was in French.

9 For the account of the meeting in Dogmersfield, Katharine's journey to London and her wedding to Prince Arthur, see Grose, II, pp. 249–322 and Leland, 2nd ed. Vol. V, pp. 352–373.

10 *Ibid.*

11 The City of London was reckoned as a square mile then as it is today.

12 *Correspondence of Sir Thomas More,* E. F. Rogers, ed., (Princeton, 1947), p. 4.

13 Grose, II, loc. cit., and Leland, *loc. cit.*

14 *Sp. Cal.,* I, p. 265.

15 *Sp. Cal.,* Supplement to I and II, p. 6.

[16] For the accounts of Arthur's funeral and how the news of his death was broken to the King and Queen, see Grose, *op. cit.,* pp. 322–331; Leland, *op. cit.,* pp. 373–381; and Polydore Vergil, *Anglica historia 1485–1537.* Camden Society third Series, LXXIV, (London, 1950), p. 123.

Chapter 3

[1] *Mem. H. VII,* p. 246.
[2] *Sp. Cal.,* I. p. 278.
[3] *Ibid.,* p. 294.
[4] *Ibid.,* p. 295.
[5] *Ibid.,* p. 306.
[6] *Ibid.,* p. 309.
[7] Their grandson, Charles V, later built a magnificent tomb for them in the city below. The remains of his parents, Philip and Juana, were also buried there. Today, all four of them, carved in marble, lie side by side, at peace in death as they never were in life.
[8] For Ferdinand's sentiments on Isabella's death expressed in his letter of announcement to Henry VII, see *Mem. H. VII,* p. 416.
[9] Wood, p. 139.
[10] *Sp. Cal.,* I, 425.
[11] Wood, p. 131.
[12] *Mem. H. VII,* p. 419.
[13] *Ibid.,* p. 240 ff.
[14] Hall, p. 500.
[15] *Mem H. VII,* pp. 282–303 for *a narrative of King Philip of Castile in England in 1506.*
[16] *Ibid.,* p. 288.
[17] *Sp. Cal.,* Supp. to I and II, p. 131.
[18] Wood, p. 140.
[19] *Sp. Cal.,* Supplement to I and II, p. 27.
[20] *Ibid.,* p. 25.
[21] *Sp. Cal.,* II, p. 19.

Chapter 4

[1] Thomas More in a poem he wrote in Latin to celebrate the Coronation (to be seen in the British Museum).
[2] Hall, p. 508.
[3] *Ibid.*

4 Henry's armor with its decorations can still be seen in The Tower of London.

5 Skelton J., *Complete Poems 1460–1529*, P. Henderson, ed. (London, 1959), p. 131.

6 Dickens, Charles, *A child's history of England*, Chap. 27.

7 *L. & P.*, II No. 395.

8 *Epistles of Erasmus*, I, p. 457.

9 Erasmus, *Epistles* II, 24 paraphrased in *L. & P.*, II 2, No. 4340 (1518).

10 Forrest, p. 27.

11 *Sp. Cal.*, II, p. 20.

12 *Ibid.*, p. 41.

13 Halliwell, I, p. 198; *L. & P.*, I, rev. ed. No. 45.

14 Wood, p. 159.

15 *Sp. Cal.* II, p. 21.

16 *Ibid.*, p. 38.

17 The original *Great Tournament Roll* is kept in the College of Heralds, London, but there is now a collotype reproduction of the whole manuscript, although not all the illustrations are in color: *The Great Tournament Roll of Westminster*, edited by Sidney Anglo. Oxford, 1968.

18 Hall, p. 519.

19 *Ibid.*

20 *Music composed by Henry VIII*, reproduced from British Museum ms. 31922. Collected and arranged by Lady Mary Trefusis, Oxford, 1912.

21 *Sp. Cal.*, II, p. 52.

22 *L. & P.*, I (2nd ed.) No. 1436.

23 Hall, p. 539.

24 Ellis, 1st series I, p. 79.

25 *Ibid.*, p. 84.

26 Pol. Vergil. The numbers taking part in the battle of Flodden differ in different accounts, as do the reports of the numbers killed.

27 Ellis, p. 83.

28 *Ibid.*, p. 88.

29 *Ibid.*

30 *Calendar of State Papers, etc. Milan.* A. B. Hinds, ed. (London, 1912), I, Nos. 654 and 669.

31 *L. & P.,* I. 2 (2nd ed.) No. 3163, p. 1349. The records are not clear whether she is E(tiennette) or G. la Baume.

32 Hall, p. 567.

33 *Ven. Cal.,* II, p. 188.

34 *Ven Cal.,* II, p. 56.

35 A. F. Pollard, *Henry VIII* (London, 1963), p. 48.

36*Music Composed by Henry VIII, op. cit.,* p. 63.

37 *Ven. Cal.,* II, p. 201.

38 *Sp. Cal.,* II, p. 248.

39 *Ibid.*

40 *L. & P.,* I, 2, No. 2704.

41 *Ibid.,* No. 3041.

42 *L. & P.,* II, 1, No. 1282.

43 *Ven. Cal.,* II, p. 563.

44 *L. & P.,* II, 1, No. 411. Henry VIII was an inch or two over 6 feet in height. At that time his waist was 35″ and his chest 42″. By 1536 they had expanded only an inch or two, but fifteen years after that, judging by his armor, his waist had grown to 54″ and his chest to 57″.

45 *Ven. Cal.,* II, p. 248.

46 *Ibid.,* p. 529.

47 *Ibid.,* p. 559 from "Report of England by Giustinian, The Venetian Ambassador," *Four years at the court of Henry VIII.*

Chapter 5

1 *Reliquae Antiquae,* T. Wright and J. O. Halliwell, eds. (London, 1841), I, p. 258.

2 *Ven. Cal.,* II, p. 285.

3 *L. & P.,* II, part 2, No. 3976.

4 It is interesting to note that the same ringleaders later organized another rebellion on board one of Cabot's ships.

5 A copy of Henry's book is to be seen in Windsor Castle. Another is in the Houghton Library of Harvard University.

6 The title is still held by British monarchs and appears on the coin of the realm.

7 R. W. Chambers, *Sir Thomas More* (London, 1935), p. 152.

8 *L. & P.,* II 2, No. 4279 (and Ellis I, p. 125).

9 *Ibid.,* p. 1515: "Expenses of the Household, October 7, 1518."

[10] *Hall,* p. 703.

[11] H. Clifford, *The Life of Jane Dormer* (London, 1887).

[12] *L. & P.,* IV 3, No. 5750, p. 2558.

[13] Hall, who is at his most eloquent about pageantry, filled papers of his Chronicle with detailed descriptions of the gorgeous costumes, jewels, furnishings, feastings, joustings, masques and other revelries at the Field of Cloth of Gold.

[14] *Ibid.,* p. 621.

[15] William Shakespeare, *Henry VIII,* Act I, Sc. II.

[16] *Hall,* p. 635.

[17] *Ibid.,* p. 640.

[18] *Sp. Cal.* Further Supplement to I and II, p. 74.

[19] *L. & P.,* IV, 1, No. 1484.

[20] Dr. A. S. McNalty's opinion, with which I agree, has recently been contradicted by Professor J. J. Scarisbrick. But this is a point which cannot be definitely proved either way.

[21] *Ven. Cal.,* III, p. 455.

[22] *L. & P.,* IV 3, No. 5807.

[23] *Ibid.,* No. 5806.

[24] *Ibid.*

[25] *Oxford Book of English Verse,* (London, 1950), p. 79.

[26] F. Madden, *Privy Purse Expenses of the Princess Mary* (London, 1831).

[27] For this section on Vives and his contemporaries including quotations see Foster Watson.

[28] Ellis, II, p. 19.

Chapter 6

[1] *L. & P.,* IV 1, No. 1939.

[2] *Ibid.*

[3] *Sp. Cal.,* III, 2, p. 186.

[4] *Ibid.,* p. 276.

[5] *Ibid.*

[6] *Ibid.,* p. 845.

[7] Leviticus, 18:16.

[8] Deuteronomy, 25:5. Both these quotations are taken from the King James version of the Bible which was not published until almost eighty years later. Leviticus and Deuteronomy, together with

the other books of the Pentateuch, had however been translated into English and printed by Caxton in the *Golden Legend* in 1493. Henry and his advisers also had access to the Vulgate. For a discussion of canon law and the divorce see J. Gairdner and H. Thurston, *English Historial Review,* Vols. XI, XII, XIX.

⁹ *L. & P.,* IV 1, No. 1484.

¹⁰ Harpsfield.

¹¹ Cavendish, [Wolsey's gentleman usher from 1526–1530], p. 46.

¹² Leland, p. 703: "M. Boleyn", *L. & P.,* 2nd ed., I 2: "Mademoiselle Boleyn."

¹³ Cavendish, p. 29.

¹⁴ *Crónica del rey Enrico Otavo de Inglaterra,* by an unknown author.

¹⁵ Crapelet. See *E. H. R.,* Vol. VIII.

¹⁶ *Sp. Cal.,* V 1, p. 344.

¹⁷ Most of Henry's love letters to Anne Boleyn, some in French, some in English, are to be seen in the Vatican Library. How they came to be there is a mystery, though it has been suggested that the papal legate Campeggio (see p. 220) somehow obtained possession of them and took them away hidden in his luggage when he left England.

¹⁸ *Ven. Cal.,* IV, p. 365.

¹⁹ *Sp. Cal.,* III 2, p. 432.

²⁰ *L. & P.,* IV 2, No. 4990.

²¹ *Ibid.*

²² Hall, p. 755.

²³ *L. & P.,* IV 2, No. 4875.

²⁴ *Ibid.,* No. 7545.

²⁵ *Ibid.*

²⁶ *Sp. Cal.,* III 2, p. 842.

²⁷ Hall, p. 756.

²⁸ Cavendish, pp. 79 ff.

²⁹ Cavendish, p. 82. Griffiths had been in Katharine's service since the early days in Ludlow.

³⁰ *Ibid.,* p. 88.

³¹ *Ibid.*

³² *Ibid.,* p. 90.

33 *Sp. Cal.,* IV 2, i, p. 177.
34 Cavendish, p. 178.

Chapter 7

1 *L. & P.,* V, No. 112.
2 *Ibid.,* No. 105.
3 *Sp. Cal.,* IV 2, i, p. 153.
4 *Ibid.*
5 *Ibid.,* p. 172 for the whole of this incident.
6 *Ibid.,* p. 279.
7 *Ven. Cal.,* IV, p. 292.
8 *Ibid.,* p. 293.
9 Hall, p. 784.
10 *Sp. Cal.,* IV 2, i, p. 473.
11 *Ibid.,* p. 495.
12 *Ibid.,* p. 256.
13 *Ibid.,* p. 510.
14 *Ibid.,* p. 524.
15 *Ibid.,* p. 554.
16 Holinshed, R., *Chronicles, etc.* (London, 1577).
17 *Sp. Cal.,* IV 2, i, p. 739.
18 Harpsfield, p. 200. Buckden Palace is today a school for train-
ing young priests. Katharine's room has become a dormitory.
19 *Sp. Cal.,* IV, 2, ii, p. 756.
20 *Ibid.,* p. 788.
21 *Ibid.,* p. 693.
22 *Ibid.,* p. 882.
23 *L. & P.,* VI, No. 1126.
24 *Sp. Cal.,* V, 1, Supplement, p. 603.
25 For an account of this dramatic incident, see *Sp. Cal.,* IV, 2, ii,
pp. 895 ff.
26 Thomas Abell had already been imprisoned in 1532 for publishing a book in Katharine's favor.
27 *Sp. Cal.,* V, 1, p. 118.
28 Kimbolton Castle today is a boys' boarding school set in a
pleasant park. The moat has disappeared without trace and the outside of the building was remodeled by Vanburgh in the seventeenth
century. The room where Katharine lived and died is now the head-
master's study.

[29] *Sp. Cal.,* V, 1, i, p. 221.

[30] *Ibid.,* pp. 595 ff.

[31] *L. & P.,* IX, No. 1050.

[32] *L. & P.,* X, No. 28.

[33] For Chapuys's account of Katharine's death, see *Sp. Cal.,* V, 2, pp. 2–6.

[34] For Bedingfield, see *L. & P.,* X, No. 28, 37. Bedingfield's report to Cromwell and Chapuys's to the Emperor of the events of the next few days vary only in details. Bedingfield tends to play down the amount of time the ambassador spent with Katharine. The ambassador is obviously not quite accurate in his dates.

[35] *L. & P.,* X, No. 28.

[36] *Sp. Cal.,* V, 2, pp. 10 ff.

[37] *Ibid.,* p. 18.

[38] *Ibid.,* pp. 16, 17.

[39] *Inventories of the Wardrobe . . . of Katharine, Princess Dowager,* I. G. Nichols, ed., Camden Society, Miscellany III (London, 1835).

[40] The letter itself has been lost but its contents are known from sixteenth-century copies. Chapuys also reported its existence.

[41] Harpsfield, p. 177.

[42] Chapuys, *L. & P.,* X, No. 141; *Sp. Cal.,* V, 2, p. 19.

[43] *Ibid.*

[44] There are two accounts of Katharine's funeral: One is from the Vienna archives (see *L. & P.,* X, No. 284); the other from Peterborough (see "Obsequies of Katharine of Aragon at Peterborough" in *Archeological Journal,* XI (1854), pp. 265–74).

SELECTED READING LIST

GENERAL

1. Read, Conyers, ed. *Bibliography of British History: Tudor Period 1485–1603,* 2nd ed. Oxford, 1959.
2. Levine, Mortimer, comp. *Tudor England 1485–1603.* Cambridge, 1968.
3. Victoria History of the Counties of England, London, 1901 (in progress) or see volumes in Bedfordshire, Huntingdonshire, Shropshire, Worcestershire.

LETTERS AND PAPERS OF THE PERIOD 1485-1536

4. *Memorials of King Henry VII* (Rolls Series), ed. James Gairdner. London, 1858. Includes part of Bernard André's history (probably the only strictly contemporary history of the reign of Henry VII), the journals of Roger Machado, and a description of the visit of Philip and Juana of Spain to England in 1506.
5. *Letters and Papers illustrative of the reigns of Richard III and Henry VII.* Rolls Series. Vols. I & II, ed. James Gairdner. London, 1863.
6. *Letters and papers, foreign and domestic, of the reign of Henry VIII.* Vols. I–XI, ed. John S. Brewer, James Gairdner. London, 1862–1887.
7. *Calendar of letters, despatches and state papers relating to the negotiations between England and Spain.* Vols I–V, supplement and further supplement to Vols. I and II, ed. G. A.

Bergenroth, Pascual de Gayangos, Garrett Mattingly. London, 1862–1886, 1947.

8. *Calendar of state papers, Venetian.* Vols. I–V, ed. Rawdon Brown. London, 1864–1873.

CHRONICLES, HISTORIES AND LITERARY WORKS OF THE PERIOD

9. *Antiquarian Repertory.* Vols. I & II, ed. Francis Grose. London, 1807 and 1808.

10. Cavendish, George. *The life and death of Cardinal Wolsey,* ed. A. S. Sylvester. Early English Text Society, orig. series, CCXLIII. London, 1959. First separate biography in English. Written about 1557 by a gentleman usher of Wolsey's household who did not forget that to offend the King might mean death.

11. Erasmus, *Epistles.* 3 vols. Translated from Latin by F. M. Nichols. London, 1901–1918.

12. Forrest, William. *The history of Grisild the Second: a narrative in verse of the divorce of Katharine of Aragon,* ed. W. D. Macray. Roxburghe Club, London, 1875. An account very sympathetic to Katharine written after her death toward the end of her daughter's reign.

13. Hall, Edward. *The triumphant reigne of King Henry VIII.* London, 1809. This history was first published in 1548 and was intended as a glorification of the House of Tudor; references to Katharine are therefore sometimes lacking.

14. Harpsfield, Nicholas. *A treatise on The Pretended Divorce between Henry VIII and Katharine of Aragon.* Camden Society New Series, XXI, ed. N. Pocock. London, 1878. Another account very sympathetic to Katharine, written after her death during Mary's reign.

15. Leland, John. *Collectanea (de Rebus Britannicis).* 2nd ed. Vols. IV & V, ed. Thomas Hearn. London, 1770.

16. Stow, John. *Annales or a general chronicle of England.* London, 1605.

17. Vergil, Polydore. *The anglica historia 1485–1537.* Camden Society, third series, LXXIV, ed. Denys Hay. London, 1950.

LETTERS

18. *Original letters illustrative of English history,* Vols. I–III, ed. H. Ellis. London, 1824.
19. *Letters of the Kings of England,* Vols. I & II, ed. J. O. Halliwell. London, 1846.
20. *Letters of royal and illustrious ladies,* Vol I, ed. M. A. E. Wood (Green). London, 1846.

LATER WORKS (useful for Background Reading)

21. Brewer, J. S. *The reign of Henry VIII from his accession to the death of Wolsey,* 2 Vols., ed. J. Gairdner. London, 1884.
22. Childe-Pemberton, W. S. *Elizabeth Blount and Henry VIII.* London, 1913. A useful, though biased, account of Henry VIII's known mistress, written by a descendant of her father.
23. Condé, J. A. *Arabs in Spain.* Vol. III. Translated from the French by Mrs. J. Foster. London, 1853.
24. Friedmann, P. *Anne Boleyn, a chapter of English history 1527–1536.* London, 1884.
25. Froude, J. A. *The divorce of Katharine of Aragon.* London, 1897. An account unfavorable to Anne and complimentary to Henry.
26. McNalty, A. S. *Henry VIII, a difficult patient.* London, 1953. Henry VIII's behavior interpreted by a doctor who did not consider him to be syphilitic as has sometimes been suggested.
27. Pollard, A. F. *Henry VIII.* London, 1905.
28. ———. *Wolsey.* London, 1929 (Fortuna Library, ed. G. R. Elton, London, 1965. Both these books by Pollard are essential to a knowledge of the period.
29. Prescott, W. H. *History of the reign of Ferdinand and Isabella The Catholic.* Edited and abridged by C. Harvey Gardiner. London, 1952.
30. Watson, Foster. *Vives and the Renascence education of women.* London, 1912. For information on the education of Princess Mary.
31. Williamson, J. A. *The Tudor age,* 2nd ed. London, 1957.

BIOGRAPHIES

32. Claremont, Francesca. *Catherine of Aragon.* London, 1939. A sympathetic, readable, though not always accurate story.

33. Mattingly, Garret. *Catherine of Aragon*. Boston, 1941. The best biography so far, only spoiled by an unsuitable would-be dramatic style.
34. Paul, J. E. *Catherine of Aragon and her friends*. London, 1966. Gives interesting sidelights on the minor characters.
35. Prescott, H. F. M. *Mary Tudor,* London, 1962. For further details on the upbringing and history of Princess Mary.
36. Strickland, A. *Lives of the Queens of England*. London, 1857. For many years the standard biography but now out of date in many details.

ARTICLES IN JOURNALS

37. *American Catholic Quarterly Review*. Vols. VIII and XXIX. For articles on Henry VIII and Mary Boleyn.
38. *English Historical Review*. Vols. XI, XII, and XIX. For articles on canon law and the divorce by J. Gairdner & H. Thurston.
39. *English Historical Review*. Vols. VIII and X. For articles on Mary and Anne Boleyn by J. Gairdner.

ADDITIONAL BOOKS

40. Woodward, G. W. O. *King Henry VIII*. London, 1967. An illustrated biography.
41. Luke, M. M. *Catherine The Queen*. New York, 1967.
42. Heer, F. *The Holy Roman Empire*. Translated from the German by J. Sondheimer. London, 1968.
43. Scarisbrick, J. J. *Henry VIII*. London, 1968.
44. Simons, Eric N. *Henry VII, The first Tudor King*. London, 1968.
45. Russell, J. G. *The Field of Cloth of Gold*. London, 1969.
46. Chapman, H. W. *The sisters of Henry VIII*. London, 1969.
47. Richardson, W. C. *Mary Tudor, the white queen*. London, 1970.

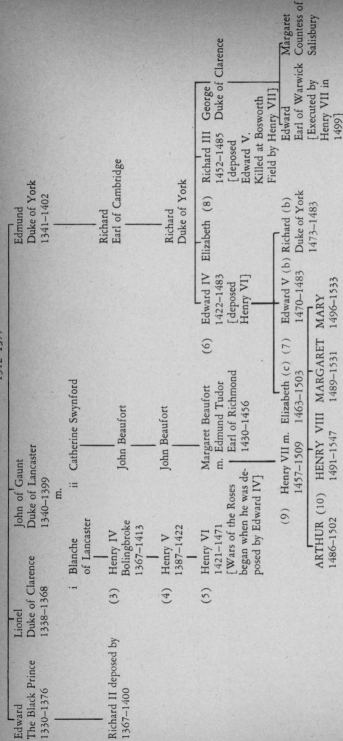

(1) EDWARD III (a)
1312–1377

Edward The Black Prince 1330–1376

Lionel Duke of Clarence 1338–1368

John of Gaunt Duke of Lancaster 1340–1399
m.
i Blanche of Lancaster
ii Catherine Swynford

Edmund Duke of York 1341–1402

(2) Richard II deposed by 1367–1400

(3) Henry IV Bolingbroke 1367–1413

John Beaufort

John Beaufort

Richard Earl of Cambridge

(4) Henry V 1387–1422

(5) Henry VI 1421–1471 [Wars of the Roses began when he was deposed by Edward IV]

Margaret Beaufort m. Edmund Tudor Earl of Richmond 1430–1456

Richard Duke of York

(6) Edward IV 1422–1483 [deposed Henry VI]

Elizabeth

(8) Richard III 1452–1485 [deposed Edward V. Killed at Bosworth Field by Henry VII]

George Duke of Clarence

(9) Henry VII m. Elizabeth (c) 1457–1509 1463–1503

Edward V (b) 1470–1483

Richard (b) Duke of York 1473–1483

Edward Earl of Warwick [Executed by Henry VII in 1499]

Margaret Countess of Salisbury

ARTHUR 1486–1502

(10) HENRY VIII 1491–1547

MARGARET 1489–1531

MARY 1496–1533

(a) Edward III had seven sons and five daughters, some of whom died in infancy.
(b) Both thought to have been murdered in The Tower on Richard III's instructions.
(c) Elizabeth had four sisters.

*   *   *   *   *

Simplified plan of the Royal Houses of York (White Rose) and Lancaster (Red Rose). Numbers in brackets indicate order in which Kings reigned. Dates are of lives, not reigns.

PORTRAITURE OF KATHARINE

The following is the only known list of all the portraits of Katharine of Aragon. Portraits 1a, 2a, 3a and 6 can be found in this book.

A   PORTRAITS AND MINIATURES

KATHARINE AS A YOUNG GIRL

The identification of all portraits in this section is disputable.

1a Portrait by Sittow (also known at Maître Michel, court painter to Ferdinand and Isabella).
Kunsthistorisches Museum, Vienna.

1b Later copy of same portrait.
Kunsthistorisches Museum, Vienna.

1c The Sittow *Madonna* in Berlin and

1d *Magdalene* in the Detroit Institute of Arts have similar features and may have been inspired by the same subject.

2a Portrait of a young girl with a rosebud in her hand

by Juan de Flandes (also court painter to Ferdinand and Isabella).
Thyssen-Bornemisza Collection, Lugano. Formerly identified as Juana, now claimed (by Charles Sterling) to be Katharine.

2b Apparently identical version in the Sedgwick Collection, University of California at Santa Barbara.

KATHARINE IN LATER LIFE

Identification acceptable of all these miniatures and portraits which are of a similar type.

3a National Portrait Gallery, London, and

3b Practically identical version in The Fine Arts Museum, Boston.
Both thought to have been painted during her lifetime from a lost original by Johannes Corvus.

4 National Trust: Duke of Devonshire Collection, Chatsworth.

5 Royal Collection, Windsor Castle.

6 John Guinness Collection (formerly Northwick Park).

7 Merton College, Oxford, commemorating a visit Katharine paid to the College on April 17, 1518.

8 Petworth, Sussex. Portrait catalogued as Duchess of Abergavenny. Portrait of a young woman holding a ring in one hand, catalogued as Katharine, bears no resemblance to any other portrait of the Queen and may be one of her ladies-in-waiting.

9a The Deanery, Ripon, Yorkshire. Thought to have been painted in the 17th century.

9b A second version of the same portrait, probably painted later in the same century in the Deanery.

10 Nonsuch Park: Mrs. Eric Thompson, Helmsley, Yorkshire. A portrait of the same type as the others but perhaps not painted until the 18th century.

MINIATURES

11 With monkey. Duke of Buccleuch.

12 Head and shoulders only, similar to No. 11. Duke of Buccleuch.

13 Newly-discovered miniature, thought to be by Lucas Horenbout. Acquired in June 1969 by National Portrait Gallery, London.

B OTHER LIKENESSES

14 Woodcut. *A joyful meditation to all England of the Coronation of our most natural sovereign lord, King Henry The Eight,* London, 1509 by Stephen Hawes, formerly a groom to Henry VII.

15 Stained glass representations of Arthur and Katharine in the east window of St. Margaret's, Westminster.

16 Stained glass representation of Henry VIII and Katharine in the east window of the Chapel of the Vyne in Hampshire.

17 Reproduction of portrait, date unknown, of Arthur

and Katharine in the Victoria County History for
Hampshire, Vol. 12.
The boy is undoubtedly King Edward VI, but the
girl could be Katharine.

18   Great Tournament Roll of Westminster to celebrate
the birth of Katharine's first son in 1511. College of
Heralds, London.

Four other portraits of Katharine were listed in sixteenth
century inventories; but they have either been lost or remain
unrecognized:

1   among Katharine's possessions listed after her death
as "one table peyntid representing the pictours of the
King and the Princess Dowgier";

2   in the inventory of Margaret of Austria made in
1524: a small picture of the Queen of England with
bare head and wearing a robe of crimson velvet;

3   in Lord Lumley's inventory of 1590;

4   among Juana's pictures left behind in Tordesillas.

The portraiture of Katharine has been a controversial subject for just over fifty years. There are known to be in
existence today about twenty portraits, miniatures and illustrations which are possible likenesses of her. Of the
portraits and miniatures only two depict a young girl and
the attribution is a matter of dispute. The rest are of Katharine probably between the ages of forty and forty-five. The
National Portrait Gallery miniature is the only likeness believed to have been painted from life.

THE YOUNG KATHARINE

It is tempting to regard the excellent Sittow portrait in Vienna (1a) as a genuine likeness of Katharine about the time she left Spain. It is indeed the one that has most often been chosen to represent her. Because of the facial resemblance it has also been claimed that she was the sitter for two of Sittow's religious paintings (1c and 1d). There is, however, no conclusive proof that the Vienna portrait is of Katharine though persuasive arguments have been brought forward both to support and contradict the attribution since 1915 when it was first made. The recently discovered miniature now in the National Portrait Gallery may however swing the balance in favor, as it is not difficult to see a resemblance between the two.

The Juan de Flandes portraits (2a and 2b) were until recently considered to be of Juana. When the Thyssen Collection was shown in New York some years ago, it was claimed in the catalogue that the subject was Katharine. The strong resemblance between this portrait of a girl with a rose and the one of Juana (plate 8), companion picture to one of Philip (plate 9) in Vienna, justifies the assumption that it is, at any rate, a portrait of one of Isabella's daughters.

KATHARINE IN LATER LIFE

The portraits of Katharine as a middle-aged woman are acceptable as being more or less her likeness. They are different versions of the same type. Any contemporary portraits that were not destroyed at the time of her downfall have been lost during the following centuries. When her daughter Mary succeeded to the throne, Katharine, however,

again became an important historical figure, not as the first
of Henry VIII's six wives but as mother of a ruling monarch.
She, together with Jane Seymour, took her place alongside
Henry VIII in the Long Galleries of the great houses where
they were later joined by Anne Boleyn. Most of the portraits
extant today belong to this category. Only the London
(plate 28) and Boston (3b) versions are thought to have
been painted during Katharine's lifetime, copied from some
lost original by Johannes Corvus. The rest are later copies
of the same type differing only in regard to details of dress,
quality of workmanship and the kind of overpainting they
received. The most interesting are the Chatsworth portrait
which is inscribed in Latin, *Katharine, Dowager English
Queen* (4) and the Guinness portrait with psalter (plate 27),
which may be the missing Johannes Corvus.

MINIATURES

All three known miniatures are thought to have been painted
during Katharine's lifetime and the newly-discovered miniature in the National Portrait Gallery may have been painted
from life. With its Latin inscription *Queen Katharine his
wife* it is obviously a companion to a miniature of Henry
VIII, perhaps the one of Henry without a beard at the age
of 43 in the Fitzwilliam Museum, Cambridge. If this is correct, in spite of the fact that the miniature has been much
overpainted, it is possible to see Katharine as she looked at
about the age of 40.

The other portrayals of Katharine are too stylized to give
any idea of her true appearance. She and Arthur are said to
be the figures in the east window of St. Margaret's, Westminster (16). The story is that the window was commissioned by Ferdinand and Isabella for Henry VII's chapel in

Westminster but, as the glass did not arrive until after the death of Arthur, it was never put in place. After having been moved at least twice it was bought by St. Margaret's in the seventeenth century. The stained glass windows of Katharine and Henry VIII in the Chapel of the Vyne (17) are said to have been given by Henry VIII to commemorate a visit he and Katharine paid to the house in 1510, though they were not put in place until after 1520.

Finally, the Westminster Roll, a glorious piece of decoration nearly sixty feet long, was made to honor Katharine the young Queen and celebrate the birth of her first son. It must, therefore, have been made in 1511 between January 1, when he was born, and February 22, when he died. The Roll is remarkable for the color and gaiety of its pictures more than for the accuracy of its representation. It marks one of the happiest interludes of Katharine's life. She and Henry are proud parents, young and joyful. She sits with her ladies in a pavilion decorated with Tudor roses. Henry goes to the joust on a horse draped with a blue cloth embroidered with *K*s, declaring himself her noble royal heart. The rose and the pomegranate grow as one.

Index